Aromas of Asia

Perspectives on Sensory History

Books in the Perspectives on Sensory History series maintain a historical basis for work on the senses, examining how the experiences of seeing, hearing, smelling, tasting, and touching have shaped the ways in which people have understood their worlds.

Aromas of Asia

Exchanges, Histories, Threats

Edited by Hannah Gould
and Gwyn McClelland

The Pennsylvania State University Press
University Park, Pennsylvania

Library of Congress Cataloging-in-Publication Data

Names: Gould, Hannah (Anthropologist),
    editor. | McClelland, Gwyn, editor.
Title: Aromas of Asia : exchanges, histories, threats /
    edited by Hannah Gould and Gwyn McClelland.
Other titles: Perspectives on sensory history.
Description: University Park, Pennsylvania : The
    Pennsylvania State University Press, [2023]
    | Series: Perspectives on sensory history |
    Includes bibliographical references and index.
Summary: "A multidisciplinary collection of essays
    exploring the interconnections and disjunctures
    in Asian cultural histories of scent. Examines
    how scent functions as a category of social
    and moral boundary-marking and boundary-
    breaching within, between, and beyond
    Asian societies"—Provided by publisher.
Identifiers: LCCN 2023017588 | ISBN 9780271095417
    (hardback) | ISBN 97802710954 (paper)
Subjects: LCSH: Odors—Social aspects—Asia—History.
    | Smell—Social aspects—Asia—History. | Odors in
    literature. | Smell in literature. | LCGFT: Essays.
Classification: LCC GT2847 .A76 2023 |
    DDC 306.4—dc23/eng/20230420
LC record available at https://lccn.loc.gov/2023017588

Printed in the United States of America
Published by The Pennsylvania State University Press,
University Park, PA 16802–1003

The Pennsylvania State University Press is a
member of the Association of University Presses.

It is the policy of The Pennsylvania State University
Press to use acid-free paper. Publications on
uncoated stock satisfy the minimum requirements
of American National Standard for Information
Sciences—Permanence of Paper for Printed
Library Material, ANSI Z39.48–1992.

GPSR Authorized Representative: Logos
Europe, 9 rue Nicolas Poussin, 17000 La
Rochelle, France, contact@logoseurope.eu.

Contents

Illustrations

Acknowledgments

The editors acknowledge the seed funding from the Japanese Studies Association of Australia, which supported the production of this book and the "Workshop on Cultures of Sense," held at the University of Melbourne in February 2020. At the workshop, we met with multiple experienced researchers in the field of sensory studies, discussed future possibilities for the work, and shared in the sensory experience of vegetarian South Asian curry and rice. The workshop developed into our call for a volume exploring the "olfactory cultures of Asia," and we were gratified to receive so many excellent contributions from scholars around the world. We are appreciative of the support and opportunities offered by our institutions, the University of Melbourne and the University of New England. Specifically, we would like to thank the following colleagues for their significant assistance along the way: Tamara Kohn, Richard Chenhall, Carolyn S. Stevens, Francois Soyer, Richard Scully, David Chapman, and Diana Barnes.

Hannah Gould: I would like to thank my partner, Daisuke, my family, and my friends for supporting me throughout the past few years. I am very lucky to be part of a vibrant Melbourne academic community, including my colleagues in the DeathTech Research Team and the School of Social and Political Sciences, who have supported and challenged me intellectually in the development of this work. I completed this project while living in Naarm (Melbourne), on the sovereign lands of the Wurundjeri Woi Wurrung People of the Kulin Nation, and I extend my respect to their Elders. Finally, I must extend my deep gratitude to Gwyn McClelland, for his dedication and enthusiasm for this project, despite all the hurdles—personal and global—that the past few years have thrown at us. I could not have wished for a better academic collaborator, mentor, and friend.

Gwyn McClelland: I am grateful to Keren, Lydia, and Geordie, for their steadfast support of my new academic calling in the period of time working on this book, involving a move to a new city and state in the middle of a global pandemic. In Armidale, Keren and I were humbled to be welcomed by Uncle Steve Widders at a eucalyptus-scented smoking ceremony carried out by the Anaiwan community at the Aboriginal Keeping Place in Armidale. My generous colleagues in the "Work-in-Progress" Languages, Literatures,

Linguistics, and Cultures Research group at the University of New England, Armidale (Anaiwan Country), Australia closely read an early draft of my chapter in this volume, and I appreciate their incisive comments. Thanks to Joelle Tapas of Harvard University for the opportunity to speak on this topic at the Modern Japan History Workshop, Tokyo, in June 2021 and to those who offered questions and comments at this occasion. Van C. Gessel and Mark Williams opened up the world of Endō Shusaku for me, Masako Fukui donated additional Endō books, and I wish to acknowledge my scholarly debt to colleagues Shijō Chie and Chad Diehl in the world of Nagasaki studies. It has been a pleasure to learn so much from scholars, including Constance Classen, Kelvin Low, and Mark M. Smith, in the unfolding of this project. Last but not least, thanks and appreciation to my colleague Hannah Gould, for her acumen and enthusiasm in engaging in this long-term project. Occasionally, despite COVID-19, we were able to work together, usually with the assistive scents of coffee and chocolate, and a research assistant puppy nearby.

Introduction

Scents, Sensory Colonialism, and Social Worlds in Asia

Gwyn McClelland and Hannah Gould

The transformation of global olfactory experience is one of the less remarked-upon effects of the COVID-19 pandemic that spread rapidly across the globe from its first identification in Wuhan, China, in late 2019. By May 2020, the medical condition of *anosmia*, or loss of a sense of smell, was recognized as a key clinical indicator of infection with COVID-19 (the SARS-CoV-2 virus), sometimes independent of other symptoms. The condition is estimated to affect nearly half of all diagnosed patients.[1] Although most patients regain their sense of smell within a month, for some, a condition of anosmia, or even paranosmia (phantom smells), lingers. Walker et al. quote one patient with this condition: "Anosmia is like experiencing the world in two dimensions. I dearly miss the energising aroma of strong morning coffee and the soothing effect of spring scents. Appetite has dampened and fine wines which I loved have lost their depth and complexity. There are no smells to evoke good memories and I have lost an important coping mechanism. . . . Friends trivialise this condition and show no empathy."[2] This testimony speaks to the tricky nature of olfaction: its profound impact in shaping one's everyday experience of the world and the popular dismissal of its significance. Western cultural hierarchies and intellectual traditions tend to elevate the reliability and importance of vision and hearing while dismissing other senses like smell, taste, or touch.[3] Philosophers from Plato to Descartes have aligned vision with rationality, and Immanuel Kant once bemoaned smell as the most ignoble of the senses; he described it as "animalistic," "fleeting," and thus unworthy of cultivation.[4]

Beyond an acute condition of anosmia, COVID-19 has more fundamentally shifted how people imagine and experience the air around them. As breath is expelled from somebody's lungs, aerosolized particles travel through the air and can enter another's nose, mouth, and lungs. The confirmed airborne transmission of COVID-19 thus reconfigures the visible boundaries between bodies, such that the air becomes enlivened with a potentially threatening force. In efforts to mitigate transmission, face masks have become a common feature of everyday olfactory experience around the world. Of course, for many communities across Asia, masking is a relatively common practice, for reasons of fashion or courtesy, or due to past experiences with H1N1 and SARS.

Strong-smelling miasmas, or drifting clouds of noxious air, have been central to human understandings of disease transmission since before the emergence of germ theory. Miasma theory remains salient in writing on COVID-19, particularly where the virus crosses cultural or ethnic borders. Several Western commentators, for example, appear to give olfactory evidence when positioning Chinese "wet markets" as the origin site of the virus. In *The COVID-19 Reader* (2021), one writer describes the markets as "various covered stalls on a walkway with pungent smells where different kinds of animals were caged in close proximity . . . including bats, civets, snakes, frogs, ferrets, and others. A lack of hygiene was obvious from the smells and scattered wastes."[5] Given this olfactory experience, the authors describe their lack of surprise that a pandemic might emerge from this context. Their description of the wet markets, however, stands in contrast to Zhong, Crang, and Zeng's 2020 ethnography, which shows how freshness is constructed and valued in people's sensory experiences of markets in China.

What the sensory experiences of COVID-19 so powerfully illustrate is how olfaction is simultaneously an intimately embodied, individual experience and a social phenomenon that travels between bodies and communities—and even around the globe. In *Aromas of Asia: Exchanges, Histories, Threats* we are concerned with this specific question: how does the mobility of olfactory sense make social worlds? Our analysis privileges flows, exchanges, and encounters to identify prejudices, accusations, and power games of scent and odor. This not only helps us chart new dimensions of people's lived experiences and histories but also invites us to rethink the category of Asia itself, not as a preexisting entity but as one that emerges through sensory exchange.

What some have called the *"sensual revolution* in the humanities, social sciences and the arts,"[6] emerging in the late 1990s and early 2000s, challenged the assumed ascendency of psychological or medical approaches to the study of perception, inviting scholars to explore the sociocultural construction of the senses, and thus our foundational experience of the world. This theoretical turn did not emerge from nowhere; as scholars such as Mark M. Smith have articulated, it stands on the work of early historians like Johan Huizinga and Lucien Febvre, among others.[7] Fundamentally, sensory studies asks us to move beyond cursory treatments of the senses as natural tools of perception or cultural epiphenomena to consider how the senses constitute, and orient people within, social and material worlds. Now, over fifteen years since the publication of the first issue of the *Senses and Society* journal, the sensory revolution has proved a fertile one, with scholars across multiple disciplines working variously to articulate multisensorial experiences, to challenge sensory hierarchies, and to broaden our understanding of what constitutes a "sense." A significant driving force behind this work, particularly in cultural anthropology, has been to critique and dismantle Western "commonsense" ideas about the senses.[8] For example, the Roman-Grecian categorizations of the senses into five modalities (vision, hearing, smell, taste, touch) has been shown to be a rather parochial configuration, one that is frequently contradicted by sensory cosmologies and vocabularies around the world and through time (see, for example, Marinucci, Jia, Khoo and Duruz, and Tang, in this volume).[9] Other sensory categories also challenge the aforementioned Western hierarchies and the privileging of vision: for example, in Chinese philosophy, the eyes and the ears are described as of equal significance.[10] As a result of the sensual revolution, scholars working today must acknowledge the importance of the senses in understanding seemingly all lines of inquiry, and they must not dismiss sensory perception as a neutral, shared mode of encountering the world.

Despite this significant body of work and decentering efforts, recent critiques show how contemporary scholarship on the senses remains wedded to Western and English-language scholarly contexts and concerns.[11] Kelvin Low points out that scholarship is bifurcated between "Euro–American contexts" and "non-industrial societies," where the latter tend to be presented primarily as a counterexample or foil to Western sensory cultures and hierarchies.[12] Comparatively, there has been remarkably minimal analysis of sensoria in Asian contexts, and few existing works analyze olfaction.[13]

Studies of sense, then, retain a distinct center-periphery relationship between the West and the "rest." While illuminating the distinctiveness of multiple sensory cosmologies can work to destabilize an idea of human sensory perception as "natural" or universal, such studies can also reinforce ideas of radical alterity or otherness. Thus, they have historically contributed to constructing and maintaining unequal structures of power. Part of the problem is a predilection toward describing discrete sensory cultures as relatively stable worlds that are "rooted" in place and essentialized to a particular population. Scholars frequently focus on the minutiae of everyday life without explaining what happens when sensory orders come into contact, not only in one-to-one encounters but also on larger scales and within broader sensory landscapes, shaped by deep histories of trade, colonization, and migration (see, for example, Khoo and Duruz, also McClelland in this volume). The former approach constructs cultures as "sensory isolates," denying the histories of exchange through which sensory worlds merge and diverge through forces of imposition, appropriation, and rejection. Any attempt to maintain sensory isolates becomes impossible when we consider key "sensory highways" that have historically run across and shaped Asia, such as economic exchange along the Silk Road, the diffusion of dharmic religious traditions out of South Asia, and the waves of invasion, colonization, and forced relocation that shaped the history of the continent. In recent decades, the speed and number of interconnections of sensory worlds have only intensified, whether by the diffusion of global popular culture, the spread of pandemics, or environmental devastation via clouds of industrial smog.

Seeking to conceptualize Asia and its borders as a dynamic space of olfactory exchange, this collection responds to recent provocations about (Asian) "transnational sensescapes" by Kelvin Low, Devorah Kalekin-Fishman, and others.[14] Low argues that localized sensoria should be studied on their own terms, utilizing their own terminologies, to properly understand symbolisms and the theoretical importance of the senses.[15] The language of "sensescapes" that we deploy here originates and extends upon the work of Arjun Appadurai in conceptualizing global interconnectedness in modernity via the structure of "scapes" (e.g., "technoscapes," "ethnoscapes" and "ideoscapes").[16] Scapes have the quality of being observable from both emic and etic perspectives (insider and outsider). They position people in the world and give it meaning, but they also depict sensory environments. However, as Dennis, Dawson, and Behie, recent critics of this concept and its abuses, argue,[17] we must be careful to avoid seeing "scapes" as fixed or preexisting the act of perception. Rather, they are always emergent, arising through human encounters with the environment, as J. J. Gibson's work on the affordances of perception originally suggests.[18] In this manner, the delineation of "Asian scentscapes" in this volume does not suggest that there is a single or unified plane of olfactory perception that crosses or exhausts the borders of Asia. Indeed, our deployment of the scapes metaphor is intended to destabilize the idea of set or impermeable borders in order to describe, as Appadurai originally described, "a complex, overlapping and disconnected order that is highly unpredictable."[19]

Although the "scapes" metaphor easily evokes visual perception, the contributions in this collection draw attention to the particular qualities and agencies of olfaction as a mode of exchange. Smell is a powerful boundary marker that has been used to enforce—sometimes violently—differences in dimensions, including ethnicity, gender, caste, and class (see McClelland and Kapoor in this volume). It shapes individual, collective, and state-based memory, as well as discourses about heritage, language, and power. Olfaction enables a pervasive intimacy; smell cannot be "undone" or "unsmelled," yet it fades beyond notice or even perception upon prolonged exposure. That is, people become encultured to scent, unable to consciously perceive its character until a contrasting phenomenon is introduced. This makes smell a potent metaphor for thinking about relations between self and other, evoking how unfamiliar "new smells" provoke strong reactions, both positive and negative. It is perhaps for this reason that Koichi Iwabuchi chose the metaphor of odor to discuss how products of popular culture are produced and received as they travel across Asia and into the West. In his seminal 2002 work *Recentering Globalization*, Iwabuchi suggests that popular consumer commodities originating from Japan are intentionally made "culturally odorless" so that they can be easily appropriated into local contexts. But making something odorless is a difficult task, and smell can be difficult to ward against or keep out. Through its potency, smell can reconfigure borders, unsettle official histories, and create new social-sensory realities from emerging contexts, such as environmental degradation, pathogen outbreaks, and shifting racial politics. Such exchanges operate through time and at multiple scales to constitute personal, local, national, and regional scentscapes. For these reasons, we propose that smell is not simply an undertheorized dimension of life in Asia but also a particularly generative phenomenon to think with when attempting to theorize the dynamics of transnational exchange.

Historicizing Olfactory Asia

Asia is home to a heterogeneous and changing complex of scentscapes that have blended together and come apart throughout history. It is an olfactory context that exists in relation to, and is defined by, its encounter with external cultures. Conversely, Western sensory superiority has long required, and continues to require, an olfactory other. Famously, Edward Said described a science of imperialism justifying exploitation and domination by European powers and ascribing inferior and negative characteristics to the "Orient."[20] Interacting with enduring frames of Orientalism, Western ocularcentrism has historically enacted a kind of sensory colonialism, by aligning Asia and its peoples with more "debased" or "primal" senses.[21] All scholars, therefore, must consider colonial encounter as a condition for exploring their field or subject matter from the historical position of today, even where that may be precolonial in nature.

The olfactory tropes of Orientalism present as extremes. At one pole, Asian cultures have been cast as pungent, populated by "stinky" foods and bodies: see, for example, Mallapragada[22] on curry, or Khoo and Duruz (chapter 4) on durians. This pungency emits a dangerous sensuality that effects an unwanted intimacy across the boundaries of the self and other. It can be both alluring and threatening. An American diplomat, Bayard Taylor, wrote in his journal in 1853 of the "sickening smell of opium" that marked the streets of Shanghai. At the other extreme, Asia is subject to readings of a stringently sanitized, antiseptic, or odorless character. Pop-science articles dissect differences in deodorant use due to East Asian genes said to determine sweat production,[23] while travelogues wax lyrical about Singaporean public transport, with its stringent cleaning regimes, "orchid-tea fragrance," and new anti-COVID ventilation systems.[24] Ultimately, tropes of both pungency and sanitation work to dehumanize by casting Asian peoples and cultures as unnatural bearers and producers of scent.[25] Most notably, there is an unequal distribution of olfactory stereotypes across different communities in Asia, demonstrating how localized sensory hierarchies and imperial histories beyond the West-Orient bifurcation intersect with more global frames.

This volume contests Orientalist olfactory tropes while identifying their continued significance and potential to do real harm across multiple scales. Working against the reductive opposition of "West-rationality-vision" and "Asia-irrationality-smell," our contributors commit to taking scent seriously as an analytic instrument and dimension of lived experience. By paying attention to historic and ethnographic detail, the authors in this volume break down simple readings of a monolithic "Asia" as either pungent or sanitized, to articulate how olfaction is deployed within specific sensory orders, and how these orders intersect across local, regional, and transnational scales. This work therefore engages with stubborn historical projects of sensory colonialism that continue to shape the region, not least the sanitary civilizing campaigns of the Japanese Empire in colonial Seoul,[26] the British Empire in colonial Bengal, or the reach of the Singaporean state (see Toulson in this volume).[27] The contributors thus complicate sensory power structures within Asia beyond the center-periphery tensions of the East-West divide, revealing, in the words of Arif Dirlik, "societies globally in their complex heterogeneity and contingency."[28] It is this dynamic and emergent nature of "Asia" that we revisit in this book through the lens of sensory transnationalism.

An additional common thread across many of the chapters in this collection that deserves mention is the connection between religious or spiritual movements and olfaction. Scent and smell are frequently said to "materialize" or "manifest" the transcendent, and religious movements explore, employ, and nurture the olfactory sense as a matter of spirituality. In particular, see Marinucci, Jia, McClelland, Tanada, and Toulson in this volume.

Introducing the Contributions

Just as scent exceeds attempts to contain it within the discrete borders of a community or locale, single disciplinary approaches appear insufficient in the study of Asian scentscapes. Put simply, smell transgresses disciplinary boundaries and is best approached through methodological and theoretical pluralism. This is the interdisciplinary approach we adopt in the contributions to this collection, drawing upon different methodologies, theoretical lineages, and disciplines including anthropology, art history, economics, history, religious studies, and media studies, sparking conversation between the different disciplines. By bringing multiple perspectives together, we argue, for example, that the historical sets the anthropological in context and that the sensory worlds of literature and film amplify the philosophical and the poetic. The contributing scholars come from a range of locations within, between, or beyond an Asian geographical region. As editors, we do not claim this spread to be representative or exhaustive, but the chapters do provide a robust cross section of the "scentscapes" that traverse the region.

The book is divided into three sections, each organized around a theme: "Poetics and Philosophies," "Making Sensory Boundaries," and "Bodies—Life, Work, and Death."

Olfactory culture in many parts of Asia is shaped by a shared history of exchange across the Silk Road and the influence of varied forms of imperial or court culture, alongside ancestral cults and dharmic religious practices that utilize incense. In "Poetics and Philosophies," the historic philosophies of China and Japan are brought to the fore. Lorenzo Marinucci considers scent as the "hybridization of bodies and selves." Marinucci examines phenomenological olfactory paradigms within Japanese culture—those of *nioi* and *ka*—to disrupt an opticentric European modern sensibility, describing poetics "on a trail of incense." The author also reviews "Europe's problematic relationship with sense." Mark M. Smith has pointed out, in response to the work of Lucien Febvre and Robert Mandrou, how poets and poetry were highly concerned with the olfactory in European contexts, and in East Asia we may observe a similar trend raised by both Marinucci and later author Jia.[29] In the essay that follows, Peter Romaskiewicz relocates us to the continent, where he investigates Emperor Wu's "strange aromatics" and the intricate scentscapes of medieval China, by focusing on a compilation known as the *Materia Aromatica* (*Xiang pu*), created by Hong Chu in the eleventh and twelfth centuries. Qian Jia revisits the discussion of poetics while adding layers to consideration of scent in medieval China. While incense is usually assumed to be burned, Jia shows how in Song China *xiang* (the ideograph used for incense; *ka* in Japanese) is not only burned but also seen, touched, and tasted. She also discusses how in poetry aromas act as an "image," evoking spirituality, eroticism, and the transcendence of boundaries.

In "Making Sensory Boundaries," Gaik Cheng Khoo and Jean Duruz continue the inter-Asian expansion of scentscapes by following "whiffs" of pungent and sometimes stereotyped smells of everyday life—kopi (coffee) and durian—in changing contexts, from Southeast Asia to China. Khoo and Duruz contemporize the patterns of transnational consumption and elaborate on how they are regulated by politics, race, ethnicity, social cultures,

and emerging mainland Chinese consumer desire. Gwyn McClelland continues this section by discussing olfaction in the literary world envisaged by
the Catholic Japanese fiction writer Endō Shūsaku, whose well-known book
Silence was originally titled *The Aroma of Sunshine*. In Endō's fiction,
McClelland argues, aroma and scent are associated with othering in the colo-
nial-influenced nineteenth-century Japanese context. Smell as a marker of
class in the nineteenth century is evidenced not only in a European context[30]
but also in Asia. Olfaction is often employed to enforce boundaries, but such
boundary setting may be undercut by aromas themselves, and this is Endō's
yearning—for the place(s) that transcend East and West. Through the lens
of Dalit autobiography, Shivani Kapoor writes that odor transcends boundaries, speaking in "defiant, messy" terms and "challenging the Brahmanical
hegemonic sensorium." Kapoor urges consideration of "words that smell."
Moving from literature to the cinematic, Aubrey Tang explores how a Hong
Kong detective comedy shot from the perspective of a blind man undercuts
a dependence on the visual by showing olfaction as the "most persistent and
ineluctable" of senses. By adopting the lens of a sensing body, she argues,
we may effectively examine the ongoing idiosyncrasy of Hong Kong's post-
1997 historical situation.

Finally, in "Bodies," we move through the themes of "Life, Work, Death,"
from the island of Lombok in Indonesia to contemporary China and the
island state of Singapore. Saki Tanada describes the world of childbirth in a
Sasak world in which odor is associated with making sense of the world, a
world between Sasak Islamic hybridity and modern medical cosmologies. By
opening up the experiences from her ethnographic work, Tanada articulates
how differences in sensing and in bodily experiences may be acknowledged,
indicating synesthetic and olfactory encounters and how they are understood, especially in relation to women. Adam Liebman interrogates human
bodies' olfactory sense, returning to the contemporary world of the Chinese
mainland, in which waste politics tends to elide the regional and promote
a hygenized modern urbanity. His work directs our attention to the role of
smell in mediating human and nonhuman interactions within the context
of environmental degradation and the Anthropocene. As Mark M. Smith
suggests, "The environment . . . when under duress . . . stretches and rear-
ranges the senses."[31] In the last chapter, Ruth Toulson's ethnographic work
on a Singaporean funeral home describes people's attempts to contain the
smell of "leaky," decaying human remains while confronting the ever-present
possibility that these carefully constructed boundaries will be overwhelmed.

In drawing connections between intimate olfactory relations with bodies and the work of the Singaporean state, her contribution reinforces how smell works on multiple scales to negotiate borders.

Aroma has long been used to describe and define the region, peoples, and cultures of Asia. All too frequently, as in the context of a global pandemic, this approach has produced negative stereotypes that reinforce the alterity of Asia as the other to the West. Rather than turn away from sensory inquiry in the region, we suggest that it is only by engaging with and breaking down persistent regimes of sensory colonialism that the power of olfaction to enforce borders can be understood. Accordingly, a transnational approach to Asian aromas, or scentscapes founded on mobility and exchange, offers a chance to rethink this region through its diverse and shifting olfactory cultures.

Notes

1. Walker et al., "Anosmia and Loss of Smell."
2. Ibid.
3. Classen, Howes, and Synnott, *Aroma.*
4. Kant, *Anthropology,* §22, 50–51.
5. Cockerham and Cockerham, *Covid-19 Reader,* 4.
6. Bull et al., "Introducing Sensory Studies," 5.
7. Smith, *Sensory History Manifesto.*
8. A paradigm-shifting early example of this effort is Paul Stoller's *Taste of Ethnographic Things,* which also demonstrates the connection between the sensory turn and the embodiment or praxis turn in theory.
9. For example, see Low, "Theorising Sensory Cultures," 618–36.
10. Ibid., 622.
11. Gould et al., "Interrogation of Sensory Anthropology," 231–58.
12. Low, "Theorising Sensory Cultures," 618.
13. For example, Kalekin-Fishman and Low, *Everyday Life in Asia;* McHugh, *Sandalwood and Carrion;* Moeran, "Making Scents of Smell," 439–50.
14. Kalekin-Fishman and Low, *Everyday Life;* Low, "Theorising Sensory Cultures"
15. Low, "Theorising Sensory Cultures," 625.

16. Appadurai, "Disjuncture and Difference," 295–310.
17. Dennis, Dawson, and Behie, "Little Fear," 17–24.
18. Gibson, *Ecological Approach to Visual Perception.*
19. Salazar, "Scapes," 753.
20. Green and Troup, *Houses of History,* 279.
21. Scott, "Kipling, the Orient, and Orientals," 307.
22. Mallapragada, "Curry as Code," 263–75.
23. Guo, "Aiming at China's Armpits."
24. Mustafa, "Singapore's Endless Pursuit of Cleanliness."
25. Such dehumanizing frames are by no means unique to Asia but a product of colonialist expansion more globally.
26. Low, "Theorising Sensory Cultures," 629.
27. Prasad, "Sanitizing the Domestic," 132–53.
28. Quoted in Green and Troup, *Houses of History,* 281.
29. Smith, *Manifesto.*
30. Ibid.
31. Ibid., 72.

Bibliography

Appadurai, Arjun. "Disjuncture and Difference in the Global Economy." *Theory, Culture and Society* 7 (1990): 295–310.

Bull, Michael, Paul Gilroy, David Howes, and Douglas Kahn. "Introducing Sensory Studies." *Senses and Society* 1, no. 1 (2006): 5–7.

Classen, Constance, David Howes, and Anthony Synnott. *Aroma: The Cultural History of Smell*. London: Routledge, 1994.

Cockerham, William C., and Geoffrey B. Cockerham. *The Covid-19 Reader: The Science and What It Says About the Social*. London: Routledge, 2020.

Dennis, Simone, Andrew Dawson, and Alison Behie. "A Little Fear: Rethinking Scapes, Structures, Time and the Ordinary." *Journal of Futures Studies* 25, no. 2 (2020): 17–24.

Gibson, James J. *The Ecological Approach to Visual Perception*. Classic Edition. New York: Taylor & Francis, 2014.

Gould, Hannah, Richard Chenhall, Tamara Kohn, and Carolyn S. Stevens. "An Interrogation of Sensory Anthropology of and in Japan." *Anthropological Quarterly* 92, no. 1 (2019): 231–58.

Green, Anna, and Kathleen Troup. *Houses of History: A Critical Reader in Twentieth-Century History and Theory*. Manchester: Manchester University Press, 1998.

Guo, Owen. "Aiming at China's Armpits: When Foreign Brands Misfire." *New York Times*, February 2, 2018. https://www.nytimes.com/2018/02/02/business/china-consumers-deodorant.html.

Kalekin-Fishman, Devorah, and Kelvin Low. *Everyday Life in Asia: Social Perspectives on the Senses*. London: Routledge, 2010.

Kant, Immanuel. *Anthropology from a Pragmatic Point of View*. 1798. Edited by Robert B. Louden with an introduction by Manfred Kuehn. Cambridge: Cambridge University Press, 2006.

Low, Kelvin, "Theorising Sensory Cultures in Asia: Sociohistorical Perspectives." *Asian Studies Review* 43, no. 4 (2019): 618–36.

Mallapragada, Madhavi. "Curry as Code: Food, Race, and Technology." In *Global Asian American Popular Cultures*, edited by Shilpa Davé, LeiLani Nishime, and Tasha Oren, 263–75. New York: New York University Press, 2012.

McHugh, James. *Sandalwood and Carrion: Smell in Indian Religion and Culture*. Oxford: Oxford University Press, 2012.

Moeran, Brian. "Making Scents of Smell: Manufacturing and Consuming Incense in Japan." *Human Organization* 68, no. 4 (2009): 439–50.

Mustafa, Faris. "Singapore's Endless Pursuit of Cleanliness." *BBC Travel*, April 9, 2021. https://www.bbc.com/travel/article/20210407-singapores-endless-pursuit-of-cleanliness.

Prasad, Srirupa. "Sanitizing the Domestic: Hygiene and Gender in Late Colonial Bengal." *Journal of Women's History* 27, no. 3 (2015): 132–53.

Salazar, Noel B. "Scapes." In *Theory in Social and Cultural Anthropology: An Encyclopedia*, edited by R. Jon McGee and Richard L. Warms, 753. Thousand Oaks, CA: Sage, 2013.

Scott, David. "Kipling, the Orient, and Orientals: 'Orientalism' Reoriented?" *Journal of World History* 22, no. 2 (2011): 307.

Smith, Mark M. *A Sensory History Manifesto*. University Park: Penn State University Press, 2021.

Stoller, Paul. *The Taste of Ethnographic Things: The Senses in Anthropology*. Philadelphia: University of Pennsylvania Press, 1989.

Walker, Abigail, Gillian Pottinger, Andrew Scott, and Claire Hopkins. "Anosmia and Loss of Smell in the Era of Covid-19." *BMJ* 370, m2808 (2020).

Zhong, Shuru, Mike Crang, and Guojun Zeng. "Constructing Freshness: The Vitality of Wet Markets in Urban China." *Agriculture and Human Values* 37 (2020): 175–85.

PART I

POETICS AND
PHILOSOPHIES

CHAPTER 1

On a Trail of Incense

Japan and Olfactory Thought

Lorenzo Marinucci

In this opening chapter, I will address the issue of olfactory thought—thinking *of* scent and thinking *with* scent—through a mostly Japanese cultural context. As my background is philosophical, and especially phenomenological, I will also try to understand why, for most of its history, European philosophical thought has either ignored or disparaged scent, while the history of colonial modernity strongly identified smells and perfumes with a far, feminine Orient, which included Japan. It is only after acknowledging the underlying logic of this projection that a study of the two core olfactory paradigms in Japanese culture—*nioi* 匂い and *ka* 香—can help us break through it, offering us precious perspectives on a cultural study of sensitivities and a novel approach to key problems of philosophy.

Perfumed Japan

It is not hard to find mentions of perfume in stereotypical depictions of Japan in European or North American sources: the sweet and subtle scent of flowers falling in the wind, praised in *waka* or *haiku* poetry; the bitter, refined tang of *matcha* in tea ceremony; the spiritual fragrance of incense of a quiet temple; or the subtle perfume of the "way of incense" (kōdō 香道), possibly the least known among Japanese ways of refinement. Japan, according to some fantasies, is a mystical land of perfume. Scent is often preeminent in the descriptions of travelers; in fact, since living for a long time in a smellscape tends to make it nonthematic, our strongest olfactory impressions are often those of foreign lands or bodies.[1] The otherness of scent, its paradoxical conjunction of sensuality and transcendence, timelessness and impermanence, ultimately speaks of the otherness of Japan itself in the following memorable description by Lafcadio Hearn:

> I see rising out of darkness, a lotos [*sic*] in a vase. Most of the vase is invisible; but I know that it is bronze, and that its glimpsing handles are bodies of dragons. . . . The reason that I see the lotos—one memory of my first visit to a Buddhist sanctuary—is that there has come to me an odor of incense. Often when I smell incense, this vision defines; and usually thereafter other sensations of my first day in Japan revive in swift succession with almost painful acuteness.
>
> It is almost ubiquitous,—this perfume of incense. It makes one element of the faint but complex and never-to-be-forgotten odor of the Far East. It haunts the dwelling-house not less than the temple,—the home of the peasant not less than the *yashiki* of the prince. . . . Many experiences of travel—strange impressions of sound as well as of sight—remain associated in my own memory with that fragrance:—vast silent shadowed avenues leading to weird old shrines; mossed flights of worn steps ascending to temples that moulder above the clouds;—joyous tumult of festival nights;—sheeted funeral-trains gliding by in glimmer of lanterns;—[and] the murmur of household prayer in fisherman's huts on far wild coasts.[2]

To discuss scent in such a context, it is necessary to introduce in their own terms two complex Japanese olfactory paradigms, *nioi* 匂い and *ka* 香.

(See also *xiang* as described in Romaskiewicz's and Jia's contributions in this volume.) We ought to be particularly aware of Hearn's double cultural projection, by which both "scent" and "Orient" are made into something other from the perspective of a world centered on sight, on the idea of the "West," and associated categories. As the Japanese psychologist Adachi Hiroshi remarked, "When we ask for the essence of scent, the first necessary thing is to avoid borrowing concepts cultivated in the world of sight and hearing, to escape from their bonds."[3] But most of this borrowing is unconscious and ideological. In other words, before discussing the particular relevance of scent paradigms in Japan and in Asia, we must understand how and why this "scent as otherness" plays an important role in the history of modernity and Eurocentrism.

European Ocularcentrism

A genealogy of Europe's problematic relationship with scent may be traced to Greek philosophy. With its distinct bias in favor of sight, Greek philosophy considered olfaction as a lower sense, too deeply involved with the body to afford clear cognition.[4] The second intellectual downgrading of scent was an effect of the modern European scientific revolution, which, by its "secondary mathematization" of the world, further reduced scents to the rank of subjective illusion, impossible to understand and measure objectively.[5] The French Revolution, with its new model of state and citizenship, and the rapid urbanization of the Industrial Revolution, which concentrated new masses of working poor in European cities, were also complicit in creating the new ideal of modern embodiment: "As the public health movement began to get under way around midcentury, and as life became cleaner, Europeans began to become more sensitive to smells, both to body odor and to foul air. The possibility of keeping streets and bathrooms, as well as one's body, clean, led to a growing sensitivity to smells."[6]

It is in this period that the *deodorized* body of the virtuous bourgeoisie became distinguished from effete, perfumed noblemen on one side and the stinking proletarians on the other. New concerns for public health also made miasmas a much-feared specter in the smellscape of a city. Both the civilized man and the ideal city had to be odorless: soap became one of the first global commodities, a concrete, powerful symbol of *white* imperialism.[7] To summarize this process, as Tsuboi Hideo puts it, "within the pull towards ocularcentrism (*shikakuchūshinshugi* 視覚中心主義) of European modernity, olfaction has been degraded, becoming a sign for the losing side within the different paradigms of class (poor vs. rich), geographic discrimination, gender and so on."[8]

Scents obviously lingered but became signifiers of otherness in two major ways. *Spatially*, they were associated with the sensual, irrational, mystical landscapes of the Orient. In part, this was the result of the actual historical-geographical patterns of perfume and the spice trade: odoriferous substances had mostly come from the Arabic and Indian peninsulas, and their trade played no small role in the process of exploration and conquest that opened global modernity (see Jia in this volume). But the association between scents and the "losing sides" of Eurocentric ideology also made them inextricably associated with the bodily, the animal, the savage, and the feminine. The suppression and loss of scent were thus also results of a *temporal* process of hominization, the detachment of (above all white) men from their animality[9] and their uncivilized pulsional states.[10] We can see these two sets of prejudices (with their underlying fascinations) act out in Flaubert's meeting with the Egyptian *alemah* Kuchuk Hanem: "She was surely the prototype of several of his novels' female characters in her learned sensuality, delicacy, and (according to Flaubert) mindless coarseness. What he especially liked about her was that she seemed to place no demands on him, while the 'nauseating odor' of her bedbugs mingled enchantingly with '"the scent of her skin, which was dripping with sandalwood.'"'[11]

The association of scent and femininity is also a by-product of the ideological identification between sight and the male perspective. Sight has been consistently cast within European intellectual history as a sense of clarity, light, scientific inquiry, and rational detachment. It is a sense of divisions and hierarchies: first, that between subject and object, and then between different objects, which can be compared and linguistically identified. Sight, once removed from the actual occurrence of ecological perception[12] and transformed into the "point of sight" (視点 *shiten*) of camera obscura, allows gazers to make their own bodies nonthematic entities, to penetrate things without being affected by them in return.[13] No longer bound to the sexual, ethnic, emotional, and cultural particularities of a subjective existence, this disembodied gaze claims to be universal. But this supposed universality does not allow for its own process of abstraction to be also appreciated or understood—neither phenomenologically nor in terms of power. The gaze remains therefore often male, white, colonial. Other subjects are free to learn this style of vision but risk reproducing the divisions that first put them on the "losing side." Japan itself, from the early Meiji years, started to frantically deodorize itself and show a concern about the newly perceived stinks of city outcasts and rural areas.[14] On the other hand, there was an ambivalent pride in Japan's own scent tradition, rich, but dangerously feminine—especially in the eyes of the westerners. After all, in 1904, Pinkerton described Butterfly in these terms:

> She is a flower, a flower, indeed!
> Her exotic scent
> has unsettled my brain.
> She is a flower, a flower, indeed!
> And in faith, I plucked it.[15]

Scent and Its Phenomenology: Space, Time, Imagination

Acknowledging this history, we have a better chance of grasping why the phenomenology of olfaction can be a foil to the hierarchical, reified kind of perception based on such a style of vision.

Sight allows for a clear definition of the self and the world, but olfaction is a sense of blurring, a bridge between what is external and internal to the body, into which odors will seep. This last trait led Kant to define it "most ungrateful" and "most dispensable,"[16] out of a clear disgust for its trespassing of physical and moral boundaries and its disrespect of individual autonomy. In olfaction, the forgotten openness of the body, its reciprocal interpenetration with and dependence on its surrounding environment, becomes evident. Olfaction is an embodied sense also from another perspective: the body produces odors, beyond our will and often without our awareness (out of assuefaction). Body odor has a character at once sexual and scatological in most mammals: it is when the human race acquired an erect position, argued Freud, that genitality and excretion became severed and, in parallel, repressed as "inferior" functions of the newly verticalized body.

Sight is spatially three-dimensional and temporally linear, allowing us to build up a world characterized by stable, quantifiable coordinates. Olfaction is instead spatially unidimensional, signaling itself only through the qualitative, relative coupling of strong or weak, not necessarily corresponding to closer and farther in an absolute sense, but rather manifesting through the "surfaceless space" arising and coinciding with our embodiment.[17] Scents can orient us through embodied, ecological perception, but they are not stable, and the scents in an environment will soon become nonthematic if we are exposed to them for a long time. The great intimacy of scent perception is moreover counterbalanced by the fact that the *within* of the scent is also a *yonder*, the intentional quality of consciousness. By scent, embodied consciousness is also "there," something occurring in the world rather than on the side of a pure ego. Ōhashi Ryōsuke notes how both in Japanese and in European languages the grammatical expression of scent constitutes not as subject-object but instead as an impersonal, intransitive, subjectless "world-place": "In the constitution of the Welt-Ort of 'it smells' [*nioi ga suru* 匂い がする, *es reich*] noetically we forget our 'I smell.' And noematically, within the arising of a scent other scents shift and disappear."[18]

Scent also upsets the linear, pragmatic understanding of time. Odors cannot be freely recalled as objects by an act of will. They are rather *revenants*: "The peculiar thing about smell cannot be that it evokes memories, because just about everything does," observes Turin. What characterizes it is that it is "idiotic in the proper sense of the word, namely unique."[19] Olfactory time is in this sense different from that of a "past" opposed to "present" and "future." Scents are cross-temporal phenomena, bringing us back to the time of their first appearance thanks to their sameness: "It is not that the fragrance triggers the memory . . . we smell in the fragrance the memory of the past."[20] These olfactory repetitions belong to what the Japanese philosopher Kuki Shūzō called "vertical time," the "discontinuous," "mystic," "imaginary" aspect of our experience of temporality, characterized by an "eternal return of the same."[21]

Odors share with imagination another important set of phenomenological features. Visual phenomena appear as objects standing out from their background and covering a portion of it, without abrupt shifts between different moments or angles of sight. But in the case of olfaction, a scent is a nonlocalized, unstable something effused in a medium: it might emanate from an object, but it does not present it directly. When we see a rose, we take it as the presentation (*Gegenwärtigung*) of the actual object: the rose "is there." When we smell a rose, or a rose-scented perfume, the thematic element is instead just suspended in an undefined medium and rather works as a "presentification" (*Vergegenwärtigung*), its mutable "phantasm."[22] The rose could be withered, be gone, or never have been here. Thus, we can say that the scent of a flower is *not* the flower, but holds the flower within it as *image*, as a "nothing." This phantasmatic representation is, just like imagination, unstable: a manifold of different aspects emerging or sinking without regular pattern. This lack of stable outlines gives scent a dreamlike quality and makes it impervious to linguistic descriptions (at least in prose). Multiple scents can fuse into the singular, recognizable as single elements and as an emergent whole that goes beyond the sum of its components. The scent of something, because of this open and unstable character, will often evoke other images and times. Hearn's incense-triggered recollection of Japan is a good example of this peculiarity: what is plural and separate under the profile of reality overlaps in a transspatial and transtemporal fashion, "freely abiding" (*jizai* 自在) within the "sur-real" (*chōrearu* 超レアル) atmosphere of incense, in a state of "non-obstruction" (*muge* 無礙), to borrow the formulations of Nishitani Keiji.[23]

Nioi: Japanese Synesthetic Consciousness

These preliminary observations can help us approach the first autochthonous notion of "scent" in Japanese culture, that of *nioi*—yet we immediately face a surprising fact. *Nioi* defies the absolute opposition of sight and olfaction active in a modern Eurocentric context. In its original uses, *nioi* meant both "color" and "scent," suggesting a paradigm of sensation in which the visual and the olfactory registers are not opposite realms but are rather appreciated as the unitary synesthetic field preceding the division of different senses.

A Blur of Scent and Color

The word *nioi* におい or *nihohi* にほひ, often also in the verbal form *nihohu* にほふ, is a staple of ancient Japanese descriptions of natural landscapes, seasonal feelings, and interpersonal encounters. Today, it is mostly written with the character 匂. The character 匂 is not an originally Chinese character, but a *kokuji*, one of the relatively few ideographs created in Japan. This is significant: it suggests that the notion of *nioi* was important enough to warrant the creation of a new and unique character. The indistinction between chromatic and olfactory in *nioi* was, therefore, due not to a lack of attention or sensitivity but to the necessity of expressing something radically different from an already long series of scent-related Chinese characters also welcomed in Japan. (See also Romaskiewicz's and Jia's contributions in this volume, and consider 香, 馨, 薫, 芳, 臭, 嗅.[24])

The character 匂 was formed by combining the radical 勹 and the right part of the character 韵 (韻) *in*, "resonance," "rhyme." The radical 勹 is found in other characters such as *tsutsumu* 包, "envelop," *ku* 勺, "poetic strophe," *shaku* 勺, "scoop," and *nakare* 勿, an ideograph that acquired the sense of "negation" from the original one of "blur": it represented a colored flag becoming indistinct in the movement of wind, warding off evil presences. This spiritual, shamanic sense is, according to Tada, also present in the word *nihofu* itself. The Chinese characters associated with the sound *ni* was 丹, referring to the rich, warm color of red earth, and visually, *nihou* was often associated with red flowers and leaves. Red things were thought to be vessels of supernatural spiritual energy, as is still evident in bright-red Shintō architecture.[25] The *ho* could express "standing out" (秀), or the *hofu* could come from *hafu* 這ふ "expanding." Typical of the dynamogenic, penetrating effect of red-yellows is indeed their tendency to engulf and stimulate the observer as an actual force. Goethe described this effect of red in his *Zur Farbenlehre*: "The active side is here in its highest energy, and it is not to be wondered that impetuous, robust, uneducated men, should be especially pleased with this colour. Among savage nations the inclination for it has been universally remarked, and when children, left to themselves, begin to use tints, they never spare vermilion and minium. . . . In looking steadfastly at a perfect yellow-red surface, the colour seems actually to penetrate the organ."[26]

This association between color and the primitive, infantile, or feminine is another common feature of Orientalism, a manifestation of Western "chromophobia."[27] But even while decrying its primitive, almost demonic effect ("Red cloth disturbs and enrages animals. I have known men of education to whom its effect was intolerable"), Goethe recognized that, phenomenologically, the radiance of color is not an external phenomenon but a "world-place"[28] prior to the absolute division between subject and object. Defining this tendency as "primitive," without examining its internal logic, is, however, an epistemic oversight. As Uchino points out, "In ancient times people would basically take in the stimulus of the external world a total sensation. . . . [T]his does not show the unclarity of their perception, its numbness. On the contrary, we can say that their perception was actually keener than that of us moderns."[29]

Nioi was meant to express an environing presence, something equally perceived as color and scent, the general resonance between things before their division and categorization into distinct senses. It is not some precise perception datum *within* the scheme of five separated senses (noema) but a (noetic) *style* of perception that allows them to resonate and overlap: "In the distant past *nioi* originally belonged to a field in which what related to sight [*shikakutekina mono* 視覚的なもの] and what related to olfaction [*kyū-kakutekina mono*嗅覚的なもの] could not be divided. *Nioi* was not an event unfolding in a neatly distinct, objectified world but one arising in the chaotic world that comes before such a division. Is not the joy of scent the joy of being enveloped by the world, the joy of the primordial unity with the world?"[30]

We can see an expression of this deep, unitary feeling—which, due to its chaotic nature, can be both joyful and disturbing—in one of the most quoted lines of Japanese literature:

色は匂へど散りぬるを我が世誰そ常ならむ有為の奥山今日越えて浅き夢見じ酔ひもせず

Iro wa nioedo chirinuru o wa ga yo dare zo—Tsune naramu ui no okuyama kyō koete asaki yume miji ei mo sezu

Colors are fragrant, and yet
they will all scatter:
who in this world
is eternal?
The deep mountains of karma
we will cross today
without getting lost
in shallow dreams.

This is a poem using—just once each—all the *kana* of the Japanese sylla-bary, traditionally attributed to Kūkai and still used as syllabic equivalent of the alphabet. A literal translation of its first verse, *iro wa nioedo*, is almost impossible. *Iro* is another complex manifold of meanings: it is "color," espe-cially that of flowers, but also the beauty of phenomena, sensual desire and passions, and in a Buddhist context, it can refer to the totality of the phenome-nic world.[31] Here the worldly manifestation of *iro* expands itself into *nioi*, a process that is at the same time fragrance, radiance, and disappearance.

In which sense are colors *nioi*? Is not color a mere visual property of an object? Phenomenologically, and to the empathetic understanding of natu-ral phenomena typical of Japanese poetics, the answer is no. Colors are not stable, like visually abstracted forms. They are the concrete, qualitative mode of manifestation, constantly shifting in different conditions of light and atmosphere: "Color breaks open the forms and the unity of phenomena from the inside, it exposes itself within the world."[32] The color of flowers is not the property of a surface, the static, passive layer over an object that modern European philosophy considered a "secondary quality." Acknowledged as *nioi*, it is active "radiance" and "fragrance," a force expanding itself into atmosphere and into one's feeling body: a word like "aura," referring at the same time to light and to air, to a worldly atmosphere and to its incorporation as breathing, is perhaps the closest to *nioi* in European languages.[33]

Impermanence and Nostalgia

While stable forms can be easily thought of as independent from our engagement with the world, neither the radiance of color nor the halo of scent suggests such separation: they coincide with a nebulous field of embodied existence. Another distinctive trait of the chromatic-olfactory elements of *nioi* is thus also their impermanence. In *nioi*, this general rule of existence becomes evident; the beauty of vibrant life is often surrounded by a halo of sadness:

ちるとみて又さく花の匂ひにもおくれさきたつためし有りけり
*Chiru to mite mata saku hana no niohi ni mo okure saki tatsu
tameshi arikeri*

About to fall
or still blooming:
in the fragrance of flowers
we feel once again
that all is impermanent.
(Saigyō, *Sankashū* 772)

秋の菊 にほふかぎりはかざしてむ花よりさきと知らぬわが身を
*Kiku no ka nihofu kagiri wa kazashitemu hana yori saki to shiranu
waga mi o*

An autumn chrysanthemum
still fresh and fragrant
will go on my hat
Who knows if my life will
last less than this flower.

(Ki no Tsurayuki, *Kokinshū* 277)

While, on the one hand, *nioi* is an impermanent experience, always connected to specific moments and interactions, on the other this atmospheric color-scent is able to seep and linger into bodies and spaces:

引馬野ににほふ榛原入り乱れ衣にほはせ旅のしるしに
Hikuma no ni nihofu haibara irimidare koromo ni niowasete tabi no shirushi ni

In the fields of Hikuma
through bright hazel plains
keep wandering
till their sheen will seep in your vest
a sign of your journey.
(*Man'yōshū*, 1–57)

Hazel fruits and bark were used as a black-brown tincture,[34] but in this case, the intransitive *nihofu* and the transitive *nihowase* directly refer to the bright yellow of leaves, which lingers and remains suffused on the robes of the traveler. What remains after "confusing oneself into" nature—*irimidare* has this sense of a chaotic movement, a blur—is the "air" of those places, a mood: ineffable, unique, emotionally charged like travel itself.[35] If *nioi* is considered an atmospheric experience—here this expression is metaphorical—but in many other *waka*, what seeps into the fabric of clothing is *nioi* as perfume, the particular coexistence of fleeting and lingering that we can refer to as "permanescent."

散るとみてあるべきものを梅の花うたてにほいの袖にとまれる
Chiru to mite aru beki mono o ume no hana utate nihoi no sode ni tomareru

Without regrets
I watch the fall
of plum blossoms
but how painful is their scent
lingering on my sleeves.
(Sosei *Kokinshū* 47)

折りつれば袖こそにほへ梅の花有りとやここにうぐひすのなく
Ori tsureba sode koso nihoe ume no hana ari to ya koko ni uguisu
no naku

Plucking an armful
on my sleeves lingered
the scent of plum blossoms
A bush warbler sings
wondering if they're here.
(*Kokinshū*, 32)

Nioi as Embodiment

The common stress on sleeves and scent in old Japanese sources warrants
further reflection. In the modern, European discourse on olfaction, the deodorization of the human body is a precarious balance between the artificiality of
perfumes and the primitive, erotic aggression of body odors, which have to be
kept in check in civilized society. (In relation to concepts of filth and sexual
repression, see also McClelland in this volume.) The ideal is therefore that of
an odorless, self-enclosed body, coinciding with the somatic volume of *Körper*
(the body qua object). But, as shown by Rajyashree Pandey, in ancient Japan,
bodies were rather perceived as open texts, whose salient features were not
full and stable traits but their liminal, expressive textures, such as "tangled
hair" and "perfumed sleeves." *Nioi*, as the general and recognizable style of
someone's presence, their atmospheric expansion in time and space, was in
many ways more relevant than flesh and bones. We read in *Genji monogatari* of two lovers exchanging robes to affirm an intermingling of perfumes
more significant and powerful than sex itself: "How could the fragrance
attached to his incomparable robes not transfer itself and dye her thoughts
and feelings as well?"[36]

Even when the body of the other was apprehended visually, what was
conceived to be beautiful was not its stable shape but the shifting emotions
coloring it in single instants. The eroticism of *nioi* was characterized by an
open presence, a reciprocal permeation of spaces, objects, bodies, and subjec-
tivities.[37] "Body and clothing are metonymically linked to one another in a
relationship that is marked by contiguity, proximity, and association, each
taking on the characteristics of the other. The distinct odors of the body transfer themselves to and mingle with perfumed robes. All the senses—haptic,

visual, and olfactory—are involved in experiencing clothes, not as dead objects but rather as living entities, suffused with the essence of the one to whom they belong, and it is this link with the loved one that gives them the power to produce desire and affective intensity."[38]

By this sensibility, there is no absolute division between embodied existence and the world but rather a porous interface inhabited by perfumes. Not only does this atmospheric body absorb the *nioi* of the external world, but the scent seeps into objects or spaces holding something essential of it, a kind of "spirit" (*tama*), even when the original is gone.

From *Nioi* to *Ka*: Metonymy and Metaphor

I have stressed how *nioi* is a visual-olfactory experience, presenting an atmosphere before its division into different modes of sense. But there are two fundamental aspects in the phenomenology of scent. The first one, as we have seen, is this "condensation"—the atmospheric totality of a trip or of an erotic meeting is expressed as a whole in olfaction. A scent can therefore be "erotic," "melancholic," "vibrant," and so on. When separate things float together as *nioi*, heterogeneous elements of reality are held together as "mutual metaphors."[39] But scents can also be "transferred," show a tendency to freely float, announce and signify something by expanding their most subtle aspect (the "essence" *sei* 精) beyond their actual presence, both in time and in space. Notoriously impervious to analytical language, scents can be talked about only through the *like* of metaphor and simile ("There are perfumes fresh like the skin of infants / Sweet like oboes, green like prairies," writes Baudelaire) and the *of* of metonymy (the scent *of* plum blossoms, *of* wood, *of* incense), which says nothing about the scent itself but rather points to the possible origin of its *ekstasis*. Scents may be possible, or even imaginary: often a scent can suggest something that will remain unseen, absent, visually unrevealing like incense.

Jakobson described the metaphorical and metonymic (syntagmatic) axes as the two fundamental operations of language: we can see how scent, far from being a totally nonlinguistic sense, as Kant disparagingly remarked, shows both these processes at work in their original form of tropes. Scent should be therefore considered not antilinguistic but rather "prelinguistic," not simply in terms or antecedence but in that of constitution.[40] This poetic, genetic function of metaphor and metonymy has been described by Lacan as that of *condensation* (*Verdichtung*) and *displacement* (*Verschiebung*): the two key operations of unconscious.[41] Freud himself, for his part, had already noted how the way in which a smell can announce itself even after its originating object is gone, has disappeared, or has been hidden marks a structural similarity with the unconscious.[42]

If we turn to premodern Japanese sources, we can see that this distinction between condensation/metaphor and displacement/metonymy is drawn with great acuity through the differentiation between *nioi* and *ka*, a Japanese word associated with the sinograph 香 (see Jia in this volume). According to Kōda Rohan, the sound *ka* often indicated some kind of subtle, spiritual effect at distance: like the oldest readings of *ki/ke* 気, it was something spiritual and invisible lingering in the air, which would be breathed in and have physical or emotional effects.[43] The word *kaori* 香居り, now used as "perfume," literally means "there is *ka*," and thus originally pointed to the presence of this invisible power in the air.[44] While *nioi* refers to a deep metaphorical unity between subject-object and different sense modes, *ka* describes the displacing effect of scents, their floating beyond what is "present" in a spatial and, even more remarkably, temporal sense. There is a certain overlap between the two notions (the aforementioned "permanescence"), but if we look at poems stressing emanation and temporal depth, it is *ka* that appears more often:

> 色よりも香こそあはれとおもほゆれたが袖ふれしやどの梅ぞも
> *Hana yori mo ka koso aware to omohoyure taga sode fureshi ya dono ume zo mo*
>
> More than the color of flowers
> it is their perfume
> that fills me with longing:
> whose sleeves have touched
> the plums near my house?
> (*Kokinshū* 33)

> 五月待つ花橘の香をかげば昔の人の袖の香ぞする
> *Satsuki matsu hana Tachibana no ka o kageba mukashi no hito no sode no ka zo suru*
>
> Waiting July
> when I will breathe in

the flowers of tangerine
the perfume on the sleeves
of someone long gone.
(Kokinshū 139)

Scent bears a unique connection to time and nostalgia: no other sense mode can suggest so clearly ghosts and absence, holding a fleeting moment alive within a noncontinuous temporality. In European literature, this repetition of the past in olfactory memory is most famously associated with the iconic *madeleine* episode opening Proust's *Recherche*.[45] In Japan, as in China (see Qian Jia's chapter) or Korea, the temporal quality of scents is a mainstay of poetry and has been an aesthetic expression since antiquity. In particular, the flowers of *tachibana*, wild mandarin, are connected to an indefinite past lived again through olfactory perception.[46] But the displacing quality of 香 is also the point at which scent is not anymore something simply natural and can become an artistic object.

Japanese Traditions of Fragrances

Besides *ka*, the other reading of the ideograph 香 is in fact *kō*, "incense." The two readings of the same character thus refer to both the effect in the air and to the physical object from which it emanates. There are *ka* of many things, among which natural substances, but *kō* refers to odorants as objects that have been selected and refined and have thus become artified, if not artificial. While in Europe, the main object of scent craftsmanship in a nonreligious context was perfumery—that is, the appliance of artificial scent to human bodies—in Japan, olfactory art was chiefly meant as production of a common atmosphere.[47] Even within the wider context of East Asia, olfactory arts in Japan have assumed unique shapes, up to the flourishing of *kōdō* during the Edo period (1603–1868), a world-unique example of a formalized art experience based on the sense of olfaction.

Incense

The word "incense," referring to many kinds of burned odorants, is vague. But this ambivalence is also significant as an effect of the metaphorical-metonymical relationship between language and olfaction that we have described. While many odors will evoke a specific source in image, "incense" and 香 are relatively open signifiers, revealing almost nothing of their components in their nondescript visual forms. Hearn, in his atmospheric reminiscence of Japan quoted at the beginning of this essay, perceived incense as a transtemporal landscape, the cultural object within which the variety of places and sights met through his stay in Japan could be held together in transcendental unity. Incense presents us with this paradox: it is an artistic object that is never meant to be appreciated in its physical presence (its being, *u* 有) but, ironically, has to be destroyed and consumed to become "non-being" (*mu* 無), an open-ended sensual field that unfolds with its mood, hues, images. We might say that incenses are metaphors in a physical state.

Another peculiarity of incenses is their existing on the threshold between natural and artificial. The odorants used to craft incense are of organic origin, but they are not strictly natural substances: they are often mixed, refined, diffused through indirect or direct burning, typically indoors. On the one hand, incense aesthetics cannot be defined as a simple appreciation of natural beauty, given how these substances are subject to manipulation, concentration, and removal from their original habitats, often traveling huge distances. On the other hand, it is also hard to include incense among fine arts as well: if we compare the use of fragrances to the role of stone in sculpture or that of pigments in painting, we see that the latter become the material components of newly created forms, while the lack of any stable formal construction keeps olfactory aesthetics closer to its hyletic aspect.

Even if we restrict our inspection of "incense" to Japan, we find many varieties of it. Today, one can find incense as powder or pressed in shapes, as sticks, spirals, in satchels, or, more rarely, pellets (*nerikō* 練香): these products are generally mixtures of different odorants, ranging widely in cost, quality, innovation, and creative research. But the word 香 *kō*, "incense," is also used as shorthand for *jinkō* 沈香 (aloeswood, agarwood, oud), the rare natural material used in pure form within *kōdō*, the "way of incense." *Jinkō* is the result of a complex and still not completely understood process involving aloeswood (*Aquilaria*). When a branch of this tropical tree is damaged or falls to the ground, the combination of resin secretions and of a specific microbiome in hot, humid regions of Southeast Asia transforms the aloeswood (light and nonodorous) into *jinkō*, a much heavier, darker material that emits a rich, complex scent. *Jinkō* is currently one of the most expensive natural substances of the world, and *Aquilaria* trees face severe depletion because of increasing demand. Given the great commercial value of *jinkō*, there have been many attempts to create *jinkō* through human intervention: any trained incense expert will recognize an artificial one, however, due to its lack of character. There are also other aromatic woods or materials sometimes used in a pure form, like sandal or camphor, but they do not have the same aesthetic value of *jinkō* and are therefore not used in *kōdō*.

Buddhist Perfumes

If we look at incense not simply as an object but as part of a life-form and of Japanese history, we must first of all understand its inextricable connection to Buddhism. While olfactory, atmospheric sensitivity characterized ancient Japanese culture in general, incense was a foreign product, which reached Japan shrouded in this religious aura. Today, there is still an important distinction between the incense offered in a Buddhist context (*kyōkō* 供香), that burned in daily life, and that appreciated in the crafted environment of incense ceremony. Historically, the first one holds precedence over the other two.

Jinkō entered Japan with Buddhism, in the sixth century, as an exotic material (Japan does not produce aloeswood) associated with the foreign religion. In a mythical episode from 595, described in the *Nihon shoki*, a big branch of *jinkō* floated up to the coast of Awaji. When the local fishermen used the driftwood to light a fire, they were shocked by the heavenly scent arising from the flames. They therefore offered the piece of wood to the Empress Suiko, who immediately recognized its origin thanks to her acquaintance with Buddhist rituals.[48] To this day, incense and Buddhism are strongly related: while in Shintō there is a stress on ritual purity, but usually no odorants are offered, Buddhist temples are surrounded by clouds of incense. Huge metal censers are used to burn incense sticks along the main passage of the temple, and pilgrims inhale the smoke and let it impregnate their clothes during their visit.

One of the great historical functions of incense and odorants has been the crafting and strengthening of religious atmospheres; from this perspective, neither Buddhism nor Japan are exceptional. Rare and precious substances referred to as "incense" played an important role in the history of Hebraism and Christianity as well, despite a sometimes ambivalent attitude. (See also McClelland in this volume. Leviticus 16:12 prescribes perfume offerings; Isaiah 66:3 compares them to idolatry.) The passage from materiality to immateriality that characterizes incense and scent makes scents powerful agents of sublimation, and an interreligious study of odorants, from hallucinogenic smokes to frankincense in churches, is a valid line of inquiry.[49] In the case of Mahayana Buddhism, however, with its stress on impermanence, emptiness, and the interconnection of phenomena, there is an adherence between olfactory perception and doctrinal content that does not characterize theistic religions (outside of their mystic traditions, at least).

In the tenth section of the *Vimalakīrti Sūtra* (維摩経 Jp. *Yuimakyō*), the layman Vimalakīrti, to illustrate to his audience a standpoint of nondualism going beyond conventional language, sends his emanation to Sarvagandha-sugandha (衆香国 *Shūkōkoku*, "Land of Omnipresent Perfume"), a faraway world under the protection of the Buddha Sugandhakuta (香積如来 *Kōshaku Nyorai*, "Buddha of Gathered Perfume") where "the houses, the avenues, the parks, and the palaces are made of various perfumes, and the fragrance of the food eaten by those bodhisattvas pervades immeasurable universes." Bringing back some of the miraculous food of that land, he is accompanied by a host of bodhisattvas. The whole city is filled with perfume; the fragrant hosts are made to sit on "ninety million lion thrones," which miraculously fit in one room; and Vimalakīrti is able to satiate everyone with a small morsel of the fragrant meal.[50] When an earthen guest asks these perfumed beings how Dharma is taught in their holy land, they answer, "The Tathāgata does not teach the Dharma by means of sound and language. He disciplines the bodhisattvas only by means of perfumes. At the foot of each perfume-tree sits a bodhisattva, and the trees emit perfumes like this one. From the moment they smell that perfume, the bodhisattvas attain the concentration called 'source of all bodhisattva-virtues.'"[51]

This visionary style is typical of Mahayana sutras, but here the erasure of boundaries and distances produced by perfume is used to illustrate a mode of consciousness close to the heart of Buddhist teaching. What sight and our sense of reality would consider distant (the pure land and this world), mutually obstructive (the bodies of the congregation), or fixed and exhaustible (food), once transfigured into perfume is revealed to be a transcendent "here-yonder," nonobstructive, and endless. Language, the strongest paradigm of division, is surpassed by the nondual permeation of perfume. It is significant how in East Asian Buddhism a metaphor of perfume was used to represent also the fundamental relationship between action and karma, which was described as *kunjū* 薫習, seeping through the self as perfume would a fabric.[52] This surpassing of duality in olfactory experience is well expressed in another Buddhist source, the Chinese encyclopedia *Fayuan Zhulin* 法苑珠林. Another legendary perfume of enlightenment is described, and a single line summarizes its effects: once breathed in, "one will cease to distinguish self and other, and thus begin to teach the Dharma."[53]

Listening to Scents: From *Takimono* to *Kōdō*

While the introduction of incense coincides with Buddhist ritual, the aristocratic society of the Heian court quickly developed an interest in incense also outside of a religious context. We have seen through poetic examples how deeply ancient Japanese aristocrats were attuned to olfactory stimuli and ambiances: the sensual quality of this involvement was not in contrast to the vertical transcendence of its religious use but rather complemented it as a horizontal involvement with nature and others through the creation of socially shared atmospheres.

The major incense tradition of Heian period was that of *takimonoawase*, revolving not around pure *kō* but on *nerikō*, pellets obtained mixing different odorants, a use originally imported from Tang China. As reported in a well-known chapter of *Genji monogatari*, "Plum Branch," Heian aristocrats would gather and organize contests of this fragrance making.[54] While individual recipes would vary, and were often family secrets doubling as proof of status, there were six main categories of *takimono*, each associated with a season and a mood: *baika* 梅花, "plum blossoms"; *kayō* 荷葉, "lotus leaves"; *rakuyō* 落葉, "fallen leaves"; *jijū* 侍従, "chamberlain"; *kikka* 菊花, "chrysanthemum"; and *kurobō* 黒方, "black." Even when names of actual plants were used, the relationship was metaphorical: each *takimono* was meant to suggest a specific atmosphere, a shared "field"[55] that included not only its represented object but also lingering emotional overtones.

With the beginning of the Kamakura (1185–333) and then the Muromachi (1336–573) period, the emergence of the warrior class led to a different approach to olfactory arts. The impermanence of perfume could be easily cast as a metaphor for life's fragility, and among *bushi* (the warrior class), the focus on *jinkō* became predominant. Its unadulterated simplicity allowed a more sober, virile approach to incense, while its scarcity and preciousness also made it a strong sign of status: a famous example is that of Dōyo Sasaki, a warrior-aesthete who once burned 600 grams of *jinkō* in a gesture expressing grandeur and nonattachment at the same time.[56] Two high-ranked retainers of the Ashikaga shogun, Sanetaka Sanjōnishi and Shino Sōshin, compiled a first compendium of *jinkō* types, and alongside more direct incense burnings, ludic forms of appreciation in which different types of *jinkō* had to be compared and recognized were gradually introduced. This is the first core of *kōdō*. Here we see a particular intersection of social meeting, in which the scent of incense becomes a focus of interpersonal attunement and a gamified process, in which the participants engage in friendly competition to recognize the correct pattern of the burned incenses. The surprising difficulty of this feat arises from the unavailability of scent to voluntary memory and linguistic descriptions as well as from the nuanced subtlety of *jinkō*.

While *kōdō* arose from within the highest echelons of warrior culture, its greatest flourishing occurred during the Edo period, as it became more popular among townspeople as well. This development pattern is paralleled by the two other Japanese "arts of everydayness," ikebana (*kadō*) and tea ceremony (*sadō*). The three are often considered together, as arts of proximity commonly influencing each other. They all happen indoors, in a cozy closeness in which the difference between both the performer and public, and the artistic object and performance, is practically erased. At their core is a unique aesthetic dialectic: taking everydayness, formalizing it into aesthetic patterns, and reintroducing them into the daily lives of practitioners.[57] Together with *haikai*, the other exemplary art of the Edo period, *kōdō* borrows from higher, older traditions (courtly, religious, and warrior aesthetics) to "perfume" the common everydayness of city life. One of the most popular *kōdō* formats emerging during the Edo period, the *Genjikō*, consists of identifying the recurring or new kinds of five consecutive incense burnings, tracing on paper vertical lines, and connecting them horizontally when the incenses are understood to be the same. The resulting fifty-two patterns, the *genjizu* 源氏図, are all named after chapters of the *Genji monogatari* (with the exception of the first and last): the nameless experience of scents is therefore expressed through the image of an old, perfumed literary world, bridging court and city across almost a thousand years of history (fig. 1.1). The resulting glyphs, with their highly decorative quality, can in turn be used as decorations on kimono, *ukiyo* illustrations, other *kōdō* tools, and so on. The seeping of perfume, as the essence of things past, here expands into visual culture: once a *genjizu* pattern is inscribed in a kimono, even an Edo-period courtesan, tea seller, or libertine can borrow the perfumed flair of a character of the Heian classic, in a reference game that is in part parody, in part genuine homage.

There are many different styles and kinds of *kōdō*, from simple sequences of three perfumes to ornate games involving decorated boards (*banmono*), which can transform the fragrance game into an archery competition, a horse race, a trip through Japan.[58] Compared to the flower arrangement art

帚木 Hōkigi	空蟬 Utsusemi	夕顔 Yūgao	若紫 Wakamurasaki	末摘花 Suetsumuhana	紅葉賀 Momijinoga	花宴 Hana no en
葵 Aoi	賢木 Sakaki	花散里 Hana chiru sato	須磨 Suma	明石 Akashi	澪標 Miotsukushi	蓬生 Yomogiu
関屋 Sekiya	絵合 Eawase	松風 Matsukaze	薄雲 Usugumo	朝顔 Asagao	乙女 Otome	玉鬘 Tamakazura
初音 Hatsune	胡蝶 Kochō	蛍 Hotaru	常夏 Tokonatsu	篝火 Kagaribi	野分 Nowaki	行幸 Miyuki
藤袴 Fujibakama	槇柱 Makibashira	梅枝 Umegae	藤裏葉 Fuji no uraba	若菜上 Wakana jō	若菜下 Wakana ge	柏木 Kashiwagi
横笛 Yokobue	鈴虫 Suzumushi	夕霧 Yūgiri	御法 Minori	幻 Maboroshi	匂宮 Nioumiya	紅梅 Kōbai
竹河 Takekawa	橋姫 Hashihime	椎本 Shiigamoto	総角 Agemaki	早蕨 Sawarabi	宿木 Yadorigi	東屋 Azumaya
浮舟 Ukifune	蜻蛉 Kagerō	手習 Tenarai				

of ikebana and the tea ceremony of *sadō*, *kōdō*'s expensive nature and the limited supply of its prime materials makes it far less practiced and studied outside of Japan. But the situation seems to be changing, at least academically, with the first comprehensive volumes on *kōdō* recently appearing in European languages.[59]

The participants of a *kōdō* session are "listening to the perfume" (*monkō* 聞香), an expression already found in Mahayana sutras.[60] If *nioi* is akin to the visual experience of color, the temporal and shapeless enjoyment of scent in *kōdō* is metaphorically close to that of music and natural sounds. Yamagata Hiroshi stressed how this listening is not simply nonlinguistic: rather, the experience of scent challenges our ordinary understanding of language and static things. The passive side of *kōdō* immediately corresponds to a transformative, performative one: "To name and articulate as language a non-articulated scent, we employ metaphor, we compose poetry, we transform into an object-body the scent/atmosphere (*nioi*) that lingers within the living subject: by transforming it into an object, we also face our effort to bring this scent towards expressive connection (*renshū* 連衆) and sharedness."[61]

Kōdō might be unique as the only codified olfactory art in world history; but it is a coherent expression of Japanese aesthetics at large, addressing what for Yamagata is its core concern: "The problem of an activity transforming the body into an expressive medium."[62] It is a mature fruit of a cultural tradition focused on, to borrow the words of Nishida Kitarō, "seeing the form of what is formless."[63]

Conclusion

This chapter has highlighted not only the extreme relevance of scents in Japanese culture but also how this relevance does not unfold within a single paradigm or context. A cross-cultural, interdisciplinary reflection on scent offers an important stepstone not only toward the "sensual turn" that is increasingly invoked across different fields of the humanities but also toward their general decolonization and interdisciplinary communication. A non-Eurocentric philosophy of scent reveals many hidden assumptions of the Eurocentric mindset. The modern, male, European and North American contempt for scents, of which I offered a short archaeology in the first sections, is a bias that should be addressed and dispelled if we want to experience scent as a rich, meaningful aspect of our world. This cultural-historical embeddedness also implies that a full recognition of scent *must* pass through an appreciation of otherness, in terms of an approach to the nonhuman (landscape, plants, animals), to other human beings within our immediate cultural surroundings, and to people and spaces that at first appear as distant and distinct from us. Scent is, in the most literal sense, "the other in us," not as an appropriation but as a process of open-ended hybridization of our bodies and selves. Scent, with its resistance to clear boundaries and its love for transference, is a "sense" in the two entwined meanings of the word: at once sensual and intellectual, a meaningful intersection of individuals and worlds.

Notes

1. Porteous, "Smellscape," 358; Shindo, *Nioi to kaori no bungakushi*, 91–92.

2. Hearn, *In Ghostly Japan*, 19–20.

3. Adachi, *Nioi no shinrigaku*, 3.

4. Plato, *Timaeus* 66d; Aristotle, *De anima* 421a.

5. Husserl, *Crisis of European Sciences*, 33.

6. Kern, *Anatomy and Destiny*, 46.

7. McClintock, "Soft-Soaping Empire," 304–16.

8. Tsuboi "Kaguwashiki tekusuto," 105.

9. Darwin, *Descent of Man*, 17.

10. Freud, *Standard Edition*, 100.

11. Said, *Orientalism*, 186–87.

12. Gibson, *Ecological Approach to Visual Perception*, 1, 72.

13. Yamagata, "Daisan kankaku," 82.

14. Tsuboi, "Kaguwashiki tekusuto."

15. Puccini, Giacosa, and Illica, *Madama Butterfly*, 58. I wish to thank Federica Scassillo for pointing out to me how the whole libretto of Butterfly systematically links the figure of Butterfly, and in general the atmosphere of her relationship with Pinkerton, to the scent of different flowers.

16. Kant, *Anthropology*, 50.

17. Schmitz, *New Phenomenology*, 56.

18. Ōhashi, *Kyōsei no patosu*, 180.

19. Turin, *Secret of Scent*, 14.

20. Nara and Kuki, *Structure of Detachment*, 17.

21. Kuki, *Kuki Shuzo zenshu*, 1:58–9.

22. Husserl, *Phantasy, Image Consciousness, and Memory*, 18.

23. See Nishitani et al., "Bashō kenkyū," 51. For a study of Nishitani's atmospheric take on imagination, its affinity with the notion of atmosphere, and its analogies with the phenomenology of scent, see also Nishitani, "Emptiness and Sameness," 179–217; Marinucci, "Images of Wind," 220–50.

24. Uchino, *Nihon o irodoru kaori no kioku*, 37.

25. Tada, "Kodaijin no kankaku," 18.

26. Goethe, *Theory of Colors*, 309–10.

27. Batchelor, *Chromophobia*.

28. Ōhashi, *Kyōsei no patosu*, 180.

29. Tada, "Kodaijin no kankaku," 19.

30. Adachi, *Nioi no shinrigaku*, 50.

31. Marinucci, "Iro," 193–226.

32. Ogawa, *Phenomenology of Wind and Atmosphere*, 23.

33. Uchino, *Nihon o irodoru kaori*, 45.

34. Tada, *Kodaijin no kankaku*, 17.

35. Tada also notes how the *manyōgana* (Chinese characters with a strictly phonetic value pre-dating *hiragana* syllabic script) for the word *tabi*, "travel," are 多鼻, "many noses," a highly unconventional way to represent these two syllables. Tada, *Kodaijin no kankaku*, 17.

36. Pandey, *Perfumed Sleeves*, 41.

37. Ibid., 43.

38. Ibid., 37.

39. Shirane, "Matsuo Bashō," 82.

40. Yamagata, "Daisan kankaku," 64.

41. Grigg, *Lacan, Language, and Philosophy*, 151.

42. Freud, *Complete Letters*, 280.

43. Kōda, *Rohan zenshū*, 19:476–77.

44. Ibid., 19:481.

45. Gilbert, *What the Nose Knows*, 209.

46. Ōtani, "Mukashi no hito," 77.

47. Sekiguchi, *Nioi kaori zen*, 19.

48. Aston, *Nihongi*, 123.

49. See, for instance, Harvey, "St. Ephrem," 109–28; Habkirk and Chang "Scents, Community, and Incense," 156–74; Pickett, "Idolatrous Nose," 19–39.

50. Thurman, *Holy Teaching of Vimalakīrti*, 80–81.

51. Ibid., 81.

52. Ōhashi, "On the Idea of the Aesthetics," 61–72.

53. Ariga, *Kō to Bukkyō*, 19.

54. Gatten, "Wisp of Smoke," 36.

55. Uchino, *Nihon o irodoru kaori*, 59.

56. Boudonnat and Kushizaki, *Voie de l'encens*, 25.

57. Geijitsushi, *Nihon no koden geinō*, 8.

58. Gatten, "Wisp of Smoke"; Voytishek, "Historical and Ethnological Analysis," 122–32.

59. Vogel, *Erleben mit allen Sinnen*; Jaquet, *Philosophie du kôdô*.

60. Ariga, *Kō to Bukkyō*, 187.

61. Yamagata, "Daisan kankaku," 67.

62. Ibid.

63. Uehara, "Japanese Aspects of Nishida's Basho," 153.

Bibliography

Adachi, Hiroshi 足立博. *Nioi no shinrigaku* 匂いの心理学. Tokyo: Kōbundō, 1995.

Ariga, Yōen 有賀要延. *Kō to Bukkyō* 香と仏教. Tokyo: Kokusho Kankōkai, 1990.

Aston, William George. *Nihongi: Chronicles of Japan from the Earliest Times to A.D. 697*. Vol. 2. London: Allen and Unwin, 1986.

Batchelor, David. *Chromophobia*. London: Reaktion, 2007.

Boudonnat, Louise, and Harumi Kushizaki. *La voie de l'encens*. Arles: Picquier, 2000.

Corbin, Alain. *The Foul and the Fragrant Odor and the French Social imagination*. Cambridge, MA: Harvard University Press, 1982.

Darwin, Charles. *The Descent of Man: Selection in Relation to Sex*. London: John Murray, 1896.

Freud, Sigmund. *The Complete Letters of Sigmund Freud to Wilhelm Fliess, 1877–1904*. Translated by Jeffrey M. Masson. Cambridge, MA: Harvard University Press, 1985.

———. *The Standard Edition of the Complete Psychological Works of Sigmund Freud*. Vol. 21, (*1927–1931*). Translated by James Strachey. London: Hogarth, 1964.

Gatten, Aileen. "A Wisp of Smoke. Scent and Character in The Tale of Genji." *Monumenta Nipponica* 32, no. 1 (Spring 1977): 35–48.

Geijitsushi Kenkyūkai. 芸術史研究会. *Nihon no koden geinō 5 cha—ka—kō* 日本の古典芸能〈5〉茶・花・香. Tokyo: Heibonsha, 1970.

Gibson, James Jerome. *The Ecological Approach to Visual Perception*. Hillsdale, NJ: L. Erlbaum, 1986.

Gilbert, Avery N. *What the Nose Knows: The Science of Scent in Everyday Life*. New York: Crown, 2008.

Goethe, Johann Wolfgang von. *Theory of Colors*. Translated by Charles L. Eastlake. Cambridge, MA: MIT Press, 1970.

Grigg, Russell. *Lacan, Language, and Philosophy*. Albany: State University of New York Press, 2008.

Habkirk, Scott, and Hsun Chang. "Scents, Community, and Incense in Traditional Chinese Religion." *Material Religion* 13, no. 2 (2017): 156–74.

Harvey, Susan Ashbrook. "St. Ephrem on the Scent of Salvation." *Journal of Theological Studies, New Series*, 49, no. 1 (1998): 109–28.

Hearn, Lafcadio. *In Ghostly Japan*. Boston: Little, Brown, 1899.

Husserl, Edmund. *The Crisis of European Sciences and Transcendental Phenomenology*. Translated by David Carr. Evanston: Northwestern University Press, 1970.

———. *Phantasy, Image Consciousness, and Memory (1898–1925)*. Translated by John B. Brough. Dordrecht: Springer, 2005.

Jaquet, Chantal. *Philosophie du kôdô: L'esthétique japonaise des fragrances.* Paris: Vrin, 2018.

Kant, Immanuel. *Anthropology from a Pragmatic Point of View.* Edited by Robert Lauden with an introduction by Manfred Kuehn. Cambridge: Cambridge University Press, 2006.

Kern, Stephen. *Anatomy and Destiny: A Cultural History of the Human Body.* Indianapolis: Bobbs-Merrill, 1975.

Kōda, Rohan, *Rōhan Zenshū* 露伴全集. 41 vols. Tokyo: Iwanami Shoten, 1978–80.

Kuki, Shūzō, *Kuki Shūzō Zenshū* 九鬼周造全集. 12 vols. Tokyo: Iwanami Shoten, 1990.

Marinucci, Lorenzo. "Images of Wind: A Japanese Phenomenology of Imagination as Air." In *Übergänge—Transitions—移り渉り: Crossing the Boundaries in Japanese Philosophy,* edited by Francesca Greco, Leon Krings, and Yukiko Kuwayama, 220–50. Frontiers of Japanese Philosophy 10. Nagoya: Chisokudō, 2021.

———. "Iro: A Phenomenology of Color and Desire." *European Journal of Japanese Philosophy* 5 (2020): 193–226.

McClintock, Anne. "Soft-Soaping Empire." In *The Body: A Reader,* edited by Mariam Fraser and Monica Greco, 304–16. New York: Routledge, 2004.

Nara, Hiroshi, and Shūzō Kuki. *The Structure of Detachment: The Aesthetic Vision of Kuki Shūzō,* with a translation of Iki no Kōzō. Honolulu: University of Hawai'i Press, 2004.

Nishitani, Keiji 西谷啓治, et al. "Bashō kenkyū" 芭蕉研究. *Gakkai 学海*₃, nos. 1–4 (1945).

———. "Emptiness and Sameness." In *Modern Japanese Aesthetics: A Reader,* edited by Michael Marra, 179–217. Honolulu: University of Hawai'i Press, 2000.

Ogawa, Tadashi. *Phenomenology of Wind and Atmosphere.* Translated and edited by Lorenzo Marinucci. Milan: Mimesis International, 2021.

Ōhashi, Ryōsuke 大橋良介. *Kyōsei no patosu: Konpashiōn hi no genshōgaku* 共生のパトス：コンパシオーン

(悲)の現象学. Tokyo: Kobushishobō, 2018.

———. "On the Idea of the Aesthetics of Scent-Transmission (*Kunjû*) According to the Tea-Ceremony in Japan." *Associazione Italiana per gli Studi di Estetica* 6 (1998): 61–72.

Ōtani, Masao. 大谷雅夫. "Mukashi no hito no sode no ka zo suru" 昔の人の袖の香ぞする. *Bungaku* 5, no. 5 (September 2004): 2–15.

Pandey, Rajyashree. *Perfumed Sleeves and Tangled Hair: Body, Woman, and Desire in Medieval Japanese Narratives.* Honolulu: University of Hawai'i Press, 2017.

Pickett, Holly Crawford. "The Idolatrous Nose: Incense on the Early Modern Stage." In *Religion and Drama in Early Modern England: The Performance of Religion on the Renaissance Stage,* edited by Jane Hwang Degenhardt and Elizabeth Williamson, 19–39. Farnham: Ashgate, 2011.

Porteous, J. Douglas. "Smellscape." *Progress in Physical Geography: Earth and Environment* 9, no. 3 (1985): 356–78.

Puccini, Giacomo, Giuseppe Giacosa, and Luigi Illica. *Madama Butterfly: Tragedia giapponese in due atti.* Venice: Fondazione Teatro La Fenice di Venezia, 2012.

Said, Edward W. *Orientalism.* New York: Random House, 1979.

Schmitz, Hermann. *New Phenomenology: A Brief Introduction.* Translated by Rudolf Owen Müllan. Milan: Mimesis International, 2019.

Sekiguchi, Shindai. 関口真大. *Nioi, kaori, zen: Tōyō no chie* 匂い・香り・禅：東洋人の知恵. Tokyo: Nichibō Shuppansha,1972.

Shindo, Masahiro. 真銅正宏. *Nioi to Kaori no Bungakushi* 匂いと香りの文学誌. Tokyo: Shun'yōdōshoten, 2019.

Shirane, Haruo. "Matsuo Bashō and the Poetics of Scent." *Harvard Journal of Asiatic Studies* 52, no. 1 (June 1992): 77–110.

Tada, Kazuomi. 多田一臣. "Kodaijin no kankaku: Nihofu no chikara kara" 古代人の感覚—ニホフと力から.

Bungaku 5, no. 5 (September 2004): 16–22.

Thurman, Robert A. F. *The Holy Teaching of Vimalakīrti: A Mahāyāna Scripture.* University Park: Pennsylvania State University Press, 1976.

Tsuboi, Hideo. 坪井 秀人. "Kaguwashiki tekusuto: Kindai no shintai to kyū-kaku hyōshō" かぐはしきテクスト—近代の身体と嗅覚表象. *Bungaku* 5, no. 5 (September 2004): 30–52.

Turin, Luca. *The Secret of Scent: Adventures in Perfume and the Science of Smell.* London: Faber and Faber, 2006.

Uchino, Hana. 内野花. *Nihon o irodoru kaori no kioku* 日本を彩る香りの記憶. Suita-shi: Ōsaka Daigaku Shuppankai, 2019.

Uehara, Mayuko. "Japanese Aspects of Nishida's Basho: Seeing the 'Form Without Form.'" In *Frontiers of Japanese Philosophy 4: Facing the 21st Century,* edited by Wing Keung Lam and Ching Yuen Cheung, 152–64. Nagoya: Nanzan Institute for Religion and Culture, 2009.

Vogel, Benedikt. *Erleben mit allen Sinnen Inszenierung von Duft und Ästhetik in den Traktaten zur Duft-Kunst des frühneuzeitlichen Japan.* Munich: Iudicium, 2019.

Voytishek, Elena E. 2008. "A Historical and Ethnological Analysis of Intellectual Play in the Japanese Art of Incense Blending: The Banmono Board Play." *Archaeology, Ethnology and Anthropology of Eurasia* 34, no. 2 (June 2008): 122–32.

Yamagata, Hiroshi. 山県 熙. "Daisan kankaku: Nioi no bigaku no tame ni" 第3感覚＝匂いの美学のために. *Shisō* 824 (February 1993): 58–71.

——— 山県 熙. "Nioi no bigaku: Sairon" 「匂いの美学」再論. *Bungaku* 5, no. 5 (September 2004): 76–88.

CHAPTER 2

The Shifting Smellscape of Early Medieval China

Emperor Wu's Strange Aromatics

Peter Romaskiewicz

In the first decade of the twelfth century, the Northern Song (960–1127) literatus Hong Chu 洪芻 (1066–ca. 1127) had begun in earnest to compile his specialized treatise on incense, perfume, and aromatics in a work known today as the *Materia Aromatica* (*Xiang pu* 香譜). While not the progenitor of the genre, the *Materia Aromatica* is widely considered to be the earliest extant Chinese work of its kind. In its current form, Hong Chu's treatise comprises four chapters: aromatic products, strange aromatics, affairs of aromatics, and aromatic recipes.[1] The focus of our examination will be on the second chapter, which catalogs thirty-eight anomalous aromatics and odd odors drawn principally from older works often categorized as tales of the strange (*zhiguai* 志怪). The tales of the strange genre first flourished during the Six Dynasties (220–589), and many of these stories took shape as records of strange customs, marvelous flora and fauna, and other odd phenomena concerning ghosts and spirits.[2] By incorporating these anecdotes into his specialized work on aromatics, Hong Chu added a fascinating layer of cultural lore into a treatise that also doubled as a utilitarian manual for identifying raw aromatic materials and directions on blending perfumes and incense. A close reading of the thirty-eight entries in the second chapter reveals that one individual was more often associated with these anomalous aromatics, approximately one quarter of the total, than any other figure: Emperor Wu 武 (r. 157–87 BCE) of the Western Han (202 BCE–9 CE).

The appearance of a definable discourse on strange aromatics, around which Hong Chu could devote an entire chapter, was at the confluence of two historical trends. First, during the period of the Six Dynasties, there was a tendency to use Emperor Wu as a lens to explore the exotic and marvelous.[3] This was justified not only by his fame as a flamboyant ruler of critical historical importance but also by his territorial expansion into regions outside the immediate sphere of Chinese cultural influence. If we add to this list of qualities Emperor Wu's documented proclivities for dabbling in the occult, we can find the motivational foundations for the accretion of legends to his name under the guise of tales of the strange. The early medieval lore of Emperor Wu presented him as someone with dominion over the margins of the world and who had access to the wealth and power those regions represented. One of the signs of this access was Emperor Wu's collection of novel aromatics, some of which possessed supermundane powers, such as the ability to cure the sick or revive the dead. Since many of the earliest and most colorful reports of strange aromatics appear in these legends of Emperor Wu, his literary personage should be seen as crucial in establishing anomalous odors as a recurring trope within the strange tales genre in the following centuries.

Second, these fictive stories of strange aromatics were stabilized by the real-world growth of foreign tribute and trade in exotic commodities. For many of the Song (960–1279) and post-Song scholars who compiled specialized works on incense, perfumes, spices, and drugs—all of which fall under the Chinese taxon of "aromatics" (xiang 香 or xiangyao 香藥)—the Han dynasty (202 BCE–220 CE) was envisioned as a period of critical change for Chinese olfactory culture, a change that has been deemed in modern scholarship as a scent revolution.[4] Specifically, this change was seen as the result of the influx of foreign aromatics from the Western Regions and Southern Seas. The former is a term that collectively referred to the areas to the west of China, including the various countries of Central Asia, India, and the Roman Empire, while the latter referred to the countries on the tropical maritime coast running south along the Indochinese peninsula and positioned throughout the Indonesian archipelago. The kinds of aromatics that had the most enduring impact were tree resins, gums, and woods that were not only more strongly scented and durable than most native Chinese aromatics but also constituted an entirely different kind of botanical material than the herbaceous plants typically burned or worn in pre-imperial China. While the specific identification of several of the earliest foreign aromatics remain disputed, this new olfactory culture came to be affiliated in the late medieval imagination with items such as Mediterranean storax, Arabian and East African frankincense, north Indian gum guggal, Indian and Indonesian sandalwood, and Southeast Asian aloeswood.[5]

The question remains, however, to what extent this shift in material culture and smell culture occurred under the Western Han, especially during the historical reign of Emperor Wu, when contact with foreign controlled areas to the west and south demonstrably increased. There are also additional questions regarding the meanings ascribed to these new aromatics and the cultural frameworks used to make sense of them. I argue that, while nonlocal aromatics may have circulated within the imperial boundaries of the early China, the best evidence suggests this was not as commonplace during the Western Han as is often portrayed. Consequently, a smell culture largely based on local aromatics and preexisting olfactory practices and ideas persisted into the subsequent era of the Eastern Han (25–220 CE). Moreover, evidence suggests that it was only toward the end of the Eastern Han, a period with a more sustained trade of nonlocal aromatics in addition to an ever-growing presence of novel Indian Buddhist practices and beliefs centered on smell, that we find a more clearly discernable shift in the Chinese olfactory imagination. Such a shift is, I argue, exemplified through the Six Dynasties' legends of Emperor Wu who amassed a collection of anomalous aromatics with miraculous attributes, thus signifying an attempt by Chinese authors to narratively domesticate the powerful odors that were flooding early medieval markets. I will first describe several of the known odorants of the pre-imperial and Western Han eras, drawing from both textual and archaeological materials to underscore the variety of olfactory practices and different layers of meaning associated with ancient Chinese smell culture. Then I will turn to three different fictive aromatics taken from the medieval legends of Emperor Wu that most clearly exemplify the changing smellscape yet still draw upon older paradigms of medicine to help bridge this liminal period of Chinese olfactory culture.

The Smellscape of Pre-Imperial China and the Western Han

The belief that ancient China possessed a notably different landscape of smell, or what we might term a smellscape, was often noted by Song and post-Song scholars who wrote about the history and elite consumption of aromatics. J. Douglas Porteous notes that the concept of a smellscape is similar to the visual domain in that "smells may be spatially ordered or place-related."[6] In other words, there is a spatial dimension to the phenomenology of smell that correlates certain odors to specific places, just as viewing a particular landscape orients a person geographically. For the Chinese scholars of aromatics, a geography of smell also needed a history, for in their minds, China's historical past smelled differently. Overall, it was generally believed that ancient China possessed a limited set of native odorants that were greatly expanded during and after the Han dynasty.

By examining the preface to the *Newly Compiled Materia Aromatica* (*Xinzuan xiang pu*新纂香譜), which was compiled by Chen Jing 陳敬 (dates unknown) and his son Chen Haoqing 陳浩卿 (dates unknown) at the end of the Song and beginning of the Yuan (1271–1368), we can identify which fragrances were interpreted as typical in the pre-imperial Chinese world:

> When the [*Book of*] *Poetry* and the [*Book of*] *Documents* spoke of aromatics, they did not go beyond glutinous millet, panicled millet, southernwood, and [sacrificial] fat. Therefore, the graph for "fragrance" is constituted by "glutinous millet" written with "sweetness." In antiquity, besides panicled and glutinous millet, one could burn southernwood, wear thoroughwort, and [make] sacrificial ale with turmeric. Those which were called fragrant plants were scarce and at that time a catalog [of aromatics] could not have been composed. The names and items recorded in the *Songs of Chu* gradually increased, yet still did not incorporate [aromatics] from the distant frontiers. Since the Han and Tang, those who speak of aromatics must include the products of the Southern Seas. Therefore, one cannot be without a catalog.[7]

There is a lot to unpack from this short passage, but I want to highlight a few features that are commonly addressed by Chinese connoisseurs of smell. The principal undercurrent is a belief that the substances that constituted the category of aromatics had changed dramatically over time and had expanded to include supraregional commodities, highlighted above by those originating from (and potentially being transported through) the Southern Seas. By culling the textual sources of antiquity, here exemplified by the *Book of Poetry* (*Shijing* 詩經), *Book of Documents* (*Shujing* 書經), and the *Songs of Chu* (*Chuci* 楚辭), all of which were compiled in their majority between the eleventh and third centuries BCE, Chinese scholars attempted to reconstruct the ancient smellscape in order to make informed comparisons to their contemporaneous world. Even today, the two oldest anthologies of Chinese song and verse, the *Book of Poetry* and the *Songs of Chu*, can be treated as virtual regional herbariums, with the former chiefly reflecting the plants growing in the North China Plain and the latter largely reflecting those cultivated in the subtropical south. Bracketing for now the complexities in determining which plants should be deemed as "aromatics," a taxon that was not textually established until the Eastern Han, modern scholarship has enumerated twelve fragrant plants appearing in the *Book of Poetry*, half of which may be different species of *Artemesia*, and upward of thirty-four fragrant herbs and trees in the *Songs of Chu*.[8] Because of considerable geographical and climatological variability, critical scholarship should treat ancient Chinese smellscapes not as monolithic but instead as having important regional differences and involving contested olfactory significations. Nevertheless, for scholars such as Chen Jing and Chen Haoqing, such distinctions were not as stunning as those that would emerge later between the Han and the Tang (618–907) dynasties.

Most notably, even though it is not explicitly stated, and despite the large number of potential aromatics in the *Book of Poetry* and the *Songs of Chu*, the above preface defines the ancient smellscape primarily by odorants used in ritual sacrifice. This includes two types of millet, southernwood mixed with animal fats, and turmeric-spiced sacrificial ale.[9] This is subsequently underscored by the analysis of the Chinese graph for "fragrance" or "aroma" (*xiang*), which consists of two main components: the graph for glutinous millet (*shu* 黍) written above the graph for sweetness (*gan* 甘). In the context of the above passage, this graphemic analysis of "fragrance" implies the archetypal fragrant smell was envisioned as the sweet aroma of millet, one of the chief classes of state sacrificial offerings. Moreover, because such fragrant items were relatively limited in ancient China, as explained at the end of the preface, the need to compose specialized treatises on aromatics only arose due to the widespread importation of non-native goods.

Most modern scholarship has followed Song precedent in ascribing a notable break in the cultural, social, and material practices around smell due to a readjustment in the kinds of aromatics in circulation. Writing in 1956, Yamada Kentarō noted that because Chinese civilization had its geographical origin in the temperate areas of the Yellow River basin, it was isolated from regions that naturally produced more strongly scented botanicals. Consequently, it was only with the development of Central Asian trade routes to India and the emergence of maritime commerce that ran through Southeast Asia that we begin to encounter a bulk movement of goods that came to define a new and increasingly sophisticated Chinese world of smell.[10] This has been more recently elaborated by Olivia Milburn, who is prudently cautious in determining precisely when such changes manifested but still agrees that nothing less than a "scent revolution" occurred when "exotic gums and resins like camphor, benzoin, frankincense, and storax" entered early medieval Chinese markets, resulting in "an enormous impact on the development of Chinese perfumes."[11]

In his work on the smellscape of medieval India, James McHugh has noted the need for a careful approach to reading textual works that record aromatics, since they "are not simple catalogues of what was 'out there' to smell."[12] Textual works present idealized visions of the world shaped by implicit rhetorical objectives and contextually informed ideas concerning which smells are most salient. For example, as noted above, many of the scented substances presented as characteristic of the ancient Chinese smellscape are sacrificial offerings used during state rituals. This is because the texts selected to re-create that olfactory world were mostly treatises describing proper sacrificial protocol during lavish state-sponsored banquets to honor the imperial ancestors and other spirits. Consequently, a more nuanced, sociological understanding would read the odors of cooked grains, seasoned fats, and spiced ales as the aromas of sacrificial foods used strategically to both attract the sprits to the ritual site and to provide them with nourishment. In the context of the ancient sacrificial banquet, divine smelling was therefore envisioned as a higher form of tasting and eating.[13] When scholars of smell discuss shifts away from the ancient Chinese smellscape, however, they are not simply making a comparison to changes in sacrificial foods or the meanings they elicit; they are looking to the past to locate potential analogues for comparison to their contemporary world. For those living during the Song dynasty, living a life of cultured elegance meant having a specialized knowledge in perfumes and incense, substances that are discussed in far less depth in pre-imperial Chinese texts. By turning to recent archaeological finds, we are arguably in a better position than our Song predecessors to analyze these specific dimensions of ancient olfactory culture.

Material culture provides an important supplement to textual documentation; nevertheless, inventories of tomb assemblages are no less neutral in terms of representing the available aromatics that were "out there" in the world. But they can still provide useful information regarding which scented substances were readily accessible and, moreover, deemed worthy of collection and preservation. In this regard, no other archaeological find compares in importance for the history of aromatics during the Western Han than the tomb complex at Mawagdui 馬王堆 in Changsha, Hunan. Excavated between 1972 and 1973 by the Hunan Provincial Museum, the two intact tombs, dated to 186–68 BCE, have produced a number of studies devoted to the artifacts of Western Han smell culture. The most dazzling assortment of goods were recovered from Tomb 1, constructed to hold the remains of the Marchioness of Dai (d. ca. 163 BCE), the wife of the chancellor in the kingdom of Changsha. No less than nine different kinds of fragrant botanicals were discovered, including *Zanthoxylum armatum* (Sichuan pepper), *Eupatorium fortunei* (thoroughwort), *Hierochloe odorata* (sweetgrass), *Magnolia denudata* (Mulan magnolia), *Alpinia officinarum* (galangal), *Zingiber officinale* (ginger), *Asarum forbesii* (wild ginger), *Ligusticum sinense* (Chinese lovage), and *Cinnamomum japonicum* (cassia).[14] These aromatic items were found inside a variety of storage containers and scenting equipment, including a set of lacquered boxes, an embroidered aromatic pillow, six perfuming sachets, six herbal pouches, and a pair of painted ceramic incense burners.[15] The discovery of the two incense burners was particularly revealing because they contained identifiable plant remnants. One ceramic censer, identified as item number 286 in the official archaeological catalog, contained the ashen remains of thoroughwort, while the other, identified as item 433, held a mixture of galangal, sweet grass, Chinese lovage, and Mulan magnolia.[16] The Marchioness of Dai was also found clutching two of the embroidered perfuming sachets containing Sichuan pepper, cassia, sweetgrass, and galangal.[17]

The discovery of aromatics in many of the storage areas surrounding the coffin, as well as on the body of the corpse, speaks to their importance in early Han mortuary practices and are a testament to their practical uses in daily life. These uses extended beyond the aesthetics of perfuming and olfactory hygiene. Medical manuscripts recovered from Tomb 3 at Mawangdui attest to the therapeutic and apotropaic applications of aromatics, with

Sichuan pepper, ginger, and cassia appearing regularly in prescribed treat-ments.[18] Since the Marchioness of Dai is believed to have suffered from heart disease, it is possible the two aromatic pouches were related to her treatment.[19] These therapeutic applications of aromatics, more so than their sacrificial use as divine nourishment, resonate with the medieval stories of Emperor Wu.

There are two further points worth considering in terms of the cache of aromatics found at Mawangdui. The first is that all nine of the items were regionally available, with most growing within the formal boundaries of the Western Han empire. While the distribution of their native origins remains scattered—for example, cassia was most likely sourced from the southeast-ern coastal areas, sweetgrass from the temperate north, and galangal from the tropical frontiers of the far south—none of the recovered botanicals were transported over exceptionally long distances. The finds at Mawangdui thus point to a robust interregional trade in China of perfumes, spices, and drugs by the second century BCE, but not necessarily an active supraregional move-ment of goods from the Western Regions or the Southern Seas. Importantly, as Milburn has noted, galangal was not grown within the Han Empire when the tombs at Mawangdui were sealed, thus suggesting there was technically international trade with the kingdom of Nanyue 南越 in the south before it fell to Emperor Wu's military forces half a century later.[20]

The second point focuses our attention to the materiality of these native Chinese plants. Six of the nine kinds of aromatics were constituted, at least in part, by the roots and rhizomatic rootstalks of the individual plant species. This is exemplified by the unburned remnants of ginger, wild ginger, galan-gal, Chinese lovage, sweetgrass, and thoroughwort. The specific selection of roots is due, in part, to the fact that fragrant volatile oils are concentrated in the woody underground parts of such plants. When encountering the names of these plants in textual sources, it can be easy to overlook that only certain parts were prized for their fragrant qualities and medicinal attributes. In distinction to the above aromatics, Sichuan pepper was mainly represented by its aromatic seeds and husks, cassia by its scented bark, and Mulan magno-lia by its flower buds.

If we look again to the pair of censers, we find their contents comprised loosely torn bits of roots, stems, and flower buds, all of which when incin-erated would have produced billows of smoke with a gentle, and perhaps even underwhelming, scent. This would come to stand in stark contrast to the strongly scented exotic resins and resin-impregnated woods of later centuries that were more typically placed atop charcoals and left to smol-der.[21] In contrast to the incense at Mawangdui, this indirect burning method allowed the complex fragrances of things like frankincense, aloeswood, and storax to spread with substantially less smoke. This change in the materi-ality of incense also influenced the imaginary world on display in medieval tales of the strange.

The question of when these new kinds of revolutionary aromatics arrived in East Asia remains unanswered. One of the most intriguing pieces of direct evidence to suggest the early spread of exotic resins to China was the exca-vation of the tomb of the king of Nanyue, Zhao Mo 趙眜 (r. 137–122 BCE) in 1983. The capital of Nanyue at Panyu 番禺 was a significant port of trade along the northern end of the Indo-Chinese peninsula and by the second century BCE had already developed maritime contact with regions further south, potentially even extending beyond the Southern Seas into West-ern Asia. Among the goods recovered from Zhao Mo's tomb was a round lacquered box containing broken fragments of a yellowish-white resin that were believed to resemble frankincense. Further scientific analysis of the substance, however, has yielded inconclusive results regarding its identity.[22] If the granules are determined to be frankincense, this discovery would pre-date the earliest Chinese textual reference to frankincense by approximately four centuries—a rather long span for which no other textual or archaeological evidence appears. If we admit the possibility that frankincense intermittently entered into the markets of Nanyue, and potentially even into imperial China, its circulation has curiously left no trace in surviving documents and, argu-ably, failed to make a sizable impression on Western Han smell culture.[23]

A different argument, based on circumstantial evidence, has also been postulated by the modern historian of material culture Sun Ji. He argues the changes in the structure of Western Han censers suggest a sustained practice of burning exotic resins. Specifically, according to Sun, the development of deeper censer basins in order to accommodate charcoal, as well as the adop-tion of taller lids with smaller apertures to control air flow, are structural adaptations pointing to the use of new resin-based materials.[24] While censers from the early Han have been found containing charcoal, none thus far have contained non-native aromatics. As a consequence, it cannot be dismissed that changes in censer structure were the result of adopting charcoal broadly as a more efficient and longer-lasting suffumigation technique for *native* Chinese botanicals. The use of hot charcoal is attested, for example, in the Mawang-dui medical manuals for burning plant matter.[25] Thus, the use of charcoal should not be used as conclusive evidence for the widespread circulation of foreign resins, although Sun Ji's hypothesis remains plausible.

It has been previously speculated that a small amount of exotic aromatics may have entered Western Han China through the trade networks of the northern nomadic tribes.[26] Even if we take this to be the case, this theory still fails to address the fact that the most clearly discernible changes in the Chinese olfactory imagination, at least as expressed in surviving textual sources, manifests not in the Western Han but at the end of the Eastern Han, which presents far more evidence to attest to a changing smellscape. Such a desire to locate a definitive change during the reign of Emperor Wu has consequently led to several poorly substantiated and anachronistic claims. For example, it is sometimes asserted that after successfully conquering the lands of Nanyue, which included modern-day Guangdong and northern Vietnam, Emperor Wu gained direct access to the species of *Aquilaria* tree that produced the highly valued aromatic wood known as aloeswood.[27] Text entitled the *Yellow Maps of the Three Administrative Districts* (*Sanfu huangtu* 三輔黃圖) speaks to the glories of Emperor Wu's Palace for Cultivating Lychee, a construction project used to house the "odd plants and strange trees" of the far south.[28] This reputedly included one hundred specimens of the tree that yielded aloeswood. No contemporaneous Western Han documents attest to such an ambitious project, however, and while the *Yellow Maps of the Three Capitals* remains difficult to date, it is usually ascribed to the very end of the Eastern Han or the Six Dynasties period. Otherwise, the earliest accounts documenting discrete Chinese knowledge of aloeswood date no earlier than the third century, when it was known as a product of Vietnam.[29] Stories such as the above are better viewed as later legends that developed to strategically enhance Emperor Wu's reputation for territorial conquest and the aura surrounding his collection of rare tributary items. As we will see with the tales of the strange, there is little reason to regard such stories as faithful accounts of events during Emperor Wu's historical reign.

We can add a further example regarding one of the earliest reputed recipes for blending perfumes and incense. While it is claimed to be a product of the Eastern Han, the following recipe is sometimes cited as evidence of the rapid development of a new smell culture characterized by fragrant exotica.[30] Circulating under the name of "Palace Incense of the Han *Jianning* era" (*Han jianning gongzhong xiang* 漢建寧宮中香), the ingredient list and blending directions are as follows:

[Ingredients] Four *jin* of Yellow-Aged Aromatic [a type of aloeswood], two *jin* of Korean monkshood, five *liang* of clove bark, four *liang* of patchouli leaves, four *liang* of Aromatic from Lingling [sweet basil], four *liang* of sandalwood, four *liang* of wild angelica, two *jin* of sweet grass,[31] two *jin* of anise, half a *jin* of spikenard, one *liang* of frankincense (ground in a separate vessel), four *liang* of Freshly Produced Aromatic [a type of aloeswood], half a *jin* of jujubes (dried until soft). Another recipe adds one *qian* of storax oil.

[Directions] Take the above and make into a fine powder. Refine with honey and blend until evenly distributed. After storing [the mixture] in excess of a month, make pellets or burn it.[32]

This recipe bears the hallmarks of a highly advanced art of perfumery, including, but not limited to, the total number of ingredients, the combination of both native and foreign aromatics, the use of additives and agglutinants, and last, the adoption of refined processing techniques. I cannot address all of the pertinent matters in detail, but there are several reasons why we should not take this recipe as a genuine artifact of the Eastern Han *jian-ning* era (168–72), as the recipe's name boldly indicates (which itself should be a warning sign). The first suspicion is raised by the fact that this recipe first appears in the thirteenth century, specifically in the *Newly Compiled Materia Aromatica*. Throughout the Song, it was trendy to compile blending recipes that were reputedly collected from various imperial courts, and the "Palace Incense of the Han *Jianning* era" was afforded prominence in manuals due to its (perceived) esteemed age.[33] Yet the recipe includes the names of two different kinds of low-grade aloeswood, a fine distinction that was not fully established until the early eleventh century.[34] Furthermore, storax oil, a viscid golden oleoresin exported from the Southern Seas, was not a known commodity in Chinese markets until the Tang at the earliest.[35] All of this indicates a recipe born of a much later period of Chinese olfactory culture, likely as late as the mid-Song, when more robust commercial trade networks had emerged and more sophisticated arts of perfuming had developed.

Overall, while most scholars are unanimous in the belief of a scent revolution occurring in China that sundered the ancient and medieval smellscapes, the historical situation is more complex. The ancient smellscape was always regionally fractured, and the practices of food sacrifice involving grain, flesh, and alcohol continued mostly unabated throughout the medieval period—as did the therapeutic use of aromatics, which, in the eyes of the medieval Chinese, were never categorically distinct from drugs, although different discursive framings could accentuate or occlude an aromatic's identity as medicine or perfume. The clearest changes that can be charted were in the importation of dazzling new kinds of botanical aromatics that by the Song were chiefly viewed through the prism of elite taste as expressed in the collection, categorization, and appreciation of incense. In the early medieval period, such distinctions and elite cultural practices were only just forming, and the authors compiling tales of the strange were seemingly stimulated by the semiotic ambiguity of the vibrantly scented resins and woods slowly taking over their sensual domains.

The Anomalous Aromatics of Emperor Wu and the Early Medieval Olfactory Imagination

According to surviving textual accounts, early Eastern Han perfuming culture was more conservative and, with one important exception, constituted by locally available aromatics. Some of the earliest, unambiguous textual references to burning incense in China are found in Eastern Han manuals describing the protocols of the imperial court. For example, Wei Hong's 衛宏 (second-century) *Old Observances for Han Officials* (*Han guan jiuyi* 漢官 舊儀) describes the use of a single ingredient, a native species of sweet basil (*xun* 薫, often identified as *Ocimum basilicum*), to perfume the garments of members of the Imperial Secretariat, who have audience with the emperor.[36] The same protocol employing sweet basil is also described in the subsequent court manuals compiled by Cai Zhi 蔡質 (d. 178) and Ying Shao 應劭 (ca. 144– ca. 204).[37] This offers a rather stark contrast to the Song reimagination of old palace blends made with complex combinations of perfumes as seen in the "Palace Incense of the Han *Jianning* era" above.

Interestingly, elsewhere Ying Shao also indicates the adoption of what appears to be a new court practice: the use of cloves to sweeten the breath of imperial courtiers.[38] Unlike sweet basil, which was native to China, cloves had to be imported from the Moluccas of the Indonesian archipelago. Moreover, as a foreign import, cloves were likely only available to the upper echelon of Han society, thus helping explain their appearance in formal imperial proceedings. Inasmuch as we can take Ying Shao's claims at face value, this arguably makes cloves the first non-native aromatic to have an unquestionable impact on Chinese olfactory practice.

Unsurprisingly, it was Chinese poets—those who are closely attuned to the surrounding sensorium—who were some of the first to further chronicle the appearance of novel smells in China (see also Qian Jia's contribution to this volume). Oftentimes used to signify the strange and foreign, many of these exotic odorants remain unidentified, such as *dixiang* 狄香, cited in Zhang Heng's 張衡 (78–139) *Song of Concordant Sounds* (*Tongsheng ge* 同聲哥),[39] as well as *midie* 迷迭, *aina* 艾納, and *douliang* 都梁, all of which are cited in an anonymous Han-era verse.[40] The changing smellscape is also charted in several regional gazetteers from the third and fourth centuries, especially those converging on the tropical far south. Such works catalog an influx of new aromatics into southern ports, including widely traded commercial goods such as cloves, patchouli, frankincense, and aloeswood.[41] To these sources we can also add translated Buddhist scriptures, which start to reveal the fabulous Indian world of smell, highlighting sandalwood, aloeswood, and frankincense, as well as many other kinds of sweet-smelling flowers, food aromas, and divine scents.

When we turn to the legends of Emperor Wu that began to appear after the introduction of Buddhism, however, none of these foreign substances are cited by name. Instead, perhaps to amplify the wondrous qualities of largely fictitious aromatics, we principally find a catalog of descriptive appellations, such as Rousing the Numen Incense (*zhenling xiang* 振靈香), Incense from Yuezhi (*yuezhi xiang* 月支香), and *Doumo* Incense (*doumo xiang* 兜末香), with the final example approximating a pseudo-Sanskrit transcription to underscore its foreign origin. Consequently, real imported aromatics do not often explicitly appear in the cycle of legends surrounding Emperor Wu nor in other contemporaneous tales of the strange.[42] In spite of this silence, we find the shifting smellscape helped animate the ways medieval Chinese authors started to reimagine the olfactory world, a world that was increasingly punctuated by marvelous fragrances that possessed astounding power. The pre-imperial Chinese smellscape may have been awash with the scents of ritual sacrifice and native plants, but those odors remained firmly in the world of empirical knowledge. In the early medieval period, the tales-of-the-strange genre was motivated not only by traditional Chinese stories of the fantastic but also the medieval world of international trade and luxury goods (as represented in many early regional gazetteers), and the genre consequently emerged as an apt literary venue to showcase a new reconceptualization of the sensorial domain of smell.

If we turn to the stories concerning Emperor Wu, conveniently captured in Hong Chu's *Materia Aromatica*, we can start to find the contours of this new medieval olfactory imagination. First, listed under the headword for the Incense from Yuezhi, is the following episode:

> The Charts of Auspicious Correspondences [states]: In the second year of tianhan [99 BCE], the country of Yuezhi presented Spirit Incense as tribute and Emperor Wu received and inspected it. Its appearance was like swallows' eggs. Altogether there were three pellets as large as jujubes. The emperor did not burn them but had them placed in the outer storehouse. Afterward there was a great epidemic in Chang'an and the people of the palace became ill. Many envoys pleaded to burn a single pellet [of the incense] in order to dispel the miasmatic air. The emperor burned it and those who were ill within the palace were cured. [Everyone] within a hundred li of Chang'an could smell this incense and its accumulation did not disperse for nine months.[43]

In this short narrative extracted from a Jin-era (265–420 CE) text, the foreign tribute from the Yuezhi, a name most closely associated with the Indo-Scythians in the early medieval period, proves to have an unexpectedly powerful therapeutic effect when burned by the emperor.[44] Identified as Spirit Incense in the passage, the anomalous aromatic is clearly portrayed as a gift from lands outside of China. This allows the episode not only to signify the maintenance of proper deferential relations of the periphery to the imperial Chinese center but also to express the heightened efficacy of the things perceived as rare, exotic, and normally inaccessible.[45] In this case, Spirit Incense also draws from the deep well of Chinese lore regarding the existence of magical herbs and elixirs of immortality found only in the farthest reaches of the world. Furthermore, as we have seen, this episode plays into the older pharmacological tradition that treated aromatics as medicinal drugs, albeit here as an exceptionally superior variety that dispels widespread illness.

Another notable aspect of the above story is the salience of the materiality of the strange aromatic, a point that is carefully recorded in other tales beyond the legends of Emperor Wu. Spirit Incense is described as analogous to swallows' eggs and jujubes, both small rounded objects. In addition to this, the enhanced olfactory quality of the incense, in terms of both scent duration (nine months) and scent projection (ten *li*), is also precisely noted. I believe this explicit focus on materiality and fragrance quality was motivated by the increasing real-world circulation of strongly scented resins, gums, and woods, which as raw materials would have been traded as small, semitranslucent globules and hewn chunks. This contrasts considerably with the torn strips of root, seeds, and flower buds recovered from Mawangdui and the use of dried sweet basil leaves in the offices of the Imperial Secretariat. For authors to indicate the anomalous in their works, aromatic substances like Spirit Incense were marked not only by their exceptional power but also by their extraordinary scent qualities and uncommon material composition, aspects Robert Campany has classified as "anomalies of degree."[46]

A second type of special aromatic is known as *Doumo* Incense. Unlike the entry above, Hong Chu provides three different medieval sources to flesh out the characteristics of this substance:

The *Supplement to the Materia Medica* states:
Burning it drives away malign *qi* and dispels illness and epidemics.

The *Tales of Emperor Wu of the Han* states:
The Queen Mother of the West descended and the Highest [i.e., the emperor] burned this incense which was presented as tribute from the country of Douqu. It resembled large beans and when it was used to paint the palace gates its fragrance was smelled for a hundred *li*. There was a great epidemic in Guangzhong and the dead were piled atop one another. By burning this incense the epidemic then ceased.

The *Esoteric Biography* [*of Emperor Wu of the Han*] states: The dead were all raised. This is numinous incense. It is not what China produces.[47]

In many ways, *Doumo* Incense is the same as Incense from Yuezhi. It is presented as a tribute from a foreign state, here noted as the otherwise unknown Douqu, and explained as having miraculous recuperative properties. The incense also possessed a powerful fragrance and is described as the size of large beans, a traditional Chinese metrological standard for medicinal pills.[48] Two of the above works cited by Hong Chu are devoted entirely to the legends about Emperor Wu, both of which bear some of the literary characteristics of early tales of the strange.[49] In terms of dating, the *Tales of Emperor Wu of the Han* (*Han Wudi gushi* 漢武帝故事) is a product of the third or fourth centuries, while the *Esoteric Biography of Emperor Wu of the Han* (*Han Wudi neizhuan* 漢武帝内傳) was likely compiled a century later.[50]

More interesting is the fact that *Doumo* Incense was incorporated into the eighth-century catalog of herbs and drugs known as the *Supplement to the Materia Medica* (*Bencao shiyi* 本草拾遺). This text's original entry for *Doumo* Incense cites the above passage from the *Tales of Emperor Wu of the Han* to certify the efficacy of this aromatic drug.[51] As a consequence, this citation serves to anchor the anomalous aromatic in the realm of real medicine and also adds veracity to a belief that Emperor Wu was a genuine recipient of such wondrous tributes. This was not the only attempt to historically ground strange and fragrant exotica. By the tenth century, the author of the *Materia Medica of Overseas Drugs* (*Haiyao bencao* 海藥本草) had claimed Spirit Incense was similar to imported myrrh, which possessed a dark reddish color.[52] Such boundary crossing is not unique to aromatics but indicates the fuzzy logic separating religion, magic, and medicine throughout the long medieval period.

One of the more stunning religio-medical claims is made by the compiler(s) of the *Esoteric Biography of Emperor Wu of the Han*, which states that there was an aromatic drug that can raise people from the dead. This is closely tied to our next anomalous item, classified by Hong Chu as Rousing the Numen Incense:

> The *Records of the Ten Continents* [state]: On the continent of Juku there are large trees that are like the sweetgum, but the fragrance of their leaves can be smelled for several hundred *li*. They are called Recalling the Soul trees. Place the root inside a jade cauldron and boil its juice until it is like syrup. It is called Startling the Spirit Incense, or Rousing the Numen Incense, or Returning to Life Incense, or Horse Spirit Incense, or Dispersing Death Incense. This single item has five names. It is a numinous thing. Its fragrance can be smelled for several hundred *li* and the buried corpses that smell it will be promptly revived.[53]

The *Records of the Ten Continents* (*Shizhou ji* 十洲記) originally formed part of a larger narrative that included the *Esoteric Biography of Emperor Wu of the Han* and also dates to around the fifth century.[54] In the full version of the *Records of the Ten Continents*, the above episode immediately precedes a slightly different version of the tale about Spirit Incense, so we can treat these stories as largely interrelated.[55]

Rousing the Numen Incense is just one of five names for what is described as an essential oil, distilled from the roots of special trees growing on the mythic continent of Juku in the far west. It appears as if the miraculous power of these plants, named Recalling the Soul trees, is crystallized into the fragrances of the individual aromatics that are wielded to bring back the dead. In the larger narrative from *Records of the Ten Continents*, Emperor Wu burns an incense received as tribute to treat an epidemic at Chang'an. Far more than healing the sick, the special incense revives those that have been dead for less than three days.[56] Moreover, just as with the other anomalous aromatics discussed above, this substance was also incorporated into pharmacological literature in the tenth century, under the name Recalling the Soul Incense (*fanhun xiang* 返魂香), taking the name of the tree from which the incense derived.[57]

While Hong Chu listed the Incense from Yuezhi, *Doumo* Incense, and Rousing the Numen Incense as separate entries in his catalog, a distinction, albeit under different nomenclature, that was followed by compilers of *materia medica*, it is clear that early medieval authors were less rigid in establishing clear boundaries between these (largely fictional) items. For them, the world of the fantastic need not be so easily quantifiable. In any regard, this particular clustering of strange aromatics demonstrates a strong elective affinity with indigenous ideas regarding medicinal drugs, not only in their therapeutic properties but also in their pill-sized measurements.

Not all anomalous aromatics documented by regional gazetteers, tales of the strange, or other classical sources were burned; many were ingested or worn, also indicative of long-standing Chinese medical practices (the latter exemplified by the scenting sachets of Mawangdui). This suggests early medieval Chinese owners of foreign aromatics often viewed them more as drugs than as incense or perfume, a delicate relationship that would flip by the Song, if not much earlier. For example, when scholars like Chen Jing and Chen Haojing looked into the past, they not only saw a paucity in the amount of aromatics that were natively available, but they also noticed the lack of a specific kind of aromatic, incense, which for them was inextricably linked to imported products like aloeswood and frankincense. Of course, imported aromatics would never completely eradicate their associations with medicine and continued to be listed in many medieval editions of *materia medica*, but we find already by the early sixth century the Daoist polymath Tao Hong-jing 陶弘景 (456–536 CE) noting that foreign derived cloves, aloeswood, and frankincense were all prized by incense blenders and were not appropriate for use as medicine.[58]

Such claims underscore the semiotic ambiguity of many foreign aromatics in the medieval period, a point rendered more acute by the overburdened polysemantic nature of the term *xiang*, which could refer to the aromas of sacrifice, to drugs, or to incense. Such ambiguity could be addressed in the imaginary space where the tales of the strange were spun, and as I have shown, medieval authors were quick to draw upon the existing cultural framework of medicine to make sense of these fragrant exotica. Moreover, stories placing strange aromatics in Emperor Wu's possession not only worked to embellish the emperor's fame but also made the foreign appear more familiar. In time, as foreign aromatics continued to flood Chinese ports, frontier trading posts, and urban markets, they became part of the tapestry of elite Chinese identity, an identity often draped in the perfume of incense.

Notes

1. Haifeng has sorted out many of the lingering questions regarding the textual fili-ation of the variant received editions of the *Materia Aromatica*, addressing the other-wise perplexing discrepancies in terms of the total number of entries and overall struc-ture of Hong Chu's work; see Shang, "Bei Song ben Hong Chu." For a vitae of Hong Chu's rather remarkable life in spite of being an often-disfavored low-ranking official, see Romaskiewicz, "Sacred Smells and Strange Scents."

2. Campany, *Strange Writing*.

3. Schipper, *Empereur Wou des Han*; Smith, "Ritual and the Shaping of Narrative."

4. Milburn, "Aromas, Scents, and Spices."

5. I include the regions of origin only to signal the widespread geographical distri-bution for each of these substances and not to indicate where medieval Chinese authors believed them to originate, as this fluctuated throughout history.

6. Porteous, "Smellscape," 359.

7. 詩書言: 香不過黍稷蕭脂, 故香之爲字, 從黍作甘。古者自黍稷之外, 可焫者蕭, 可佩者蘭, 可鬯者鬱, 名爲香草無幾, 此時譜可無作。楚辭所錄名物漸多, 猶未取於遐裔也。漢唐以來, 言香者必取於南海之產, 故不可無譜。SKQS844:240b.

8. Wang, Qinglin, and Yanxiang, "Zhong-guo gudai xiangliao shihua," 64; Liu, *Songdai Xiangpu zhi yanjiu*, 19. It is often over-looked that the Chinese term for "aromatics," *xiang*, originally referred to the fragrant, sweet-smelling *property* of an object (most commonly, the aroma of a sacrificial object) and only later came to be used to denote a class of fragrant *objects* (e.g., aromatics). This is further complicated by the invet-erate tendency of modern scholars to read *xiang* as incense, an additional semantic layer that also does not emerge in Chinese textual sources until the Eastern Han. Curiously, this development occurred in spite of the fact that censers have been recovered from tombs distributed throughout China that date to before the Eastern Han. For a treatment on the Japanese understanding of *xiang* (or, in Japanese, *kō*) and the related native Japanese term *nioi* 匂, see Lorenzo Marinucci's chap-ter in this volume.

9. Each of these aromatic substances has a long history in terms of use in sacrificial rites as well as a variety of therapeutic and apotropaic applications. For the importance of smell in ancient state sacrifice, see Sterckx, *Food, Sacrifice, and Sagehood*, 84–95, 168–74; Milburn, "Aromas, Scents, and Spices," 441–64. While thoroughwort (often mistaken as orchid) was central to ancient Chinese religious practice, it played less of a role in state sacrifice in the North China Plain.

10. Yamada, *Tōzai kōyaku shi*, 319–20.

11. Milburn, *Aromas, Scents, and Spices*, 459.

12. McHugh, *Sandalwood and Carrion*, 62.

13. Sterckx, *Food, Sacrifice, and Sagehood*.

14. Hunan nongxueyuan, *Changsha Mawangdui yihao*, 21–42; Liu, "Changsha Mawangdui sanhao"; Lu and Lo "Scent and Synaesthesia," 43. Inadvertently repeating an identification error by Di Lu and Vivienne Lo, Milburn distinguishes Sichuan pepper (*Zanthoxylum armatum*) from *Z. bungeanum*, thus providing a list of ten total aromatics. None of the official Mawangdui catalogs list the latter. Additionally, Milburn identifies *Lingusticum sinense* as licorice root, but it should be noted that Chinese licorice (*gancao* 甘草) was not recovered at Mawangdui. For relevant (mis)identifications, see Lu and Lo, "Scent and Synaesthesia," 42; Milburn, "Aromas, Scents, and Spices," 445.

15. Chen and Li, "Cong Mawangdui yihaomu."

16. Hunan sheng bowuguan et al., *Changsha Mawangdui yihao Han mu*, 125.

17. Hunan yixueyuan, *Changsha Mawangdui yihao*, 262.

18. Harper, *Early Chinese Medical Literature*, 103–4.

19. Lu and Lo, "Scent and Synaesthesia," 43.

20. Milburn "Aromas, Scents, and Spices," 446–47.

21. Sun, *Handai wuzhi wenhua ziliao tushuo*, 415–16.

22. Mai, "Xianggang Nanyue wangmu fanying de zhu wenti," 34. For pertinent sources related to the tomb of Zhao Mo, see Milburn, "Aromas, Scents, and Spices," 447–48.

23. Yamada, *Tōa kōryō shi kenkyū*, 84.

24. Sun, *Handai wuzhi wenhua ziliao tushuo*, 413–19.

25. Harper, *Early Chinese Medical Literature*, 273.

26. Yamada Tōzai kōyaku shi, 320.

27. Fu, *Zhongguo xiang wenhua*, 123.

28. He, *Sanfu huangtu jiaozhu*, 247.

29. Yamada, *Tōa kōryō shi kenkyū*, 185–86.

30. Milburn, "Aromas, Scents, and Spices," 453–54.

31. While the *maoxiang* recovered from Mawangdui is identified as sweetgrass, which, for the sake of consistency, I have decided to retain here, there is evidence that medieval sources treated *maoxiang* as a type of citronella (*Cymbopogon* spp.).

32. 黃熟香四斤、白附子二斤、丁香皮五兩、藿香葉四兩、零陵香四兩、檀香四兩、白芷四兩、茅香二斤、茴香二斤、甘松半斤、乳香一兩(別器研)、生結香四兩、棗半斤乾焙。一方入蘇合香油一錢。右為細末、鍊蜜和勻、窨有餘作丸或蕊之。SKQS844:271b–272a.

33. The subsequent recipe in the *Newly Compiled Materia Aromatica* is entitled "Palace Incense of the Tang *Kaiyuan* era"; see SKQS844: 272b. It is worth noting that another reputed Han-era recipe, the "Incense Recipe of the Han Palaces" (*Hangong xiangfa* 漢宮香方), with annotation attributed to the famed exegete Zheng Xuan 鄭玄 (128–200), has been revealed as a Tang forgery; see Liu, *Songdai Xiangpu zhi yanjiu*, 253–58.

34. Liu, *Songdai Xiangpu zhi yanjiu*, 150–56.

35. Yamada, *Tōa kōryō shi kenkyū*, 157–60.

36. Sun, *Hanguan liuzhong*, 33.

37. Ibid., 143, 206.

38. Ibid., 116; Milburn "Aromas, Scents, and Spices," 459–60.

39. Xu, *Yutai xinyong jianzhu*, 28.

40. T2122:573c04–06. *Midie* is sometimes said to be rosemary, but there is little evidence to firmly establish this identification. Furthermore, *aina* has been identified as Malayan camphor and *douliang* as thoroughwort, but I remain skeptical of these identifications in this specific context. Medieval Chinese Buddhist sources also attest to both aromatics but treat *aina* as a plant, not a tree resin, and *douliang* as a presumably indigenous Indian plant, not a species native to East Asia. These questions should be explored elsewhere.

41. Liu, *Songdai Xiangpu zhi yanjiu*, 32.

42. Just limiting ourselves to the other seven aromatics associated with Emperor Wu in the *Materia Aromatica*, we also find *Hengwu* Aromatic (*hengwu xiang* 蘅蕪香), *Duyi* Aromatic (*duyi xiang* 都夷香), Sinking Light Incense (*chenguang xiang* 沈光香), Perfuming the Flesh Incense (*xunji xiang* 薰肌香), Spirits and Demons Incense (*qijing xiang* 祇精香), Jin Midi Incense (*jindi xiang* 金磾香), and Expelling Coldness Aromatic (*bihan xiang* 辟寒香). I have translated the names here as "incense" only when the accompanying description describes the aromatic as being burned. For a further investigation of these items, see Romaskiewicz "Sacred Smells and Strange Scents."

43. 瑞應圖：大[=天]漢二年，月支國貢神香，武帝取看之，狀若燕卵，凡三枚，大似棗。帝不燒，付外庫。後長安中大疫，宮人得疾，眾使者請燒一枚以辟疫氣，帝然之。宮中病者差，長安百里內聞其香，積九月不散。SKQS844:224b.

44. The *Charts of Auspicious Correspondences* likely refers to the lost apocryphon by Sun Rouzhi 孫柔之 (dates unknown) who lived during the Jin. A longer version of this story is preserved in the *Treatise on the Investigation of Things* (*Bowuzhi* 博物志) by Zhang Hua 張華 (232–300); see Milburn, "Aromas, Scents, and Spices," 246.

45. Campany *Strange Writing*, 281–82.

46. Ibid., 240–45.

47. 本草拾遺曰：燒去惡氣，除病疫。漢武帝故事曰：西王母降，上燒是香。兜渠國所獻，如大豆，塗宮門，香聞百里。關中大疫，死者相枕，燒此香，疫

則止。內傳云：死者皆起。此則靈香，非中國所致。SKQS844:225a.

48. Harper, *Early Chinese Medical Literature*, 223n6.

49. Schipper, *Empereur Wou des Han*; Smith, "Ritual and the Shaping of Narrative."

50. Smith, "Ritual and the Shaping of Narrative," 133, 196. Notably, the passage cited by Hong Chu from the *Esoteric Biography of Emperor Wu of the Han* does not appear in the received edition of that text.

51. Li, *Bencao gangmu*.

52. Ibid.

53. 十洲記：聚窟洲有大樹如楓，而葉香聞數百里，名曰返魂樹。根於玉釜中，煮汁如飴，名曰驚精香，又曰振靈香，又曰返生香，又曰馬精香，又名卻死香。一種五名，靈物也。香聞數百里，死屍在地聞即活。SKQS844:224b. A slightly longer version of this story is preserved in the received *Records of the Ten Continents* in the Daoist canon; see DZ598:6a–6b.

54. Smith, "Ritual and the Shaping of Narrative," 196.

55. The *Records of the Ten Continents* version of the Spirit Incense story is closer to that which appears in the *Treatise on the Investigation of Things*; see footnote above. The *Records of the Ten Continents* divides the tale into two parts, the first covering the reception of the tribute and then its later use during the epidemic; see DZ598:6b and DZ598:8b, respectively.

56. DZ598:8b.

57. Li, *Bencao gangmu*.

58. Yamada, *Tōa kōryō shi kenkyū*, 172–73.

Bibliography

Abbreviations

DZ   Anonymous. *Zhengtong daozang* 正統道藏. Shanghai: Hanfen Lou, 1924–26. (Passages cited by text number, followed by page and register.)

SKQS Ji Yun 紀昀, ed. *Siku quanshu* 四庫全書. Shanghai: Shanghai Guji Chubanshe, 1987. (Passages cited by volume number, followed by page and register.)

T   Takakusu Junjirō 高楠順次朗 and Watanabe Kaigyoku 渡邊海旭, eds. *Taishō shinshū daizōkyō* 大正新修大藏經. Tokyo: Taishō Issaikyō Kankōkai, 1924–32. (Passages cited by text number, followed by page, register, and line number.)

Primary and Secondary Sources

Campany, Robert Ford. *Strange Writing: Anomaly Accounts in Early Medieval China.* Albany: State University of New York Press, 1996.

Dongjie, Chen 陳東傑, and Li Ya 李芽. "Cong Mawangdui yihaomu chutu xiangliao yu xiangju tanxi Handai yongxiang xisu" 從馬王堆一號墓出土香料與香具探析漢代用香習俗. *Nandu xuetan (Renwen shehui kexueban)* 南都學壇 (人文社會科學版) 1, no. 17 (2009): 6–12.

Fu, Jingliang 傅京亮. 2008. *Zhongguo xiang wenhua* 中國香文化. Ji'nan: Qilu shushe.

Harper, Donald. 1998. *Early Chinese Medical Literature: The Mawangdui Medical Manuscripts.* London: Kegan Paul International, 2008.

He, Qinggu 何清谷, ed. *Sanfu huangtu jiaozhu* 三輔黃圖校注. Xian: Sanqin chubanshe, 2006.

Hunan, Nongxueyuan 湖南農學院, eds. *Changsha Mawangdui yihao Han mu chutu dongzhiwu biaoben de yanjiu* 長沙馬王堆一號漢墓出土動植物標本的研究. Beijing: Wenwu Chubanshe, 1978.

Hunan, Sheng Bowuguan 湖南省博物館 and Zhongguo kexueyuan kaogu yanjiusuo 中國科學院考古研究所, eds. *Changsha Mawangdui yihao Han mu* 長沙馬王堆一號漢墓. Beijing: Wenwu Chubanshe, 1973.

Hunan, Yixueyuan 湖南醫學院, eds. *Changsha Mawangdui yihao Han mu gushi yanjiu* 長沙馬王堆一號漢墓古尸研究. Beijing: Wenwu chubanshe, 1980.

Li, Shizhen 李時珍. *Bencao gangmu* 本草綱目. 2 vols. Beijing: Renmin Weisheng Chubanshe, 1982.

Liu, Jingmin 劉靜敏. *Songdai Xiangpu zhi yanjiu* 宋代香譜之研究. Taipei: Wenshizhe Chubanshe, 2007.

Liu, Lixian 劉麗仙. "Changsha Mawangdui sanhao Han mu chutu yaowu jianding yanjiu" 長沙馬王堆三號漢墓出土藥物鑑定研究. *Kaogu* 考古 9 (1989): 856–60, 871–72.

Lu, Di, and Vivienne Lo. "Scent and Synaesthesia: The Medical Use of Spice Bags in Early China." *Journal of Ethnopharmacology* 167 (2015): 38–46.

Mai Yinghao 麥英豪. "Xianggang Nanyue wangmu fanying de zhu wenti" 象崗南越王墓反映的諸問題. *Lingnan wenshi* 嶺南文史 2 (1987): 20–36.

McHugh, James. *Sandalwood and Carrion: Smell in Indian Religion and Culture.* Oxford: Oxford University Press, 2012.

Milburn, Olivia. "Aromas, Scents, and Spices: Olfactory Culture in China before the Arrival of Buddhism." *Journal of the American Oriental Society* 136, no. 3 (2016): 441–64.

Porteous, J. Douglas. "Smellscape." *Progress in Human Geography* 9, no. 3 (1985): 356–78.

Romaskiewicz, Peter. "Sacred Smells and Strange Scents: Olfactory Imagination in Medieval Chinese Religions." PhD diss., University of California, Santa Barbara, forthcoming.

Schipper, Kristofer. *L'empereur Wou des Han dans la légende taoïste.* Paris: École française d'Extrême-Orient, 1965.

Shang Haifeng. "Bei Song ben Hong Chu *Xiang houpu* bianzheng jiyi" 北宋本洪芻《香後譜》辨正輯佚. *Gugong xueshu likan* 故宮學術季刊 36, no. 1 (2019): 1–36.

Smith, Thomas E. "Ritual and the Shaping of Narrative: The Legend of the Han Emperor Wu." 2 vols. PhD diss., University of Michigan, 1992.

———. "Where Chinese Administration Practices and Tales of the Strange Converge: The Meaning of *Gushi* in the *Han Wudi Gushi*." *Early Medieval China* 1 (1994): 1–33.

Sterckx, Roel. *Food, Sacrifice, and Sagehood in Early China.* Cambridge: Cambridge University Press, 2011.

Sun Ji 孫機. *Handai wuzhi wenhua ziliao tushuo* 漢代物質文化資料圖說. Shanghai: Shanghai Guji Chubanshe, 2011.

Sun Xingyan 孫星衍. *Hanguan liuzhong* 漢官六種. Edited by Zhou Tianyou 周天游. Beijing: Zhonghua Shuju, 1990.

Wang Yingzhu 王穎竹, Ma Qinglin 馬清林, and Li Yanxiang 李延祥. "Zhongguo

gudai xiangliao shihua: Liyi zhi
bang, xiangyun liuchang" 中國古代
香料史話: 禮儀之邦, 香韵流長.
Wenming 文明 3 (2014): 60–79.
Xu Ling 徐陵. *Yutai xinyong jianzhu* 玉臺
新詠箋注. Edited by Mu Kehong 穆
克宏. Beijing: Zhonghua Shuju, 1985.

Yamada Kentarō. 山田憲太郎. *Tōa kōryō
shi kenkyū* 東亜香料史研究. Tokyo:
Chūō Kōron Bijutsu Shuppan, 1976.
———. *Tōzai kōyaku shi* 東西香藥史.
Tokyo: Fukumura Shoten, 1956.

CHAPTER 3

The Poetics of Incense in the Lives of Medieval Chinese Officials

Qian Jia

Contrary to assumptions that the sense of smell is "primitive," "bestial," sensual, and nonintellectual, fragrance in China has long been associated with refinement and spirituality.[1] In antiquity, the smell of cooked food and burning herbs served as offerings for deities in sacrifices.[2] Fragrance has been used as a sign for individuals of great virtues or perfection in governance in literary texts since early periods, such as in the poem "Encountering Sorrow" ("Lisao" 離騷) and in the *Book of Documents* (*Shangshu* 尚書).[3] In medieval China, the scent of incense in particular was closely related to spirituality, cultivation, and social status.[4] Burning incense had been the privilege of religious authorities, the imperial palace, and high aristocracy in China since the first century. But it only became widely accessible in the Song 宋 dynasty period (960–1276) as a result of religious and economic developments. The Song scholar-officials (*shidaifu*, 士大夫), with their rising prominence in the political and cultural realms since the late tenth century, reconstructed the cultural image of incense and influenced understandings of scent. They turned incense into the signature of their own social class, establishing its significance for their autonomous cultivation of spirituality, the imagining of their duties to the state, and as integral to their private experience of romance and intimacy. Employing scent as an instant device to create and break spatial, temporal, social, and even gender boundaries, the *shidaifu* writings on the effects of incense had a decisive impact on the way this treasured commodity was perceived, imagined, and used throughout later centuries.

Scent's invisible and intangible meditative and transformative properties explicate why incense permeates the contemplation and composition of writing on this theme. Therefore, this chapter explores the complex poetics of incense in medieval China. The discussion also uncovers how olfactory sensation is represented in classical Chinese poetry, a genre of writing often appreciated for its mastery of visual imagery. The poetic portrayal of incense first drew inspiration from religious scriptures and palace activities but gradually diverged to center on the lives of scholar-officials. The way incense smoke diffuses, separates, disappears, and lingers provides a rich and multivalent poetic imagery that relates to many different facets of life: public and private, religious and secular, spiritual and sensual. The contradictory yet coexisting tendencies of movement serve as poignant analogy for ambivalent and indeterminate situations, for the engagement and disengagement with worldly obligations, love affairs, and memories of the past. Scents triggered not only olfactory sensations but in fact synesthetic experiences pertaining to various senses and the mind.

This chapter works chronologically through the traditions of two major poetic genres, *shi* 詩 and *ci* 詞, with a focus on the Song period, but also including the preceding Six Dynasties and Tang periods. As genre conventions in classical Chinese literature tend to prescribe the content of compositions, the major themes in *shi* and *ci* greatly differ. Regarded as a formal and public genre, *shi* poems, with regular line lengths, often evoked themes pertaining to aspirational and philosophical contemplations. Coming to maturity in the Song dynasty, *ci*, irregular in line lengths, initially appeared as lyrics written by male literati for courtesans to sing, mimicking a female voice and centering upon women's yearnings for love. Focused on romance, intimacy, and women, the genre had an informal and private nature and was thus seen as a lesser poetic form. It is only by investigating both genres of verses that one can see the full poetic portrayal of scents and olfactory sensations in the Chinese tradition.

If one searches poems with the character *xiang* 香 (meaning "incense" or "fragrance") in comprehensive anthologies of *shi* and *ci* of the time periods mentioned above, one finds thousands of relevant poems in each genre.[5] The large quantity of results from the Song period especially indicates the popularity of themes of scent in poetry at the time but also poses a great challenge for analysis. Yet the uses of scent in these poems are largely formulaic and show influences of early allusions and works by renowned authors, as one would expect from classical Chinese poetry. Below, I have grouped them into themes and selected the earliest representatives or the ones by the most influential authors in each theme. Also, because of the all-encompassing nature of the term *xiang* (discussed in detail in the next section), the selection favors poems with the image of burning incense to ensure that we focus on incense instead of on all fragrances.

Of course, Song literati wrote about incense in genres other than poetry—namely, catalogs of incense (*xiangpu* 香譜) and in narratives. Song paintings also incorporate a great interest in images of incense and censers. This chapter is part of a larger project investigating the Song scholar-officials' fascination with incense and how exquisite scents led them to gradually reconceptualize spirituality, officialdom, private life, empirical experiences, knowledge, wealth, and cultural others, as manifested in various verbal and pictorial representations. The evolving aesthetics and symbolism regarding incense in poetry, the most prominent, long-standing, and pervasive form of expression in Chinese cultural history, capture both the essence and the nuances of this significant change.

Defining Incense

Before delving into the poetry, a terminological challenge in this study must be addressed. The Chinese character for incense, *xiang* 香, has more complex implications than its usual English translation indicates (see Marinucci in this volume). In the early second-century dictionary *Shuowen jiezi* 說文解字, *xiang* is defined as "fragrance" using the character 芳.[6] In other words, the character is the general term for all fragrances, which leads to the inevitable question: What specifically counted as incense in medieval China? A clear answer does not appear until the Song period, when the commodity became widely accessible and systematic knowledge of *xiang* was gradually established in the *xiangpu* texts. Emerging at the beginning of the eleventh century, these catalogs feature entries on categories of aromatics, with information about origin, form, texture, quality, scent, and usage, as well as recipes for processing them into incense.[7] These *xiangpu* collectively redefined *xiang* by their lists of incense ingredients in various formulations, with an emphasis on aromatics from southern China and foreign states, including agarwood varieties, sandalwood, frankincense, and so on. The ingredients were sourced from plants, animals, or minerals but needed to undergo manual production or preservation. Raw materials, such as fresh flowers, were not considered incense. Furthermore, the texts instructed readers in various ways to enjoy incense: incense could be burned, worn, hung as ornaments, or consumed as medicine.[8]

By contrast, the modern English definition of incense describes it as "an aromatic gum or other vegetable product, or a mixture of fragrant gums and spices, used for producing a sweet smell when burned."[9] The broader definition in Song China displays a finer understanding of incense's source materials and a wider range of applications. Incense was enjoyed not because it offered one type of scent ("sweet") to satisfy a single sensation ("smell") via one particular means ("burning"). Instead, different *xiang* produced varied scents for different occasions. The aromas triggered not only the sense of smell but also sight, touch, and taste. Properties other than scent, such as medical benefits, were also explored.

Incense and Spirituality in Religious Texts and Pre–Song Dynasty *Shi* Poetry

In the following section, I will first introduce the origin of "images" of scent in *shi* and then analyze poems that incorporate such images. One main aspect of the poetics of *xiang* in Song *shi* derives from the crucial function of incense in Buddhist and Daoist rituals: its scent and smoke delineate a space of spiritual cultivation. Instructions and depictions on the use of incense may be found in medieval Daoist scriptures. Both bathing in water with aromatic herbs and burning incense are indispensable actions of purification within Daoist practices. Burning incense also supports the notion of contact between the divine and the mortal. Scriptures instruct adherents to burn a mixture of incense at bedside near the head during sleep to prepare for encounters with deities. The fragrance expels the rank air of the mortal world and invite deities to descend.[10] Aspiring to the heavens, incense smoke creates a portal that allows humans and gods to meet. Furthermore, lighting an incense burner is a crucial opening act in major Daoist rituals, initiating communication between the priest and the divine world while extinguishing the incense burner closes the ceremony.[11] Additionally, scriptures were regarded as sacred in Daoism, so one ought to burn incense to purify the space as a gesture of reverence before reading. Burning incense would create a sacred space and associating the act with reading later became prevalent in poetry.

There are abundant references to incense as well in Buddhist sutras. The most frequently depicted use is as offerings to deities. Influential scriptures in medieval China often mention burning incense, together with the presentation of aromatic herb water, flowers, and jeweled ornaments as offerings for the Buddha.[12] Sutras portray burning incense as an indispensable step in the preparation of ritual sites and give detailed instructions about what types of incense to burn and when and where to burn them.[13] Yet scriptures rarely directly address the significance of burning incense. The closest explanation appears to be in the phrase "incense serves as the envoy for the Buddha" 香為佛使.[14] Burning incense, in this understanding, sends a message to invite the Buddha and deities from all directions. Incense serves as a symbol of the power and virtue of Buddhas and Bodhisattvas.[15] The presence of fragrance signifies the presence of the divine, and the depiction of incense in poems on monasteries incorporates such implications.

Burning incense has always been an important part of the monastic life in China. Zanning 贊寧 (919–1001) identifies Dao'an's 道安 (312–385) regulations for monks and nuns as the first clear indication of burning incense in everyday monastic practice.[16] Teaching and chanting should only take place after the incense is burned. Zhiyi's 智顗 (538–597) instruction on practicing meditation specifies burning incense as a part of the preparation before entering (the site of) meditation or ritual performance.[17] Compiled in the Song, the earliest extant set of Buddhist monastic rules, *Chanyuan qinggui* 禪院清規, shows the prevalent use of incense in monks' daily routine.[18] Apart from assemblies, lectures, and meditation, burning incense is additionally integral to the reception of guests and before serving tea or meals, a common trope in poetry on literati interactions with monks.

The descriptions of incense in religious texts had a noticeable impact on its depiction in poetry, and by studying how poetics evolved through time, we gain an understanding of the historical development of the portrayal of incense. The religious implications of notions of scent in poetry gradually changed: instead of piety for the divine, the need to adjust to undesirable realities in secular life became a major motivation for spiritual cultivation. Images of profuse incense abounded in medieval poems on Daoist abbeys and Buddhist stupas as an indication of the copious offerings that the venues received—for example, "the stupa appears to surge from the ground; like a vertical swirl of incense smoke."[19] The most significant incorporation of evocations of scent in *shi* poetry is in their references to purification and the delineation of a spiritual space, especially common in Tang 唐 dynasty (618–907) poems regarding spiritual experiences. Poetic depictions of burning incense during individual spiritual practice without reference to religious authorities, however, did not appear until the ninth century. Prior to that, whenever the act of burning incense was mentioned, the poem described a scene either in the monasteries or in the presence of a monk or a Daoist. Wang Wei 王維 (701–761), who was one of the most celebrated elite poets in the eighth century and known for his affinity for Buddhism, is a source of representative works for this early usage. The poem "At the Scene of the Abbot's Room on a Spring Day" 春日上方即事 is an excellent example:

> He likes to read *Biographies of Eminent Monks*,
> and occasionally studies techniques of grain avoidance.
> A dove carved on the top of his staff,
> turtle shells for supporting his couch.
> Willow colors shade spring mountains;
> pear blossoms hide evening birds.
> By the northern window, under peach and plum trees,
> he sits in leisure, simply burning incense.[20]

As the title suggests, this poem describes the scene in an abbot's room. The daily objects on display indicate the age (both the dove pattern and the turtle shell signify seniority), status, and profession of the resident. The third couplet appears to picture the outdoor scenery, but the two verbs "shade" and "hide" both suggest a movement of covering, a sense of seclusion, and a toning down of the spring color and liveliness. The act of burning incense appears in the final couplet. While the plum and peach trees integrate the abbot's room with the spring hues outside, just as the burning incense closes the poem, the scent seals this spiritual space of tranquility while still allowing a connection with the outside.

The hinted-at theme of reclusion in the poem above becomes the opening mood in the following poem by the same author, "Offering Food to Monks from the Fufu Mountain" 飯覆釜山僧, whereby incense plays a crucial role in the development of his contemplation.

> Late in my years, I come to understand the principle of purity,
> day by day distancing myself from the crowd.
> Waiting for monks from the remote mountain,
> I clean my shabby hut beforehand.
> As expected, from the cloudy peaks,
> they visit my dwelling among wild grass.
> Sitting on straws, we eat pine nuts;
> burning incense, we read scriptures of the Way.
> Lighting up the lamp as daylight disappears;
> striking the chime when the night starts.

Once enlightened, one sees extinction as joy,
and this life will have abundant leisure.
Why sink deep into the thought of reclusion?
The body and the world are similarly empty.[21]

Wang Wei begins with an intention to distance himself from the mundane world and resorts to the men of spirituality, monks from the Fufu Mountain, for help. The fourth couplet encloses the main pivot of the poem. Until the end of line 7, the poem is full of actions: the poet is cleaning, and after the monks arrive, cooking and eating take place. Yet after the burning of incense in line 8, deriving from the monastic practice of greeting guests, the bustle ceases, and the space takes on a tranquil ambience. In reading, time passes, and the poet's mind, upon the realization of emptiness, is relieved from the anxiety caused by his discordance with the world and his inner debate about reclusion. The smell of incense transforms the poet's mindset and alters the space, but the change only occurs during his religious practice in the presence of monks.

In the early ninth century, poems that describe burning incense in sheer solitude—without religious figures, whose presence had been ubiquitous in such practices up to that point—started to emerge, signaling an emerging secularization of incense and spiritual cultivation. The following poem, "Sitting Leisurely by the Northern Window" 北窗閑坐, reads as Bo Juyi's 白居易 (772–846) statement on the emerging new poetics.

By the empty widow, two patches of bamboo,
in the room of stillness, incense burns.
Outside the door, red dust fuses;
in the city, the white sun is busy.
Do not bother to search for a Daoist;
need not study the transcendent method.
I have the trick to extend my life span:
when the heart is at leisure, years prolong.[22]

The opening couplet, with bamboo patches by the studio window, is reminiscent of Wang Wei's depiction of the abbot's room. Bo creates the image of a quiet and enclosed space, and the incense scent serves a similar function of separation as it does in Wang's poem. The second couplet explains what is blocked out: the busy world of dust and official duties. In the next quatrain, the poet claims that he does not need the assistance of religious authority; alone, he can keep his mind at ease and thus prolong his life span. Although Bo's playful tone on the Daoist search for transcendence does not necessarily stand in opposition to Wang's search for spiritual enlightenment with Buddhist monks, Bo's confidence in controlling his own mindset by situating himself in the privacy of his study is significant. The scent no longer serves as an offering to the divine, and the poet's spiritual cultivation is not an act of religious devotion to please the deities but rather his pursuit of a peaceful mind to help cast away his worries about public duties. The poem can thus be read as a declaration, secularizing the smell of incense and spiritual pursuits. Additionally, the immaterial sanctum created by the scent does not obstruct the physical connection to the outside world and thus allows the poet to maintain the status of "hermitage in officialdom" (liyin 吏隠), "the achievement of a detached state of mind while filling an official post and enjoying all the benefits that came with it."[23] The smell of incense thus began to transform from a symbol of religious authorities to a practice engaging in autonomous spiritual pursuits.

Burning Incense in Song Dynasty *Shi* Poetry

In the early Northern Song (960–1127), incense in China relied heavily on importation and foreign tributes and was still a luxury. Yet because of increasing domestic incense production, especially from the far south (near the present-day Guangdong, Guangxi, and Hainan) and the rapidly expanding incense trade with areas along the Arabian Sea, the price of the commodity dropped significantly.[24] The late Tang convention of using incense to demarcate a private space of spiritual autonomy consequently flourished in the Song dynasty. The scent also helped Song scholar-officials create temporary asylums in exiles.[25] Hundreds of poems with the phrase "fenxiang" 焚香 ("burning incense") can be found in *Complete Song Poems* (*Quan* Song *shi* 全宋詩). The act of burning incense and enjoying solitude became a signature in the Song literati lifestyle, a gesture of temporary withdrawal from official duties and the world of clamor. The most frequently seen catchphrase is "burning incense, sweeping the ground, and reading," deriving from the Daoist ritual progression of burning incense as a gesture of purification and reverence before reading scriptures. What they were reading were usually Buddhist or Daoist scriptures but sometimes also literary classics. Song scholar-officials' growing interest in religious texts and practices partly explains the prevalence of these descriptions in poetry, but the increasing availability of incense in daily life also contributed to its rising popularity in literary representation.

Although the usage of "burning incense" in *shi* poetry sometimes appears formulaic in the Song period, scents such as these took on new significance in the scholar-officials' lives during political vicissitudes, when they generally had little control of their destinies. The early Song political arena was dominated by factionalism, and many suffered from persecutions and exiles. Su Shi 蘇軾 (1037–1101), one of the most prestigious scholar-officials at the time, was banished to Huangzhou in 1079, which initiated a series of exiles that extended to the end of his life.[26] His brother Su Zhe 蘇轍 (1039–1112) and his close friend Huang Tingjian 黃庭堅 (1045–1105) were also punished by implication and suffered from political strife throughout their lives. Precedents in the tradition of exile poetry are replete with adversity in the place of banishment (usually in the south), longings for home, and the frustration of unfulfilled ambition. The poems by the Northern Song literati embarked rather on a new direction: they write about their efforts to adapt to and find pleasure in their undesirable situations. This emerging poetics has been interpreted as a gesture of political dissonance, which indicates the poets' alienation from their identity as officials.[27] However, the adversity was impossible to evade, and the poets could not entirely blend into the new environments or escape the distress of displacement. Creating spatial boundaries while maintaining connection to the surroundings, the incense scent in their poems embodies their ambivalence.

The following poem by Su Shi, "The Southern Hall" 南堂, was composed in his third year in Huangzhou (1083), which had become bearable compared with his earlier days there and his later exiles in the far south. After a few years of resistance, Su Shi seemed to finally build up a comfortable asylum of his own: the Southern Hall, a humble three-room residence by the Yangzi River.[28] He composed a sequence of five four-line poems for the place, the last of which is cited here. The preceding poems describe how Su Shi enjoyed life by resorting to books, farming, and friendship while confronting his experiences of hardship. The completion of the humble hut gave him a boost of joy, which distanced him from his surfacing thoughts on old age and homesickness. The fifth poem continued the theme, but with a subtle twist, and incense played a vital role in expressing the extra layer of meaning.

After sweeping the ground and burning incense, I shut the door and
   sleep,

The water-like pattern of the bamboo mat, and the smoke-like canopy.
The traveler wakes up from a dream, "where am I?"
Rolling up the curtain of the western window—waves touching the
    sky.[29]

The opening line consists of a series of movements, sweeping the ground,
burning incense, and shutting the room, preparing a pure and private space
of enclosure. As if tired from all the efforts featured in the previous four
poems, Su Shi allows himself to rest, temporarily removing himself from
the immediate reality. He can only truly relax in the comfort of a scholar-official's private room where the incense always burns. However, while
he sleeps, the mist-like canopy and water-like pattern of the mat reconnect
the isolated space with the outside world, the Yangzi River's water and mist.
The line indicates the poet's integration with his surroundings, while the
moment of confusion after the poet wakes up implies a sense of dislocation.

The scent of incense in the "Southern Hall" poem simultaneously creates
and breaks spatial boundaries. The aroma both delineates a private space
that separates him from his surroundings and extends to link the space to
the water, transforming it into a boat, allowing the poet to escape in dreams.
The sky-touching waves by the western window, echoing with the mist-like
canopy and water-like pattern of the mat, make the hut resemble a boat in
the water. The imagery resonates with a line in the *ci*, "To the Tune: Immor-
tal by the River" 臨江仙, that Su Shi wrote in the same year: "I will drift
away on a small boat from now on, / entrusting the rest of my life to rivers
and seas."[30] As a banished official, it was illegal for Su Shi to leave the place
of exile, which is why he entertains the idea of drifting away on the river.

A similar usage of scent can be found in one of Huang Tingjian's colo-
phons.[31] It was composed in 1103 when he was banished to Yizhou (in
present-day Guangxi), where he died two years later. In the account, Huang
tells us that he was forced to move to the south of the city, and his rented
place was named "Clamor and Desolation Study." The living conditions were
poor, with rain pouring, wind circling, and no shelter or cover above him.
The noise from the markets was loud and deafening. Although his difficulties
might be heightened by exaggeration, Huang experienced severe hardship
and did not bend to reality. On the contrary, he claims, "Others thought that
I could not endure the adversity. Yet my family were originally farmers. Had
I not taken the *jinshi* exam, I would be living in a hut in the field just like
this. So why would I not endure it? Setting up the couch, burning incense,

and sitting myself down, I directly face my western neighbor's chopping board for ox butchering."[32]

Despite Huang's vigorous protests, this passage shows, conversely, that he was still an elite scholar-official and unable to fully adapt to the life of the lower classes. He needed the shield of incense aroma to distance him from the reality: the butcher's chopping board and its stink. Here the boundary is not only spatial but also social—Huang distinguishes himself from the commoners with the poetic signature: the scents of the literati class.

From Wang Wei to Huang Tingjian, Tang and Song literati experienced various struggles in the life of officials, from the troubling urge for reclusion to the ambivalent divergence from the scholar-official identity in exile. Affecting both the nose and the mind, the scent of incense assists them in setting boundaries between public and private spheres, worldly duties and spiritual pursuits, reality and ideal, and social classes. Although the immaterial and temporary boundaries created by incense appear to be vulnerable, the mind as transformed by the aroma is perceived to be improving. Claiming incense outside of the authority of gods and detached from the state, medieval literati began to master their minds and seek enlightenment on their own.

Incense and the State

Just as multiple scents can both separate and connect, the poetics of incense is far from one-dimensional. Despite the implication of the previous section's discussion of scholar-officials' detachment from official duties, scent can signify state power and officialdom in traditional Chinese poetry, as it was quintessential in the imperial palace and bureaus. Since its initial importation in the first century, incense was burned in various venues in the palace. For example, it was burned in the assembly hall where the emperor gave audience to ministers as well as in the imperial libraries, offices of ministries, and women's quarters. Poets wrote about the pervasive scent to compare the palace to the haze-filled Daoist heaven, to use it as a metaphor for the omnipresent grace of the emperor, and to celebrate imperial birthdays, as the far-extending smoke symbolized longevity.

Not all poems employed the profuse incense smoke in the palace to sing praises, however, and precise images were at times used to strike a subtle note of dissonance. The harmonizing poems on going to the court assembly by Tang dynasty literati Jia Zhi 賈至 (718–772) and Du Fu 杜甫 (712–770)

are models for such ambivalent depictions of incense. Both poems portray the imperial palace at dawn in the first quatrain. Jia then describes the officials in the assembly and their clothes infused with an incense smell from the imperial braziers:

> The sounds of waist-strung swords follow steps on the pavements of
>   jade,
> bodies in caps and gowns tease wisps of incense from imperial
>   braziers.
> Together we bathe in waves of Grace by Phoenix Pool,
>   at every dawn court dipping our brushes to serve our Lord and Ruler.[33]

The final couplet of this poem praises imperial grace and pledges to serve the emperor. The incense scent represents "the waves of Grace" that the officials all "bathe" in. This depiction of incense was widely adopted by later poets to imply desire to receive imperial appointments or gratitude for their obtained positions.

Instead of the court assembly, Du Fu turns his attention to what happens afterward, depicting his friend Jia returning home from the palace, with sleeves full of fragrant smoke, and composing poetry. "Dawn court done, the scented smoke you carry filling your sleeves; / the poem finished, pearls and jade are right on your flourished brush."[34] The intangible smoke and its "filling" of the sleeves form an almost ironic contrast, which ensures that the materiality of pearls and jade in the next line, used as a metaphor for the beauty of the poetry that Jia composes, appear more substantial. Whether Du Fu does it intentionally or not, the couplet shows an intriguing pairing of an insubstantial award from the service to the court and the substantial achievement of literary talent by the individual.

The following poem, "Thoughts While Burning Incense" 焚香有感 is by Ren Boyu 任伯雨 (ca. 1047–1119), who served in three regimes, subsequently experienced various political disturbances of the late Northern Song, and finally died in his exile in Hainan. The poem uses the trope of incense to express two opposing desires regarding the imperial court and officialdom.[35]

> Sweeping the ground, burning incense, and opening the bamboo gate;
> light smoke, profuse and fragrant, winding leisurely in the dawn glow.
> Yet I recall the past at Extending Harmony Palace Hall,
> after the assembly, carrying home full sleeves [of incense fragrance].[36]

Leisurely burning incense in his residence, the poet recalls the time when he served at court. The two couplets mirror each other, with the contrast of two types of incense smoke representing the private and the public spheres respectively. The poem appears as an odd juxtaposition of opposite sentiments. However, it is likely that incense simultaneously evokes both engagement and disengagement with official duties in the mind of the poet, as his career constantly toyed with his fate, leading him to the highest prestige and the most painful predicaments. Rather than self-contradictory, the scent's dual implications capture the official class's ambivalent attitude toward the state and life in officialdom.

Incense and Romance in Poetry Before the Song Dynasty

As mentioned earlier, classical Chinese poetry is bound by convention. Poems on different themes tend to employ different sets of images. However, due to its penetration of all spaces, scent prevails in poems of drastically different themes, from the most public and spiritual (as discussed in the previous two sections) to the most private and sensual. Indicating beauty and goodness of a person, fragrance is an essential part of Chinese love poems. There is an endless list of two-character phrases starting with *xiang* (fragrant/fragrance) in medieval poetry, such as "fragrant cloud" (*xiangyun* 香雲, referring to hair), "fragrant quilt" (*xiangqin* 香衾), "fragrant sleeves" (*xiangjue* 香袂), and "fragrant steps" (*xiangjie* 香階). It appears that anything about a desirable person could be aromatic. Although some of the phrases can be used to describe virtuous men, in the context of love poems, such terms mostly refer to women.

Incense, frequently given as a token of love, and whose fragrance fills the spaces where love affairs take place, is a popular image in the poetic depiction of romance and intimacy. The scent triggers synesthetic experiences of smell, sight, touch, and emotion. It also frames the temporal aspects of the experience, marking its duration and retrieving it from memory. The lingering aroma of incense after it burns out serves as an apt analogy for the persistent yearning and sorrow that love brings. Transgressing boundaries, the scent allows poets to challenge genre conventions on gender expression.

Such poetics is first seen in early medieval *shi* poems. The third-century ballad-style poem, "West of Chang'an" 西長安行 features incense as a token of love and expands on its resonance with the tangled feelings that love stirs:

Where is the one that I am yearning for?
He is in the west of Chang'an.
What would you use to cheer me up?
Knitted incense pouch with a double-pearled ring.
What would you use to cheer me up again?
Winged goblet with green jade beads.
Today I hear that you
have changed your mind.
Yet, the incense cannot be burnt,
and the pearl ring cannot be sunk.
But the incense will burn out one day,
and the ring will sink deeper and deeper.[37]

The female persona is experiencing the willful changes of love. The man courted her with luxurious gifts at first but has changed his mind. She wants to burn out the incense, the token of love, but it would only be a painful confirmation of the death of the romance. The incense thus becomes a heartbreaking symbol of her lingering affections and the eventual termination of their love.

Poems on the imperial harem and palace ladies often relate incense to temporality. Burning incense during the night, especially when sleeping, was common in the palace, so incense was often paired with other time markers, including the water clock or the graduated candle, and the bamboo rod in poetry.[38] The quatrain below is a typical example:

Spring window facing the fragrant isle;
beaded curtains, newly hung.
By burning incense [we] know the hour on the dripping clock;
with graduated candles [we] confirm the bamboo-rod tally.[39]

Such poems usually depict the scene of the bedroom, and the woman inside is lonely and pensive, waiting for the lover (the emperor) who rarely or never comes.[40]

Eupatory ointment burnt out and I add more;
the extinguished censer exudes fragrance once more.
Simply ask me how much sorrow I have,
then you will know how long the night lasts.[41]

THE POETICS OF INCENSE 77

The censer continues to emit fragrance because the woman is kept awake by her tears and constantly adds fuel to it. The extending smell of incense resonates with her endless sorrow and the infinite night.

The incorporation of incense in the depiction of love and yearning is further developed in Tang and Song *shi* poetry but, as one expects, truly thrived in *ci*, a genre that is mostly devoted to romantic themes. *Ci* lyrics before the Song already started to form a set of poetics pertaining to incense. Rarely the central image or topic in *ci*, incense, however, is a common element in the depiction of the boudoir and the woman inside. Often paired with images of layers, enwrappedness, and intimacy, such as the screen, the canopy, curtains, beddings, and women's apparel, incense further envelops the space with scents and smoke.

Additional to olfactory sensations, incense also triggers the sense of touch (or the craving for it). Its close association with the female body makes it an erotic stimulus. The aroma blends with the breath of the woman, such as in the line "in the soft scents of eupatory and musk, I sensed her breath."[42] The act of adding incense is also seductive because it directs attention to women's bodies—for example, "fragrant bones and slender waist change the agarwood and sandalwood,"[43] and "slim hands gently arrange / incense in the jade burner."[44] The sense of touch can also be the experience of temperature. Burning incense engenders warmth in the boudoir, such as in "glass pillows inside the crystal bead curtain, warm fragrance evokes dreams in the mandarin duck embroidered quilt."[45] Incense also turns cold after the coal burns out: "Incense cools behind the brocade screen, the embroidered quilt cold / Downcast and disheartened, I think about you, helplessly," indicating the woman's melancholy and longing for the parted lover.[46] Thus, in love poems, incense not only induces olfactory-tactile synesthesia but also emotions of unfulfilled yearning.

Incense and Romance in Song Dynasty *Ci*

Apart from the obsession with sensuality in earlier lyrics, Song poets probed deeper into various characteristics of incense and their resonance with human emotions. Also, rather than dwelling on the poetic tradition of writing romance with a focus on the male literati assumption of women's yearnings and complaints, Song writers started to uncover men's complex feelings about love, usually regarded as inappropriate and unmasculine and therefore rarely expressed in other genres or in earlier *ci*.

As mentioned above, the act of "stirring incense" in pre-Song lyrics is mostly erotic because of its association with women's bodies. In "To the Tune: 'Stirring Incense'" 翻香令 by Su Shi, however, the action conversely embodies a man's tenderest and deepest affection.

> The metal burner remains warm, with musk residue.
> Cherishing the aroma, I stir the jeweled pin one more time.
> I sniff again, and there is still fragrance.
> This time, the scent is even greater than before.
>
> Hiding from others, I cover the tiny mountain of immortality,[47]
> and secretly light agarwood together [with the musk],
> only hoping to make the dense mist last longer.
> For our love is deep, I fear that the incense might break before burning out. [48]

This piece is traditionally read as a eulogy that Su Shi wrote for his deceased wife, Wang Fu 王弗 (1039–1065). Unexpectedly, the act of stirring incense is carried out by the male poet instead of by a seductive woman. The musk might be imagined to have been left by his wife, who presumably used to burn incense for him. The poet has a dilemma: he wants to burn the musk because the aroma reminds him of her, but the musk will soon be exhausted if he does so. He solves the problem by adding agarwood to the musk to prolong the scent and thence the feeling of being with his wife. The phrase "hiding from others" discloses the poet's complex emotion. A Confucian scholar-official was not supposed to show his romantic emotions explicitly, so, embarrassed by his sentimental act of treasuring the aroma by mixing incense, he had to do it secretly to avoid being seen. The last line implies another motivation for the act: he is afraid that the incense might extinguish before burning out, which is an omen for separation from loved ones in the next life. Wishing to spend another life with his wife, Su Shi is trying to prevent losing her again.

Whereas the Su Shi lyric above turns a conventionally feminine act associated with incense into an expression of a male poet's grief for loss, in "To the Tune: 'Rest after Crossing the Brook'" 過澗歇近, Liu Yong 柳永 (ca. 987– ca. 1053) adopts incense to reveal a man's suffering in romance instead of women's. The lyric captures the moment when the poet wakes up as the incense burns out.

Sobering up, I just woke from a dream.
In the small chamber, fragrant charcoal turned into ashes.
On the door, the silver toad moves its shadow.[49]
No human sound,
the endless night, pure and cold.
On the green tiles, frost congeals;
through the loose bamboo curtain, wind wafts.
Dim is the sound of the dripping clock,
drifting to me and turning the listener sad.

What should I do with my heart?
I am dispirited recently, as if being sick for long.
The phoenix tower is only a few feet away,
but the date of reunion is far from set.
Turning and tossing, I cannot sleep.
The shiny pillow is icy;
the smoke of coiling incense has ceased,
who will tidy up the double quilts for me?[50]

As the fragrant wood turns into coal, sleep ends. The burned incense signals the termination of a period of time but simultaneously marks the beginning of another: awoken in the solitary night. The persona's gender remains ambiguous in the first stanza, and the lyric reads like a generic *ci* on lonely women. The "phoenix tower" in the third line of the second stanza, referring to residence for a woman, is the first and only clear indication that the persona is a male, since he yearns for a woman. The poet is thus employing the language and imagery that conventionally depict women's emotional turmoil to utter a love-lorn man's thoughts, a topic that almost no other male poet had embarked on.

By mentioning the ceasing smoke, the ending suggests a closure for the poet's melancholy. However, in the last line, as the yearning for the lover is concretized by the memory of the girl making his bed and the worry that no one would ever do it for him again, the poet sinks deeper into emotion. The romantic sentiments intensify and extend to shadow the future, even after the incense smoke disappears. Throughout the poem, the process of the incense burning out and the smoke diminishing parallels with the surfacing, lingering, and culmination of the poet's yearning. Incense frames the memory of romance.

Wu Wenying's 吳文英 (1200–1260) lyric "To the Tune: 'Heavenly Scents'"
天香 combines and dramatizes multiple poetics of incense in *ci* on romance,
with an interesting twist of the genre convention of gender expressions.

> Weaved pearls tinkled,
> silk sachets on the canopy of leisure.[51]
> I leaned on her soft bosom of warm musk.
> The stamens of the Forever-Together flower,[52]
> were absolutely charming.
> The phoenix chest heavy, half-full with silk gowns,
> crimson fringes hung on the four corners.
> Listless, we would not get up; spring slumber under the ruffled trim.
> The fragrance of incense drifted across the courtyard of rouge
>   crepe-myrtles;
> smoke locked the painted screen and the agarwood in.
>
> In red gauze, she tested the hot-spring water.
> Dew invaded; from her skin oozed the fragrance of eupatory.
> My eyes roam in the moonlit night by the shallow creek:
> flower aroma secretly surfaces.
> This Xun Yu is now old;
> which, however, does not lessen my Han Shou-like charm.
> I am sending my yearnings from faraway;
> the fragrance lingers in my dreams.[53]

Unreservedly erotic, the lyric greets the reader with a full spectrum of sensual
stimuli: the tinkling sound of pearls, the touch and smell of the woman, and
the sight of various furniture in her room. Scents constitute a crucial part
of this typical repertoire of sensuality in lyrics: the incense pieces in the silk
sachets, the warm musk on the woman, the floral aroma, and the smell of
burning incense. At the end of the first stanza, the incense scent frames the
entire space of intimacy by spreading over the courtyard, with its smoke
locking up the chamber.

The erotic depiction continues in the second stanza: the woman enters the
hot spring and her wet skin oozes eupatory fragrance. The poem then turns
away from the scene and to the poet's mind. He gazes into the moonlit night
by the shallow creek, a serene view in sharp contrast with the intense sensuality. Yet the "secretly surfacing" floral aroma recalls the erotic sensations. Then

the poet starts to lament his old age and evokes two historical figures that are frequently alluded to in poetry because of their association with incense, Xun Yu 荀彧 (163–212) and Han Shou 韓壽 (?–300). In earlier poetry, Han Shou, who seduced a prominent official's daughter with his handsome looks, is a name often adopted by female personas in poetry to refer to their faraway lovers and to express sorrowful yearnings.[54] Yet here it is used by the male poet to refer to himself, analogous with Xun Yu, an official who fumed his clothes with incense and used the scent as a gesture of refusal to corruption.[55] By claiming "this Xun Yu is old," the poet is admitting the decline of his public self as a scholar-official, but he soon retrieves confidence in the romantic persona, Han Shou, which is a rare and unconventional identification, as men in Confucian society should fulfill their aspiration in worldly achievements, not in romantic affairs. The poet here integrates a male voice into the corpus of feminine expressions and rebelliously claims that he finds solace and self-affirmation in romance. The ending reveals that the poet is yearning for a past lover. It is the fragrance that lingers in his dreams and arouses his memory of her. Scents frame the entire erotic experience and the memory it leaves.

Conclusion

The smell of incense, which easily travels through time and space, also transcends multiple seemingly unbreakable boundaries in Song scholar-officials' lives and poetry: the bond to the state, their social class, gender, and literary convention. Claiming this exquisite scent of multivalent uses and significances from religious and state authorities, poets employ it to express dissatisfaction with the roles that the authorities prescribe to them: as dependent devotees, as loyal officials, and as Confucian gentlemen who ought to champion public accomplishments and evade expressions of private emotions, intimacy, and femininity. Burning incense became a signature of the Song literati class and their necessary method of combating adversity in the unpredictable reality of their times, seeking spiritual autonomy, and importantly, exploring the private self with a new genre of writing. We have seen how pervasive scents infused aspects of spiritual, political, and cultural significance in Chinese history and how they were refashioned and reimagined by the Song poets to embody their multifaceted realities and subtle divergence from traditional values. Like pervasive scents, which simultaneously separate and connect, the changes among the scholar-officials are doubtlessly discernible yet circumspect.

Notes

1. McHugh, *Sandalwood and Carrion*, 11; Corbin, *Foul and the Fragrant*, 6.

2. E.g., presenting the legend of Lord Millet (Hou Ji 后稷), the *Shijing* 詩經 poem, "Birth to the People" 生民 (Mao 245), ends with a description of a sacrifice for the deity where the aromas of steaming grains, grilling fat, and burning herbs were used to draw the Lord's attention and please him. *Maoshi zhengyi*, 17.264.b.

3. The line "utmost governance exudes fragrance, sensed by the divine and the numinous" in *the Book of Documents* (traditionally attributed to Confucius) associates fragrance with perfection in governance. *Shangshu zhengyi*, 18.125a. In "Encountering Sorrow," which is attributed to Qu Yuan 屈原 (ca. 340–278 BCE), the persona, a banished official, adorns himself with fragrant herbs to separate himself from the morally polluted world and indicate his purity and worthiness.

4. The chapter uses the term "medieval China" in its widest sense, which spans from the third to the thirteenth century.

5. Lu, *Xian Qin Han WeiJin Nanbeichao shi* (hereafter Lu); Peng et al., *Quan Tang shi* 全唐詩; Fu et al., ed., *Quan Song shi* (hereafter *QSS*); Zeng et al., *Quan Tang Wudai ci* (hereafter *QTWDC*); Tang, *Quan Song ci* (hereafter *QSC*).

6. *Shuowen jiezi*, 7a.20.

7. A chapter of my dissertation (forthcoming) focuses on the *xiangpu* genre, so I do not elaborate on the topic here.

8. Shen, *Xiangpu Xinzuan xiangpu*.

9. *OED*, https://www-oed-com.stanford .idm.oclc.org/view/Entry/93377?rskey= RXdRCS&result=1&isAdvanced=false#eid.

10. See in the fourth-century scripture "Dongzhen taiyi dijun taidan yinshu dongzhen xuanjing" 洞真太一帝君太丹隱書洞真玄經 (DZ 1318). *Zhengtong Daozang*, 1030.7a.

11. Anderson, "*Falu*."

12. E.g., *Flower Ornament Sutra*, the *LongerĀgama sutra*, and *Lotus sutra*. T. 278: 9.478c24–481b13; T. 1: 1.5c24, 27c17–28b17; T. 262: 9.30c7–31a3.

13. See in *Śuraṃgama-sūtra* and *Dhāraṇī sutra*. T. 945: 19.133b4; T. 901: 18.785c14.

14. Hou, *Zhongguo fojiao yishi yanjiu*, 51–52; T. 128: 2.839c15; T. 125: 2.662a7.

15. E.g., *Vimalakīrti Sutra*, T. 474: 14.532a5–c10.

16. *DaSong seng shilue* 大宋僧史略, T. 2126: 54.241b27; Hou, 54.

17. *Xiuxi zhiguan zuochan fayao* 修習止觀坐禪法要, T. 1915: 46. 463a3.

18. X. 1245: 63.

19. Xiao Que 蕭愨 (fl. 561), "Harmonizing with Palace Attendant Cui's Poem," Lu, 2.2276. In the *Lotus Sutra*, a stupa rises from the ground as a reward for steadfast faith, so the use of the imagery also praises the temple for its exceptional dedication. T. 262: 9.32c14.

20. Chen, comm., *Wang Wei jijiaozhu*, 7.612.

21. *Wang Wei jijiaozhu*, 6.521.

22. Gu, comm., *Bo Juyi ji*, 25.573.

23. Yang, *Metamorphosis of the Private Sphere*, 36.

24. Lin, *Songdai xiangyao maoyi shi*, 72, 331.

25. Shang, "Xiang chan shi de chuhui," analyzes Huang Tingjian's poems on burning incense and reaching enlightenment in Chan meditation. I will thus not discuss these poems here.

26. Huangzhou is in present-day Hubei. The banishment was the result of the "Crow Terrace Poetry Trial." Su Shi was accused of insulting the throne at Crow Terrace (the Imperial Censorate) because he criticized the recent political reforms in his writings. *Song shi*, 338.10809.

27. Egan, *Word, Image, and Deed*, 236–37.

28. See "Fourteen Letters to Cai Jingfan" 與蔡景繁十四首, Kong, *Su Shi wenji*, 55.1663.

29. Kong, *Su Shi shiji*, 22.1167.

30. Zou and Wang, *Su Shi ci biannian jiaozhu*, 467.

31. "Inscribed at the End of My Own Writing" 題自書卷後, in *Shangu tiba, Baibu congshu jicheng* 22, 9.1.

32. The "*jinshi* exam" refers to the civil service examination, the main method of selecting officials in imperial China since the Tang.

33. "Dawn Court at Daming Palace," trans. Owen, *Poetry of Du Fu*, 1.363.

34. "A Companion Piece For Drafter Jia Zhi's 'Dawn Court at Daming Palace'" 奉和賈至舍人早朝大明宮, trans. Owen, *Poetry of Du Fu*, 1.363.

35. *Song shi*, 345.10951.

36. QSS, 18.11800.

37. Fu Xuan 傅玄 (217–78), Lu, 1.564.

38. Bedini, *Trail of Time*, 53–66.

39. Yu Jianwu 庾肩吾 (487–551), "Harmonizing with the Poem on the Spring Night under Imperial Command," Lu, 23.1992.

40. Except for erotic poems that imply intercourse between the emperor and consorts.

41. Xiao Gang 蕭綱 (503–51), "Imitating Shen Yue's 'Night After Night,'" Xiao and Dong, *Liang Jiawendi ji jiaozhu*, 2.140.

42. Ouyang Jiong 歐陽炯 (896–971), "To the Tune: Sands of the Washing Stream," QTWDC, 3.449.

43. Han Wo 韓偓 (844–923), "To the Tune: Sands of the Washing Stream," QTWDC, 1.179.

44. Mao Xizhen 毛熙震 (fl. 947), "To the Tune: The Female Daoist," QTWDC, 3.588.

45. Wen Tingyun 溫庭筠 (812–70), "To the Tune: Bodhisattva Barbarian," QTWDC, 1.100.

46. Ouyang Jiong, "To the Tune: Spring in Jade Mansion," QTWDC, 3.463.

47. The "tiny mountain of immortality" refers to the censer.

48. Zou and Wang, *Su Shi ci biannian jiaozhu*, 875.

49. The "silver toad" refers to the moon.

50. QSC, 38.

51. The silk sachets are often filled with incense.

52. The Forever-Together flower was a symbol of union and thus a common pattern of quilt cover for lovers. The phrase here may be a pun for both the quilt pattern and actual flowers.

53. QSC, 2908–9.

54. *Jin shu*, 40.1172–73.

55. *Yiwen leiju*, 70.1222.

Bibliography

Anderson, Poul. "*Falu.*" In *The Encyclopedia of Taoism*, edited by Fabrizio Pregadio, 400–401. London: Routledge, 2008.

Bedini, Silvio A. *The Trail of Time: Time Measurement with Incense in East Asia*. Cambridge: Cambridge University Press, 1994.

Chen, Tiemin 陳鐵民, comm. *Wang Wei jijiaozhu* 王維集校注. Beijing: Zhonghua Shuju, 1997.

Corbin, Alain. *The Foul and the Fragrant: Odor and the French Social Imagination*. Translated by Miriam L. Kochan. Leamington Spa: Berg, 1986.

Egan, Ronald. *Word, Image, and Deed in the Life of Su Shi*. Cambridge, MA: Harvard University Harvard-Yenching Institute, 1994.

Fang, Xuanling 房玄齡, comp. *Jin shu* 晉書. Beijing: Zhonghua Shuju, 1974.

Fu, Xuancong 傅璇琮 et al., eds. *Quan Song shi* 全宋詩. Beijing: Beijing Daxue Chubanshe, 1995.

Gu, Xuejie 顧學頡, comm. *Bo Juyi ji* 白居易集. Beijing: Zhonghua Shuju, 1979.

Hou, Chong 侯沖. *Zhongguo fojiao yishi yanjiu: Yi zhaigong yishi wei zhongxin* 中國佛教儀式研究以齋供儀式為中心. Shanghai: Shanghai Guji Chubanshe, 2018.

Huang, Tingjian 黃庭堅. *Shangu tiba* 山谷題跋, *Baibu congshu jicheng* 百部叢書集成, 22. Taipei: Yiwen Yinshuguan, 1965.

Kong, Fanli 孔凡禮, comm. *Su Shi shiji* 蘇軾詩集. Beijing: Zhonghua Shuju, 1982.

———. *Su Shi wenji* 蘇軾文集. Beijing: Zhonghua Shuju, 1986.

———. *Su Zhe nianpu* 蘇轍年譜. Beijing: Xueyuan Chubanshe, 2001.

Kong, Yingda 孔穎達. *Maoshi Zhengyi* 毛詩正義. *Shisanjing Zhushu* 十三經注疏. Beijing: Zhonghua Shuju, 1982.

———. *Shangshu zhengyi* 尚書正義. *Shisanjing zhushu*. Beijing: Zhonghua Shuju, 1982.

Lin, Tianwei 林天蔚. *Songdai xiangyao maoyi shi* 宋代香藥貿易史. Taipei: Zhongguo Wenhua Daxue Chubanbu, 1986.

Lu, Qinli 逯欽立, comm. *Xian Qin Han WeiJin Nanbeichao shi* 先秦漢魏晉南北朝詩. Beijing: Zhonghua Shuju, 1983.

McHugh, James. *Sandalwood and Carrion: Smell in Indian Religion and Culture.* Oxford: Oxford University Press, 2012.

Ouyang, Xun 歐陽詢, comp. *Yiwen leiju* 藝文類聚. Beijing: Zhonghua Shuju, 1965.

Owen, Stephen, trans. *The Poetry of Du Fu.* Boston: De Gruyter, 2016.

Shang, Haifeng's 商海峰. "Xiang chan shi de chuhui: Cong beiSong Huang Tingjian dao Riben shiting shidai shanguchao" 香禪詩的初會–從北宋黃庭堅到日本室町時代山谷抄. *Hanxue Yanjiu* 漢學研究 36, no. 4 (2018): 73–111.

Shen, Chang 沈暢, comm. *Xiang pu Xinzuan xiangpu* 香譜新纂香譜. Hong Kong: Chengzhenlou, 2015.

Takakusu, Junjirō 高楠順次郎 et al., eds. *Taishō shinshū daizōkyō* 大正新脩 大藏經. Tokyo: Daizō Shuppansha, 1960–78.

Tang, Guizhang 唐圭璋, ed. *Quan Song Ci* 全宋詞. Beijing: Zhonghua Shuju, 1965.

Tuo, Tuo 脫脫, comp. *Song shi* 宋史. Taiwan: Zhonghua Shuju, 1965.

Xiao, Zhanpeng 肖占鵬, and Dong Zhiguang 董志廣, comm. *Liang Jiawendi ji jiaozhu* 梁簡文帝集校注. Tianjing: Nankai Daxue Chubanshe, 2012.

Xu, Shen 許慎. *Shuowen jiezi* 說文解字. Beijing: Zhonghua Shuju, 1963.

Yang, Xiaoshan. *Metamorphosis of the Private Sphere: Gardens and Objects in Tang-Song Poetry.* Cambridge, MA: Harvard University Asia Center, 2003.

Zeng, Zhaomin 曾昭岷 et al., eds. *Quan Tang Wudai ci* 全唐五代詞. Beijing: Zhonghua Shuju, 1999.

Zhengtong Daozang 正統道藏. Shanghai: Shangwu Yinshuguan, 1923–26.

Zou, Tongqing 鄒同慶, and Wang Zongtang 王宗堂, comm. *Su Shi ci biannian jiaozhu* 蘇軾詞編年校注. Beijing: Zhonghua Shuju, 2002.

MAKING SENSORY

BOUNDARIES

CHAPTER 4

A Whiff of Southeast Asia

Tasting Durian and Kopi

Gaik Cheng Khoo and Jean Duruz

In this chapter, we focus on the scent of belonging in Southeast Asia. This is a region known to the Chinese as Nanyang (南洋 literally "South Sea"), a tropical place where, historically, the Chinese had come first to trade, find work, and eventually settle. As the Nanyang Chinese integrated and became habituated to local tastes and smells, they also re-created and developed new tastes and smells—like roasted kopi and cultivated durian clones—which are fiercely national or localized to Malaysia and Singapore but which also have broader regional and global appeal.[1] That said, the Nanyang is also an imaginary homeland that presents a foodscape where iconic foods and their cultures of olfaction become sources of nostalgic remembering and enterprise.[2] Drawing on earlier arguments in this volume's introduction (chapter 1) regarding hierarchies of sensory experiences and their spatialities, especially lingering colonizing perspectives such as "the West and the 'rest'"—we suggest that a focus on specific olfactory cultures in Southeast Asia and their imagined communities can provide a more nuanced, less dichotomous account of sensory remembering. In particular, we want to note an intra-Asian expansion or broadening out of Southeast Asian scentscapes to China, as a result of economic globalization and the opportunities that the world's largest market has to offer.[3] In the process, meanings of "Nanyang" are reworked in subtle ways.

Throughout this chapter, we examine food's viscerality as a means of interpreting everyday practices, together with the geopolitical framing of sensual knowledge and the significance of smelling and tasting for mapping Asian culinary cultures—a mapping that complicates and moves beyond Eurocentric hierarchies of "good" and "bad" smells and beyond "superior" and "inferior" or "commodifiable" geographies. In other words, as Tang argues in Chapter 7, this does not mean a reversed hierarchy that favors scent over the ocular-phono senses. Instead, we argue here for a different and more complex account of sensation, an account (like Tang's) where smelling (in some cases, together with tasting) results in "the disruption of ocular-centric hegemony" and democratize(s) the cultural space. In adopting this movement outside, rather than against, traditional conceptual frameworks, we anticipate that meanings of authenticity, embodiment, and nostalgic remembering, together with those associated with the valuing of imagination and "different" sensory histories, will shape our analyses in unexpected ways.

Our approach here is through a focus on two "entangled" objects—durian and kopi (the Malay word for coffee)—to unravel different yet complementary stories of local provenance and resonant scentscapes.[4] Additionally, these objects suggest how globalization and the opening up of China to trade, investments, and cheap air travel to Southeast Asia have coincided in expanding the scentscape of the Nanyang, that place of imagined Chinese belonging for Chinese abroad. Vested in nostalgia for past times and places, meanings of durian and kopi, together with their pervasive aromas, may also signify transcendence by time, place, and culinary histories. This shift, though differently imagined in each of the following accounts of origins and futures, is from the intimate and familiar histories embedded in childhood or travel memories to the shaping of communities of smelling and tasting as forms of connoisseurship across, and beyond, national borders. Consider, for example, the intra-Asian trade routes of durian and kopi going from Malaysia, Singapore, and Thailand to Hong Kong, Macau, China, and the Southeast Asian diaspora in Australia. All in all, while the olfactory cultures of durian and kopi are discussed in different ways in this chapter, together they contribute to a distinctive Southeast Asian scentscape and represent the diversity of ways particular foods can contribute to this. Certainly, as our chapter title indicates, there are only "whiffs" of this here, but, at the same time, these "whiffs" serve as hints that our tales are more complex than they first appear. More importantly, such "whiffs" remind us that these, after all, are political tales, with tastes and smells not simply naturally occurring and freely floating but invested with meaning by regimes of social relations. More broadly, these might be of class and classiness, race and ethnicity, and more specifically, of dictates of the market, consumer cultures, and differing aroma perceptions within and across the Asian region. For, as Seremetakis reminds us, "A politics of sensory creation and perception [is] a politics of everyday life."[5]

Crucially, our argument focuses on examples of distinctive smells and scentscapes that map Singapore and Malaysia more subtly rather than simply identifying places and foods through binaries of "bad" or "good" smells. The edible commercial durian (*durio zibethinus*) is a spiky greenish-brown fruit native to Borneo and Sumatra averaging the size of a rugby ball with a pungent aroma often described as "rotten garbage," and we choose it as an obvious example. It permeates Southeast Asian culinary landscapes variously—nostalgically, as the smell of childhood, "home," the orchard, tradition, or, contradictorily, with a sometimes-muted aroma, as a prized product for global markets. And then again, durian may become a source of connoisseurial pride for communities celebrating the rich, pungent aroma and numbing sensation of freshly dropped fruit. Meanwhile, kopi is a dark, syrupy coffee produced from stewed, butter-fried beans, its history a blend of colonial attachment to coffee drinking combined with local ingredients and production methods. On the one hand, kopi's aroma and taste is fetishized by some (tourists, expatriates, other local ethnic—non-Chinese—groups) as "unusual," "exotic," or excessively thick and sweet, while for others, kopi retains an iconic status, inscribed with bittersweet remembrance of "home." This is the case whether this "home" is enshrined in the remembered spaces of childhood or in "adopted" places of belonging, such as Ya Kun Kaya Toast outlets in China, celebrated by Singaporeans in online reviews.

Primarily through the vehicle of nostalgic remembering, our argument traces the ways that scent cultures both confirm and disrupt borders—local, national, and even virtual ones—and create other spaces for imagined communities. Such communities of aroma are defined by trade and international markets, by the sense memories of those with deep histories of place as well as those living in diaspora, by tourists in search of "new" and unusual

scentscapes, or by the "new" culinary bourgeoisie—hipsters and connoisseurs, together with their festivals and social media environments. A more
nuanced "take" on cultures of aroma defies analyses vested in essentialism or
rigid forms of power distribution and instead suggests myriad and complex
ways olfactory experience might be shaped by different meanings, different
everyday practices, and different politics.

We turn now to an autoethnographic account of the "entangled" objects
themselves with their pasts and futures of embedded histories and networks
of social relations. Methodologically, we largely formulate our conclusions
based on content analyses of media and some interviews and observations
from fieldwork separately conducted over the years in Malaysia and Singapore respectively by Khoo (on durian) and Duruz (on kopi). Our approach
to such scentscapes and foodscapes is both emic and etic, though we speak
from the position of insiders: nationality-wise, Khoo is Malaysian, and Duruz,
although Australian, has been drinking kopi in Singapore since 2004. Let us
begin with the haunting smell of durian.

First Whiff: Cultivating Connoisseurship in Durians

I (Khoo) went on a field trip to find out more about durians. In the month of
July, the shopping area at SS2, a residential neighborhood in Petaling Jaya,
Malaysia, comes alive with the smell of this fruit. Durian lovers flock here
in groups to enjoy the communal fruit. A newish two-story building with a
neon signboard announcing "Durian Man" greets the driver at the intersection, announcing our approach into the durian heartland.[6] Stacks of durian
line the shelves in neat rows, underneath noticeboards with detailed descriptions of each variety: Musang King (D197), Red Prawn, IOI, XO, Tekka /
Musang Queen, D24, D13, Black Thorn, Mas Johor, and more.[7] Durian Man
is only one of many shops that sell this fruit. Driving further in, we luckily
find a parking spot curbside to a field converted into lots selling durians. The
minute my car door swings open, Penny (my research assistant) and I are
greeted by a strong whiff of ripe durians. I can feel my saliva building up in
anticipation of the feast that awaits me—even though ostensibly we are here
to conduct interviews with durian sellers. Huge yellow signboards advertising
cheap durians draw my attention, and I take mental notes for which buffet to
partake in while Penny surges ahead to look for our interview subject.

Once captivated by the sweet aroma of durian, we durian lovers are
no longer agents in control of our desires, freedom,[8] or as it turns out, our

pockets! Michael Pollan raises the possibility of plants acting as agents by utilizing scent in their quest to attract animals and humans as seed dispersers in order to fulfill their evolutionary destiny.[9] Likewise, the durian's strong odor attracts not just humans but a multitude of animals, including elephants, tigers, tapirs and wild boars. Elephants, who mostly leave people alone, come into conflict with humans during durian season, as both compete for the protein-rich fruit.[10] And durian lovers who spurn holey durians are advised by durian farmers and sellers to "follow the squirrel" if they want to find the best durian.[11] This is not to reduce smell to our basest animal instincts as much as it is to elevate the olfactory in appreciation for this fruit that has been much maligned in western discourse.

The earliest account of the durian dates to 1407. Ma Huan, an interpreter for famed Admiral Zheng He on his voyages to Southeast Asia, in his book *Ying Ya Sheng Lan* writes that "the foul smell resembles that of putrid beef; inside there are 14–15 lumps, as big as chestnuts, of milk white flesh, very sweet and delicious to eat."[12] Precolonial Western accounts include some positive views of the durian's smell and taste. Venetian merchant Nicolo Conti in 1450 spotted the durian in Sumatra and described it as having "different subtleties of flavor" yet made no mention of the aroma, giving the impression that he might be discussing the less pungent species *durio graveolens*.[13] In 1583, Portuguese Garcia de Orta exclaimed that the durians of Malacca were "the most excellent fruits in the Orient," while Italian merchant Francesco Carletti found it "delightful" and, proving to be an early durian connoisseur in 1599, explained his reasons: "No other natural simple food contains as complex and as sophisticated a variety of odors and flavors."[14] As contemporary scholars have noted, the fruit's odor only began to irk European noses in the late colonial period, when Europeans began to regard the local populations' taste for durian with great puzzlement that further reinscribed the difference and maintained the racial hierarchy between colonizer and colonized.[15] Today, headlines such as "Smells like hell, tastes like heaven," support a dubious dichotomy between smell and taste and reinforce the sensational exoticism of this uniquely Southeast Asian fruit.[16] Interestingly, the Chinese description above likens it to other food that smells familiar to the Chinese nose and palate, whereas for westerners, the closest familiar food they could think of in describing the durian's smell was overly strong or moldy cheese. Other westerners adopted abject similes such as vomit, unwashed socks, rotten garbage, decomposing corpse, and more imaginatively, "a dragon's breath enough to make some people gag."[17] Such lurid descriptions create a barrier for non-Southeast Asians, as "smell plays an integral role in choosing or rejecting what ultimately goes into the mouth."[18]

When it comes to first-time eaters of durian who have heard so much about the fruit's sensory impact (its thorny exterior, the smell and the taste), judgments of what is good or bad seem to be divided between its smell, which is so potent that it can be detected a hundred feet away,[19] and its taste, which is surprisingly sweet. Tasting durian, as British novelist Anthony Burgess notes, is like "eating sweet raspberry blancmange in the lavatory."[20] In fact, many people encourage first-time tasters to get beyond the smell (bad) to get to the sweetness of the taste (good!) and then repeat. Through repeated tastings, the offensiveness of the smell recedes or turns into a good smell: "The more he eats, the sweeter the smell and the more heavenly the taste," claims the author of *Durian, The True Pearl of the Orient*.[21] The dichotomy implies that smell and taste can be separated, but like any gustatory flavors, smell, taste, touch, and visuals combine to form the identity of the spiky green durian, whose name itself derives from the Malay word *duri*, meaning thorns. We argue that the full sensory integrity of the Malaysian durian—its smell, taste, touch, and visual appearance—requires preservation, as its characteristics distinguish it from that of its neighbor Thailand—the world's largest exporter of durians (national differences explicated below). Further, we propose that, as more Chinese fans develop a taste for the Malaysian durian's complex flavors through durio-tourism, the hegemonic discourse of "bad smell, good taste" will be dismantled.

In mid-2018, the Malaysian government signed an agreement with China that allowed the export of whole nitrogen-frozen durian to China (previously only durian pulp and paste had been permitted).[22] China is the largest market for durians in the world, and with only 3 percent of the Chinese population eating durians,[23] Southeast Asian growers are confident that the market will continue to grow. Chinese demand for durian continues to rise annually: for example, despite the COVID-19 pandemic and movement restrictions and lockdowns in the first half of 2020, Malaysia saw a 128 percent and Thailand saw an 18.6 percent year-on-year increase in sales in China.[24] This opening up of the Chinese market to Malaysian whole frozen durian is important to its competitors.[25] While Thailand is working to maintain its global lead with its milder durians, Monthong (Golden Pillow) and Ganyao, the premium Malaysian durian, Musang King (Mao Shan Wang in Mandarin or, originally, Raja Kunyit in Malay) is highly popular in China and costs five times the price of Thai durians. Thus the durian, the majority grown in family plots between two to thirty acres in Malaysia to supply the local and foreign market, is now being cultivated in megaplantations of a thousand acres or more, cleared at the expense of biodiverse forests, critically endangered wild-life, and Indigenous people's land.[26]

The major difference between Thai and Malaysian durian, aside from their varieties, is that the Thai durian is cut from the branch before it ripens. This means it can withstand longer delivery times (often Thai durians are transported fresh overland into China), whereas Malaysian farmers wait until the durian ripens and falls to the ground before harvesting them. From the time it falls to the ground, the Malaysian durian only has a life span of two to four days, depending on the variety. Thus an intense hive of activity surrounds these crucial few days, as the fruits meant for export are whipped away to factories for processing either as whole nitrogen-frozen fruit (to arrest further deterioration of the whole fruit) or as pulp and paste. The majority are sold for local consumption.

The mode of harvesting affects the flavor of the durian. And by flavor, we rely on the *Encyclopedia Britannica*'s definition to describe the over-all perception that includes taste, smell, and touch, though many writers, including Korsmeyer[27] and McLagan,[28] use "taste" and "flavor" interchange-ably.[29] Thai-cut durians are not as soft and creamy in texture compared to the Malaysian tree-dropped durians. Cut durians "[give] the durian an intensely sweet frosting-like flavor and texture."[30] The alcohol content and flavor is also not as high because its natural ripening has been arrested. Lind-say Gasik, an American durian blogger who has written two books on Thai and Penang (Malaysia) durians, describes her experience tasting a rare Thai variety: "The tree-fallen Kampan Thong was INTENSE. Whereas the cut one was lightly alcoholic, the tree-fallen was intensely so—the texture was rich and fatty, with a dark caramel and rum flavor that was just like a very fancy dessert."[31]

A cut, unripe durian is similarly not as pungent and suits the taste values of Thais, which have been shaped by historical circumstances. Generally, durian aroma is valued differently across the region, with Malaysians, Indo-nesians, and Singaporeans preferring tree-dropped durian, while Thais and Vietnamese like cut durian. Therefore, pungency of smell, or its degree, is a distinguishing factor in identifying the nationality of the durian, although national varieties vary in pungency. For example, the criteria for the best durian award at the Chanthaburi Durian Festival in Thailand does not include smell, unlike the Malaysian one held at the Bangi Golf Resort in 2018–2019.

Notably, the highest percentage on the judging form at the Bangi Golf Resort Durian Festival is for taste (sweet, bitter, floral, alcoholic, and overall balance of flavors accounts for 40 percent) and aroma (pungency accounts for 15 percent). These two surpass all the other gustatory senses and suggest that Malaysians expect the aroma to be part and parcel of the gustatory experience of eating durian. Ethnic Chinese Malaysians especially prefer their durian to be bittersweet, alcoholic, and pungent, and Malaysian durian promoters in China do not feel that they should downplay its aroma while marketing the Malaysian durian. This shows they are confident that Chinese consumers who are familiar with sweet Thai durian are beginning to develop a taste for the ripened Malaysian durian.[32]

There are some historical and pragmatic commercial reasons that may explain the low value attributed to durian scent in Thailand. First, although never colonized, the fear of appearing barbaric in the eyes of westerners led to a series of modernization measures, including the self-implementation of a rigid binary sex system for Thai names and fashion in the early twentieth century, along with other western ideas such as the importance of public hygiene, using cutlery instead of eating with one's fingers, and so on.[33] Like westerners who began to distinguish themselves from locals who liked durians during late colonialism, urban Thais themselves in the later twentieth century, in an unconscious quest for *siwilai* (civilization in the European sense),[34] began to turn their noses up at pungent tree-dropped durians, regarding their custardy, soft texture and alcoholic flavor as "past [the] peak of deliciousness,"[35] "overripe [*suk suk*]," and "rotten."[36] Thus the Thai durian, like refined and "civilized" Thai culture, is cultivated to avoid offense, perhaps out of an anti-colonial and self-modernizing tendency as much as for pragmatic commercial reasons.[37] Similarly, Mariani theorizes that the bans on carrying durians in parts of public Southeast Asia (Thailand, Singapore, Malaysia) reflected in signboards found at airports, hotels, and on public transportation signify the "becoming universal" of a regulated way of thinking and describing the durian smell, which was originally based on appeasing tourists, as Southeast Asian governments chased tourist revenue.[38]

Early-cut durians only became the commercial norm in the Thai industry starting in the 1970s.[39] It would seem that as the Thai durian began to go global, its diversity narrowed from over two hundred to four commercial varieties that, aside from having desirable qualities for transportability, are more gentle to the western palate's Eurocentric-turned-universal "organoleptic" qualities: the aspects of the fruit experienced sensorially including taste, sight, smell, and touch.[40] We argue that the dominance of such a practice over half a century has reshaped the flavor preference of younger Thais for durian with a milder taste and smell and a firmer, sometimes even crunchy, texture: "Most Thais don't like too strong a smell, *except some old people*" (emphasis added).[41] Pragmatic commercial considerations to lengthen the time for transportation and distribution (the Monthong can last up to twenty days compared to the tree-dropped Musang King) and to appeal to a wider global market and its western-influenced senses may have inadvertently altered the identity of the Thai durian. For example, Thai intensive research development has also led to the creation of the odorless durian, Chanthaburi #1 to #10, by Dr. Songpol Songsri and a thornless one to facilitate easier transportation.[42]

For the Chinese, a version of durian known as Mao Shan Wang (Musang King) shot to fame in Hong Kong and China in 2010 with the widespread press coverage that Macau gambling tycoon Stanley Ho had specially chartered a flight to ship eighty-eight fresh Musang King durians from Singapore to Hong Kong. He then gifted a few to another prominent Hong Kong billionaire and philanthropist, Li Ka Shing. This "celebrity effect"[43] caused the price of Musang King to soar.[44] Since then, not only is the Musang King sought after as a luxury item by the nouveau riche, it has also been marketed as a highly nutritious fruit (with added claims of sexual potency and virility that are not widely circulated among Malaysians). But aside from novelty and curiosity, Chinese tourists are genuinely interested in the fruit;[45] some are choosing during the spring months whether to travel to Penang for durio-tourism or rather to see the Sakura trees blossom in Japan.[46] Those who do come to Malaysia on durian tours with just one name on their tongues are instead exposed to a variety in a tasting session or durian buffet that changes their minds about the Musang King being their favorite (and perhaps the only) type of durian. Tourists visiting durian-diverse orchards in Penang leave converted by their authentic experience of eating local freshly dropped fruit with different flavors and textures, most of which are not suitable for export due to their fragility.

As with Hong Kongers whose palate has developed considerably since 2012, we predict that the same will happen with Chinese consumers. Hong Kong fans describe the durian's smell as a sweet aroma in a promotional video of Pahang durians entitled "I Love Musang King." Included are photographs taken of a group of Chinese tourists, including the China Embassy trade attaché, posing with durians still hanging from a tree at a durian

orchard, and official launches of the durian at a couple of villages that are
famous for producing Musang King.[47] As one Penang durian tour opera-
tor explains about his experience introducing durians to foreign couples, he
would ask the spouse who does not like to eat durian to "'come come, come'
and get some beginner durians for them to try, the less smelly one lah, very
dry, sweet, and not too strong one. I let them try. A bit . . . a bit . . . a bit,
some of them love it. Then the husband and wife [one of whom had previously hated durian] love durians already, then they come back again."[48] It
is through getting past the whiff the nose detects, followed by taking into
the mouth the object of initial revulsion, and sensing the durian's four or
five flavors—flavors that can be detected via a combination of taste, mouthfeel, and retronasal olfaction—that the durian's smell is transformed into a
good one.[49]

This rendering of bad smell into good smell, in other words appreciation, results after repeated tastings. For fans new and old, durian tastings,
modeled after wine tastings, have been developed to form durian connoisseurship, with talk of terroir-defined varietals.[50] For example, Musang King
originates from the state of Kelantan but is best grown in Raub, Pahang;
thus tourists eating Musang King grown in Penang will taste a different
flavor. Penang has its own local varieties, like D163 Hor Lor (Gourd), D164
Ang Bak (Red Flesh), D175 Red Prawn, and the upcoming premium-priced
D200 Black Thorn. Most durian tastings begin with a blander variety and
work up to the apex, usually occupied by Musang King, or sometimes D160
Tekka (nicknamed "Musang Queen"). Chang Teik Seng, third-generation
farmer and owner of Baosheng Durian Farm in Balik Pulau, Penang is at the
forefront of cultivating durian connoisseurship. Chang has popularized the
concept of a fifth durian flavor, introducing "numb" in addition to sweet,
alcoholic, bitter, and floral. Few consumers have encountered the numbing sensation because it is only present in freshly dropped durians (within
thirty minutes to two hours) from trees forty years or older.[51] Thus, in addition to getting access to a diversity of varieties at relatively cheaper prices
than they would in the United States or China, smelling the full fragrance
of fresh rather frozen durian, and being able to experience the rare sensation of numbness on one's tongue becomes an added incentive for Chinese
and other foreigners to travel to Malaysia for durio-tourism. Their experiences may be informed by YouTube videos in English and Chinese of
durian tours and tastings posted by food bloggers and other travelers that
help promote the durian. These durian videos create a craving and nostalgia,

gastro-national pride, and even if visitors do not like the smell, respect for the commentators of Southeast Asian ancestry.[52]

Durian connoisseurship is transnational. Baosheng Farm has accommodations for durian-loving tourists (westerners, Japanese, Chinese, Singaporeans, vegans, raw-food eaters) who return annually to eat freshly dropped durians during the season. At the farm, visitors also learn about farming methods and the numerous factors that influence the durian's flavors over the course of the fruit's life cycle: the age of a tree (the older, the better), the amount of water and sun, the level of ripeness, and the time since being dropped by the tree as the sugars in the fruit begin to ferment. They also learn how to stimulate the ripening process and bring out the more complex flavors. Fruits from younger trees, as journalist Julie Wan explains, are "sweeter, creamier and gummier in texture," while those "from more mature trees are strong and tastes [sic] almost like cheese."[53] Cultivating durian connoisseurship and durio-tourism as a lifestyle choice has finally paid off for Baosheng Farm; the tasting price has almost quadrupled a decade after Wan's 2011 visit, and rooms are usually fully booked ahead of the season.

A running trope in our interviews with farmers is that good durians foster addiction. A third-generation Penang durian farmer (DW) explains his lifelong obsession in the trade and why, despite the low times in the 1990s when the prices plunged and other farmers uprooted their trees to grow other more profitable crops, he never gave up. "Durian is very unique. It's okay if you don't eat but when you eat good ones, you'll get addicted. You'll think of it all the time—the smell, texture and all linger in your mind. When the durian season is over, you'll feel sad. . . . You'll feel touched when you eat a good durian because you'll feel at the top of the world having the best durian in your mouth. This experience is mine and mine alone."[54]

DW's poetic and passionate overture to the fruit illustrates the power of sensory gustatory memory to move people and provide meaning, not just to one's identity but to one's very being: "At that moment, you'll feel very touched with the life you have and there's a purpose in life."[55] Thus the durian's uniqueness is built for true gastronomes for whom eating a thawed frozen whole fruit with only a faint aroma simply cannot compare to eating a freshly fallen durian. To savor the durian's most authentic flavor, one has to be in its natural habitat and allow the coalescing of fresh smell, taste, and touch in the mouth and at the back of the throat to trigger childhood memories or build up a sense memory of that communion with heaven that brings tourists back to Malaysia annually.

Second Whiff: Lingering Scents for Nanyang Memory-Making

> The plane lands midafternoon at Changi Airport in a monsoonal
> rainstorm. As the rain eases, the earth's ambient smells continue
> to announce yet another return to Singapore, my home away from
> home.
>   The next morning I [Duruz] walk to a market, its open-air food
> stalls nearby. An elderly worker takes my order for kaya toast and
> kopi. Yes, I reassure him, I do want kopi, the coffee with the sweet
> milk. He looks doubtful, as if I'm transgressing my own Anglo-Celtic
> boundaries, but he prepares it. I inhale the aroma of dark, strongly
> brewed coffee, cut by the viscous sweetness of condensed milk. The
> grilled toast with its pandan-flavored coconut jam and slabs of cold
> butter adds further nuances to this intimate smellscape.
>   Remember this, I tell myself sternly, as this may not last. The
> following year, I return. The stall has gone.[56]

With the above account of olfactory arrivals in Singapore and my own pleasure in ritual, we leave Malaysian durian orchards and the fruit's domestic
and Chinese markets and follow the syrupy-sweet, buttery aroma of kopi
wafting from traditional coffee stalls, boutique cafés, and upmarket malls.
In this section of the chapter, kopi becomes a distinctive Southeast Asian (or
Nanyang) form of "entangled object"—an actual object from which the social
relations in which it is positioned (time, place, class, gender, etc.) can be unrav-
eled, theoretically speaking.[57] In other words, kopi becomes a focal point for
reflecting on manifestations of material culture, evocative scentscapes, and
practices of everyday Southeast Asian placemaking—actual, remembered,
or imagined. To unravel further kopi's "entanglements," our path will take
us through a brief history of kopi and traditional *kopitiams* (coffeehouses)
in Singapore, including *kopitiams*' more recent reinventions as forms of
"yuppie" coffee shops (with their "boutique" variations) to kopi's transnational scentscapes of diasporic remembering and longing.[58]
    The origins of kopi, and of Singapore's cuisine more generally, are typi-
cally "mixed" ones. As Kong, citing Henderson, emphasizes, "Cuisines are
not fixed things . . . ; rather, they are 'dynamic phenomena' which 'evolve and
interact.'"[59] This is certainly the case for Singapore, Kong continues, with its
early history "[bringing] the mix of cuisines from different migrant ethnic-
ities that laid the foundation for Singapore's now diverse, varied and hybrid

cuisine."[60] At the same time, the more recent spread of kopi throughout Singapore is no exception to this foundational story. Lai Ah Eng, for example, charts the significance of the late-arriving (comparatively speaking) Hainanese to Singapore and their enduring contribution to the island's coffee culture.[61] Landing in Singapore during the nineteenth and early twentieth centuries, these minority-group immigrants lacked the support of clan associations that helped other ethnic groups secure employment, so the Hainanese new arrivals resorted to farm labor or domestic work. In fact, it was within Peranakan (Straits Chinese), British, and other European households that Hainanese cooks mastered the art of coffee making, though shaped by local custom as we shall see presently. Such expertise, in turn, became critical once the British and Europeans began to depart Singapore prior to the Second World War and independence. From the 1920s onward, the Hainanese were able to establish their distinctive brand of kopitiams all over the island.[62]

Selina Chan is swift to point out this was not simply the spread of European-style coffee cultures throughout Singapore based on colonial origins. Kopitiams are not simply the equivalent of Western coffee chains, such as Starbucks (see also Merry White, regarding a similar trajectory for coffee drinking in Japan).[63] Despite kopi's hybrid history, Chan is adamant in asserting its distinctiveness as a local drink of the region with its own palate of flavors, smells, ingredients, and rituals. "[In the kopitiam, t]he way in which the coffee is prepared, served and consumed is unique. Coffee beans here were fried with butter. This was different from the practice in Western Europe or the States, where beans are toasted. . . . People either added the butter or ate it separately. . . . The locals believed that coffee was a 'heaty' drink and butter a cooling food; when taken together, they would maintain the balance in the body. The coffee served here was mixed with condensed milk and sugar."[64]

The stewing of the grounds of fried beans (fried, originally, to add additional flavor to the inferior, less expensive robusta beans that were most commonly used)[65] produces an almost ink-colored liquid and a strong, enveloping aroma with warm, buttery notes.[66] Straining the grounds through a "sock" (a wire hoop with a cloth net) adds further mouthfeel to the flavor.[67] The addition of condensed milk, sugar, and sometimes evaporated milk, also needs particular mention. Condensed milk was adopted to overcome the scarcity of quality fresh milk in the tropics, with industrial processes of canning or drying also valued for this milk's keeping qualities. Additionally, the high concentration of the milk itself and of the sugar, too, acted as a preservative, as well as providing kopi with a distinctive taste and smell.[68] So, to some

extent, this "becomes firmly rooted in local gastronomy and myth-mak-
ing . . . [and] acquires its own baggage of nostalgic references and its own
fan base, as bloggers frequently attest."[69]

William Koh, documenting the "rags-to-riches" history of Ya Kun, a
traditional coffee stall established in 1920s Singapore, comments on the
cultures of nostalgia that sipping such a "cuppa" represents. "Singaporeans,
especially the working class of middle-aged men and women, will continue
to flock to Ya Kun and other similar stalls and outlets to savor not just the
coffee or tea served in traditional ceramic cups, but also the thick aroma of
strong, well-brewed coffee permeating the air, served with crispy slices of
freshly toasted bread smeared with butter and sweet-smelling kaya—reminiscent of their youthful days."[70]

"The thick aroma . . . permeating," "freshly-toasted bread smeared,"
"sweet-smelling kaya"—all these hints of ambient smells and delicious tastes
textured into this description invite a return to "youthful days" and to a past
of innocent daily ritual and conviviality. Kelvin Low claims that "the act of
'tasting memories' . . . establishes cultural connections between then and
now."[71] For our argument, we add "smelling memories" to this mix. While
taste and smell often seem inextricable (for example, in the description of
toasted bread above), a whiff may be enough to recall powerful memories
of the past, of this and other places, to remind us of memory's mobility or
even its moments of acute loss. In Singapore in 2019, the closure of an iconic,
much-loved coffee shop, Chin Mee Chin, was one such moment.[72]

Mourning the loss of nostalgic smells is a familiar trope in popular
remembering. As Iain Chambers comments, "Dishes that are the distillation
of centuries of cooking . . . not only evoke the aroma and tastes of a place; they
also register what elsewhere has been brutally canceled and institutionally
ignored. The smells from the kitchen . . . can suggest connections, collusions
and subsequent maps of meaning that the rigid grids of national geographies
are neither able to contain or recognize."[73] Here, Chambers suggests an alternative to conventional approaches to charting historical time and national
boundaries. Instead, fragmentary, and perhaps more elusive, "signs, sugges-
tions, sounds, smells and silences" might offer a different view of the world
as well as productive means to mapping its embedded cultures. The classic
example of this approach, and not incompatible with that of Chambers, is
found in Nadia Seremetakis's treatise on a peach, popularly known as "the
breast of Aphrodite"—a variety that is no longer available.[74] Recalling this

variety of peach becomes for Seremetakis "a phenomenological space in which public culture is understood and played out."[75]

Kopi, too, is such a space. However, the question remains: how might kopi's distinctive tastes and aromas, with their nostalgic associations, survive Singapore's recent waves of gentrification and, specifically, the proliferation of "boutique" coffee shops? In the last few decades, alongside Western-style cafés, such as Starbucks or Coffee Bean & Tea Leaf, it seems that a "new" version of the *kopitiam* has emerged. This is a glossier version, one with all the modern comforts and corporate presentation of Western chains. Toast Box is an example of such a "boutique" chain that blends references to the traditional and the modern. Hence, expect air-conditioning, mood lighting, shiny display cases, squeaky-clean floors and surfaces, and cutely dressed serving teams. At the same time, expect the familiar breakfast offerings of kopi and *teh* (tea) with soft-boiled eggs and kaya toast, casual hot dishes, such as *laksa*, and fusion sweetmeats, such as pandan-green chiffon cake.[76] Is this, perhaps, the best of both worlds?

Pierre Nora claims that as the sites of earlier remembering disappear, our enthusiasm for memorializing these sites and moments increases. Replacements for sources of "real" memories, Nora calls "lieux de mémoire," and claims that because "there is no longer spontaneous . . . memory . . . we must create archives, maintain anniversaries, organize celebrations . . . because such activities no longer occur naturally."[77] Perhaps the boutique coffee shop, as a stylized (and stylish) *kopitiam* with its reproduction wooden furniture, branded, thick china coffee cups, and judiciously placed artifacts and "old-world" photographs represents a "modern" example of faux nostalgia? Is this a case of Appadurai's distinction between "primary" and "ersatz" nostalgia,[78] between nostalgia based on a sense of "real" absence and that of market-driven longing for experiences one has never had?

It would be easy to criticize Singapore's rapid changes to the built environment as a tabula rasa approach to urban planning.[79] Has the loss of traditional coffeehouses and the merging of tin-shed hawker centers into artfully designed food centers, together with the creation of glitzy malls and upmarket restaurants and coffee chains in recent decades meant a deleterious change in the scentscapes, especially due to their oversanitization?[80] Does the smell of kopi still haunt the landscapes of everyday life? Lai Ah Eng, surveying the history of the *kopitiam* in Singapore, brings a hopeful note to this conversation.[81] "As Lai points out in her history of the *kopitiam*, its various forms tend to exist side by side, with each new form an addition to the landscape, rather than an erasure of older forms."[82] In fact, a study carried out in George Town, Penang, Malaysia indicates that customers of varying ages adopt the identity of "spatial omnivore" when it comes to the choice of places for drinking and eating and for "hanging out" with friends— that is, they are inclined to patronize a wide range of sites from traditional *kopitiams* and coffee chains to the more stylish artisanal cafés.[83] We imagine, therefore, that studies of kopi and coffee drinking in Singapore will suggest the same.

In the meantime, however, for traces of customer omnivorousness in local cultures of kopi drinking, we might briefly examine Daniel Ang's blog, with its recent listing, "10 Kaya Toast and Kopi Places in Singapore, for Comforting Local Breakfast." Scrolling through the entries, we find persistent reference to the smell of kopi and its accompanying kaya toast. This is the case whether the outlet is Heap Seng Liong, an "extremely old school setting that is caught in time of the 70s" with its frequently filmed Uncle in singlet and striped pajamas making toast on an old-style grill or steeping coffee grounds to produce traditional Hainanese kopi "with bitter notes," or whether the outlet is Good Morning Nanyang Coffee, positioned in the Singapore Central Business District's Far East Plaza, its kopi "aromatic and smooth, yet not overly sharp." And different again is Coffee Break in the Amoy Food Centre. With an eye to the hipster market, these second-generation owners experiment with a startling range of new flavors to blend with kopi's traditional tastes and aromas: according to Coffee Break's reviewer, "Many customers come for their flavored kopi, from 'Almond Ginger, Black Sesame, . . . Taro Milk, Mint, Melon Milk, Masala and Mango Milka.'"[84]

Pertinent to our discussion here is the intertwining of discourses of nostalgia and connoisseurship that emerge in the text of this listing. Throughout, there are linguistic markers signaling the "past" of kopi drinking and *kopitiams*, for example the appeal of Ya Kun's kopi and teh as "a magnet . . . for those who want aromatic traditional local drink" or the attraction of kopi made the "old-school way" at Tong Ah Kopitiam. As well, there are intimations of the "past" in the performances of central figures—the evocative actions of pajama-clad uncles, for example. Whether this is "real" nostalgia in the Appaduraian sense of actual experience or simply a form of collective imagining, prompted by engaging performances, complete with the props of grills, coffee "socks," and reproduction coffee cups, is, perhaps, beside the point.[85] Instead, the reality that kopi is ingested, is experienced *viscerally* by the sensorium—deeply in the nose, mouth, and gut—becomes critical. As Wong Hong Suen reminds us, it is the *sensorial* experience of food that endures in one's memory bank, long after the context in which it is consumed disappears or changes."[86]

Obviously, there are variations in methods and skills of kopi brewing and in its resulting flavors and aromas. However, in our search within the kopi cultures for nuances of nostalgic remembering, we would suggest that the crucial distinction lies not so much among different tastes and whiffs of "local" kopi but in the distinction between "local" and Western-style coffee. At the end of the day, it is Hainanese-based kopi, with its history rooted in the region—the Nanyang—that differentiates itself from the espresso-based coffee of Western chains. "For Singaporeans, kopi is a collective memory," says Pamela Chng, "The thick, bitter, yet smooth liquid can be enjoyed by everyone, regardless of age, social status, race."[87] Robert Chohan, founder of Kopi House in the United Kingdom, with its mission of "showcasing diasporic Nanyang kopi heritage," agrees, stating that kopi should be celebrated primarily for its Southeast Asian character and provenance.[88]

So it is not surprising then that Singaporeans living abroad might yearn for kopi's aromas and flavors as the taste and smell of home itself. In fact, Lindholm and Lee argue that migration (and presumably, even short-term relocation) intensifies nostalgic longings for remembered scentscapes.[89] At the same time, frequent travelers throughout the region might "borrow" kopi's visceral pleasures as a reminder of the possibility of attachment to "other" homes and "other" practices of coffee drinking than those of espresso-based cultures of so-called specialty cafés.[90] Hence, a backpacker, drinking kopi in the nostalgically styled spaces of Toast Box (with this "boutique" coffee shop itself positioned within Food Republic, Orchard Road's fashionable retro food court), notes with satisfaction that "the coffee is made, Turkish-style, poured from a long-spouted pot, and a very Southeast Asian glop of condensed milk is added."[91]

"A very Southeast Asian glop," flavoring rich, dark "Turkish-style" coffee, becomes a finely wrought detail of kopi's "entanglement" in sensory communities that spread beyond national boundaries and that defy "rigid grids of national geographies."[92] "Knowing kopi" is the testament to a form of Nanyang membership, whether this constitutes the comforts of collective memories of those "tasting the bitter black liquid as toddlers in their grandparent's lap, and hating that first experience"[93] or of those for whom the aromas and flavors of kopi represent a "world we have lost," either temporally (as in childhoods, the past) or spatially (as in erasure of a remembered built environment or in trying to make a "home" elsewhere).

However, to turn from an atmosphere of mourning and loss, we draw out briefly a second thread from the kopi listings mentioned previously. With the ways traditional, refurbished chains such as Killiney Road and Ya Kun Kaya Toast and independent coffee shops such as Coffee Hut and The 1950s Coffee (the latter, a Michelin Guide entry in 2019) are reviewed on social media come some changes. The increasing popularity of "local" coffee, in contrast to the "specialty" coffees of espresso-based chains, brings, as with the durian, the additional and loaded language of connoisseurship. Kopi drinking as the mundane, everyday activity of "the working class of middle-aged men and women"[94] now becomes invested with meanings of "distinction," as described by Bourdieu.[95] The tone of "10 Kaya Toast and Kopi Places in Singapore, for Comforting Local Breakfast" takes the reader beyond the cozy, nostalgic appeal of a "comforting local breakfast" and instead reads, at times, almost like wine tasters' notes, implying the figure of the cosmopolitan who can differentiate the different "notes" of kopi and kaya ("kopi . . . was smooth, fragrant, with the lingering delicate bitterness. . . . It has a fragrant aroma, and is not too bitter for a black local coffee").[96] Meanwhile, kaya toast receives the same sort of attention with terms like "slathered with . . . kaya" and "thick slices," "lightly . . . salted butter" urging the customer to taste and smell thoughtfully—practices of discriminating consumption.[97]

The tale of kopi and its olfactory cultures has taken us from bounded nations to the more fluidly defined Nanyang, and from "mixed" ethnically rooted culinary origins to Singapore's increasingly "diverse, varied and hybrid cuisine."[98] As well, it has traced a route through changing class meanings of kopi and its "fragrant aroma" and through relations between the past and the future, referencing both nostalgic remembering and gentrified futures shaped by increasing culinary capital. As we watch the crowds of international students queuing outside the Malaysian chain restaurant PappaRich in Adelaide's Chinatown, it does not appear that authenticity is the issue here. Instead, the mythical meanings of "home" and its olfactory nuances are themselves at stake, especially when one is seeking comfort in diaspora. It seems then that Ang's simple statement of kopi and kaya toast as "our way of life" intimates much more complexity shaping this tale than such a banal expression might suggest.[99] Like Seremetakis's mourned peach and Chambers's evocative "smells from the kitchen," the aromas of kopi persist as a critical component of Singaporean imaginaries, whether at home or abroad, or on imagined journeys of return.

Conclusion

This chapter has provided a whiff of Southeast Asia, through spaces where the aroma of durian and kopi linger. The durian orchard and the *kopitiam* hold meanings of humble comfort food and eating with the family for Southeast Asians, whose childhood memories may encompass drinking kopi and eating kaya toast for breakfast at old-styled coffee shops and, during durian season, driving with their family to an orchard in Balik Pulau, "in search of the freshest and just-drop-off-the-tree durians."[100] For those who have not have lived such childhoods, meanings of globalization, gentrification, and connoisseurship are available in the forms of durio-tourism and durian plantations catering to the mass China market. As well, these meanings inscribe either the rationalized "boutique" *kopitiam* chains promoting nostalgia throughout the region and beyond—Singapore kopi chain Ya Kun Kaya Toast has twenty-five outlets in China alone—or the disappearing traditional *kopitiam*, such as the one enshrined in the Singapore Michelin Guide. Understanding and enjoying these foodscapes and scentscapes enables travelers and gastronomes to become discriminating consumers in search of authenticity in ways that transcend simplistic or even racist discourses of "bad smells." While the aromas of both these "entangled objects'" are filtered through Western-originated judgments that either derogate (durian "stinks") or diminish (comparing kopi to specialty coffees), we have shown that there is more to these objects than simply smell. Cultural particularities exist—not only developed between Western and Asian cultures but also within Southeast Asia or the Nanyang itself, or based on Chinese migration, history, and notions of modernity and commercialism—and these shape and complicate any simplistic notions about aroma and taste.

We note that kopi and durian will continue to carry slightly different connotations for Chinese consumers: the Nanyang coffee is about a simple affordable rustic taste. It may remind some of the way traditional coffee tastes in Hainan, with a similar preparation. But the Musang King asserts the novelty of tasting something exotic and extravagant. One speaks to a humble past while the other to the conspicuous consumption of prestige and of class aspiration, best captured in Chinese artist Zhang Yong's

Fig. 4.1   Chinese artist Zhang Yong's eighteen-karat-gold-plated spiky alpaca at the 2019 Art Expo Malaysia, October 10, 2019. Photo: Gaik Cheng Khoo.

durian-inspired cutesy, cuddly animal sculptures covered in 18-karat gold plated spikes (fig. 4.1). That the durian has become a pop cultural icon in Chinese art speaks to the ubiquity and mundaneness of the Nanyang in everyday urban consumption in China: What would historic naval trader Zheng He and his translator Ma Huan think if they were to wander into a supermarket offering durian and kopi in Henan Province today?

   We therefore conclude that our olfactory experiences and the meanings we derive from kopi and durian are necessarily informed by nationality and ethnicity, class, age, and generational differences. If the young prefer specialty coffee over kopi, and eschew eating durian because its pungent smell and ways of consuming are regarded as out of trend (splitting open fresh durians and eating it with one's fingers at a roadside stall), a multitude of processes to rebrand and market durian and kopi, especially through social media, have made both popular again: witness the growth of air-conditioned coffee shops in malls, durian sellers' provision of plastic gloves and clean water to wash one's fingers after consumption, or durian dessert shops and hipster flavored kopi. At the end of the day, the merit of "entangling" these two scent products in this chapter is to trace similar effects from a generational shift and forms of gentrification that reflect increasing wealth and class consciousness. At the same time, the market recognizes the power both of nostalgic heritage and cultures of expertise and shapes their olfactory offerings accordingly.

Over the decades, everyday practices of drinking kopi and eating durian have changed and will continue to evolve and diversify as taste regimes in the region shift, depending on competing global cultural hegemonies. Hints of the "lieux de mémoire" of kopi and durian leak out of a sachet of "Musang King flavored instant White Coffee," exported by Malaysia overseas.[101] Meanwhile, a 2017 news headline proclaims "The Chinese are waking up to Malaysian coffee," noting that, just as the Chinese are importing record highs of Malaysian durian products, the export of white coffee to China hit US$51 million just in the first quarter of 2017, almost the same amount as the whole of 2015.[102] A taste for Musang King durian and kopi among members of the middle class in the world's most populous nation might very well put to rest the negative olfactory discourse of such foods, once and for all proving that taste aromas can be cultivated and shared transnationally.

Notes

1. Lewis ("Urban Dimensions") provides further detail in his study of Nanyang ethnicity and its political economy: "The overseas Chinese form a distinct nation within many different nations, within the Southeast Asian region and beyond, a nation whose only real territory was a sort of socio-cultural space within a larger regional framework and the freedom of the South China sea itself. . . . The Nanyang Chinese have been more culturally influenced by the Nanyang itself than by their common Chinese homeland."

2. Not only is "home" constituted by place, it is also the way we remember our past, for "the past is home"; Rushdie, "Imaginary Homelands," 9.

3. Appadurai, Modernity at Large.

4. Crang cited in Law, "Home Cooking," 276.

5. Seremetakis, "Memory of the Senses," 14.

6. Durian fieldwork was conducted by Khoo and her research assistant, Penny Wong from a yearlong grant provided by the Future Food Beacon at the University of Nottingham. Durian farmers, sellers, wholesalers, and other stakeholders in the supply chain were interviewed from March to August 2020.

7. Durian clones that are registered with the Department of Agriculture at the state level are given a number preceded by the letter "D" for durian, and there are two hundred varieties registered with the DOA and many more that are not. However, overlapping registration and extinct clones over the years put the actual quantity registered closer to 140.

8. In 1693, Simon de la Loubère noted that so much did the Siamese love the durian whose smell he found "insupportable" that they were willing to subject themselves to indentured slavery to eat it. La Loubère, New Historical Relation, 171, 77.

9. Pollan, *Botany of Desire*.

10. Lim, "Human-Elephant Relations."

11. "To follow the squirrel" means to follow it as it hops from branch to branch to see which durian fruit it selects to eat from. Mr. Kok, durian orchard owner, interview by Khoo, October 21, 2020.

12. Love, Gasik, and Paull, "Durian for Hawai'i."

13. West, "Knowledge of the Durian."

14. Love, Gasik, and Paull, "Durian for Hawai'i," 1–2.

15. Low, "Theorising Sensory Cultures"; Montanari, "Stinky King."

16. Bender, "Delectable and Dangerous"; David, "Smells Like Hell"; Mariani, "Odeur d'enfer"; Montanari, "Stinky King"; Small and Catling, "Blossoming Treasures."

17. Sullivan, "Ooh That Smell."

18. Wurgaft, cited in Reinarz, *Past Scents*.

19. Great Big Story, "Durian Fruit," 1:03–1:09.

20. Burgess, *Long Day Wanes*.

21. Yeap, *Durian, True Pearl*, 14.

22. The first shipment (four tons) arrived in Shanghai in June 2019. Tim, "Shanghai Yechen."

23. Dwyer, "Why China loves Durian."

24. Fruit Critic, "Chinese Import Value."

25. Thailand exports 300,000 metric tons while Malaysia only exports 17,000 tons—5.8 per cent of its total annual production, with the rest consumed locally.

26. *Malaysian Insight*, "China Demand for Durian."

27. Korsmeyer, "Introduction," 3 and 5.

28. McLagan, *Bitter*, 3.

29. Spence, "Sense of Smell," 5–6.

30. Gasik, "Chanthaburi."

31. Gasik, "Cut vs Tree-Fallen."

32. In October 2020, sixty tons of the sweet and bitter Musang King were sold online within fifty-one minutes as part of the 2020 China-Malaysia durian festival in Qinzhou city, recording 100mil RMB (approx. US$15.5 mill).

33. Jackson, "Performative Genders."

34. To stave off colonial control, the kingdom of Siam self-modernized and pursued a quest to be civilized. *Siwilai* was "a transcultural process in which ideas and practices from Europe, via colonialism, had been transferred, localized, and hybridized in the Siamese setting." Winichakul, "Quest for 'Siwilai,'" 529.

35. Suen, "Thai Fruits."

36. Mr. Wong (pseudonym), interview by Khoo, June 19, 2020, Selangor.

37. Bangkok durian taste for harder, less pungent durian predominates as embodied in the ubiquity of Monthong sold in the city but in southern Thailand, durian taste preference is closer to the Malaysian one and is reflected in varieties that are stronger in flavor.

38. Mariani, "Odeur d'enfer."

39. Gasik, "Chanthaburi."

40. Mariani, "Odeur d'enfer."

41. Songpol, cited in Fuller, "Odorless Durian."

42. Bais, "Durian Breeding"; Fuller, "Odorless Durian." More recently in 2019, after twelve years of experimentation, Indonesia has also developed a thornless durian that has a thin sweet flesh in Lombok island, though it is still in its initial phase and not quite "a game changer" yet. Fathul Rakhman, "Mengenal Si Gundul"; Cheema, "Indonesia Grows Thornless Durians." A similar thornless variety can be found in Davao in the Philippines but is deemed to have no market due to its average taste and thin flesh.

43. DW (pseudonym), interview by Khoo, July 9, 2020, Penang.

44. Kelvin, "Stanley Ho."

45. Bernama, "Durian Tours."

46. Mr. X (pseudonym), wholesaler, interview by Khoo, July 18, 2020, Penang.

47. For a promotional video that targets Chinese and Hong Kong consumers, see Family Yong, "I Love Musang King."

48. AGT (pseudonym), interview by Khoo, August 18, 2020, Penang.

49. Olfaction works through the orthonasal (what the nose detects from sniffing) and the retronasal (the smell of food eaten when air is taken in from the mouth and circulated up to the nasal cavity).

50. Airriess, "Constructing Durian Terroir."

51. This is not a guarantee because it also depends on there being a lot of gas in the fruit. Francis, "Durian Lovers Can Look Forward."

52. Great Big Story, "Durian Fruit."

53. Wan, "Smell of Success."

54. DW (pseudonym), interview by Khoo, July 9, 2020.
55. Ibid.
56. Duruz, field notes, 2015. Ethnographic research for this chapter was conducted by Jean Duruz during extended stays in Singapore at the invitation of the National University of Singapore (NUS). Duruz's research was facilitated by her attachment as Academic Visitor in NUS's Department of Geography in 2004 and as Research Affiliate in NUS's Asia Research Institute in 2008.
57. Thomas, *Entangled Objects*.
58. For more detailed accounts of the changing cultures of traditional *kopitiams* and the emergence of hawker centres and "boutique" cafes, see Lai, "*Kopitiam in Singapore*"; Lai, "Cultural Diversity and Cultural Politics"; Chua, "Taking the Street"; Duruz, "Taste of Retro."
59. Kong, "From Sushi in Singapore," 230–31.
60. Ibid., 231.
61. Lai, "*Kopitiam in Singapore*," 213–14.
62. Ibid. Lai also reminds us that while the Hainanese form was "foundational in developing the *kopitiam* into a public institution and the strong public culture of eating and drinking by the 1950s," it was not the only form of stalls selling casual food. "Paralleling the Chinese *kopitiams* and eateries were *kedai kopi* and *sarabat* stalls set up by Indians, Indian-Muslims and Malays which catered to demand for ethnic foods by the expanding Indian and Malay populations." Lai, "Cultural Diversity and Cultural Politics," 109–10.
63. Chan, "Consuming Food," 133; White, *Coffee Life in Japan*.
64. Chan, "Consuming Food," 133.
65. Yeo, "Singapore Kopi Culture."
66. Ibid., "Kaya Toast"; "Hyped!"
67. Yeo, "Singapore Kopi Culture."
68. Duruz and Khoo, *Eating Together*, 49.
69. Ibid., 49–50.

70. Koh, *Top Toast*, 2.
71. Low, "Tasting Memories," 62.
72. Ang, "Chin Mee Chin."
73. Chambers, *Mediterranean Crossings*, 130–31.
74. Seremetakis, "Breast of Aphrodite."
75. Duruz, "Rich Pickings," 379.
76. Duruz and Khoo, *Eating Together*, 54–61.
77. Nora, "Between Memory and History," 23.
78. Appadurai, *Modernity at Large*, 76–77.
79. Lim, *Asian Ethical Urbanism*, 165–66.
80. Edensor, "Culture of Indian Street," 215.
81. Lai, "*Kopitiam in Singapore*," 223–25.
82. Duruz and Khoo, *Eating Together*, 60.
83. Beh, "Chinese are Waking Up."
84. Ang, "10 Kaya Toast Places."
85. Duruz, "Taste of Retro," 153.
86. Wong, "Taste of the Past," 121.
87. Chng, cited in Yeo, "Singapore Kopi Culture."
88. Chohan, cited in Yeo, "Singapore Kopi Culture."
89. Lindholm and Lee, "Eat What You Are," 53.
90. Yeo, "Singapore Kopi Culture."
91. Roy, "Cup of Coffee."
92. Chambers, *Mediterranean Crossings*, 131.
93. Yeo, "Singapore Kopi Culture."
94. Koh, *Top Toast*, 2.
95. Bourdieu, *Distinction*.
96. Ang, "10 Kaya Toast Places in Singapore."
97. Ibid.
98. Kong, "From Sushi in Singapore," 231.
99. Ang, "10 Kaya Toast Places in Singapore."
100. Bee, "Durian, the King."
101. White coffee is a type of kopi and describes a roasting method originating from Ipoh, a town in Malaysia.
102. Beh, "Chinese Are Waking Up."

Bibliography

Airriess, Christopher. "Constructing Durian Terroir and Geographical Indications in Penang, Malaysia." *Singapore Journal of Tropical Geography* 41 (2020): 6–22.

Ang, Daniel. "Chin Mee Chin—Famous Old School Confectionary Permanently

Closed?" *DanielFoodDiary*, 1 February 2019. https://danielfooddiary.com
/2019/02/01/chinmeechin. Accessed 2
February 2021.

———. "10 Kaya Toast and Kopi Places
in Singapore for Comforting Local
Breakfast." *DanielFoodDiary*, June
5, 2020. https://danielfooddiary.com
/2020/06/05/kayatoast.

Appadurai, Arjun. *Modernity at Large:
Cultural Dimensions of Globalization.*
Minneapolis: University of Minnesota
Press, 1996.

Bais, Karolien. "Durian Breeding in Thailand." *UTAR Agriculture Journal* 2,
no. 4 (2016): 4–6.

Beh, May Ting. "Space, Identity, and Food-
scapes in the Coffee Houses of George
Town, Penang, Malaysia." PhD diss.,
Monash University Malaysia, 2019.

Beh, Yuen Hui. "The Chinese Are Waking
Up to Malaysian Coffee." *The Star*,
August 28, 2017. https://www.thestar
.com.my/news/nation/2017/08/28
/the-chinese-are-waking-up-to-malay
sian-coffee.

Bender, Daniel. "The Delectable and Dangerous: Durian and the Odors of Empire
in Southeast Asia." *Global Food
History* 3, no. 2 (2017): 111–32.
https://doi.org/10.1080/20549547
.2017.1355651.

Bernama. "Durian Tours Gaining Popularity
with Chinese Tourists." FreeMalay-
siaToday.com, July 16, 2018. https://
www.freemalaysiatoday.com/category
/nation/2018/07/16/durian-tours
-gaining-popularity-with-chinese
-tourists.

Bourdieu, Pierre. *Distinction: A Social
Critique of the Judgement of Taste.*
Cambridge, MA: Harvard University
Press, 1984.

Burgess, Anthony. *The Long Day Wanes: A
Malayan Trilogy.* New York: W. W.
Norton, 1993.

Chambers, Iain. *Mediterranean Crossings:
The Politics of an Interrupted Moder-
nity.* Durham, NC: Duke University
Press, 2008.

Chan, Selina Ching. "Consuming Food:
Structuring Social Life and Creating
Social Relationships." In *Past Times:*

A Social History of Singapore, edited
by Chan Kwok Bun and Tong Chee
Kiong, 122–35. Singapore: Times
Editions, 2003.

Cheema, Sukhbir. "Indonesia Grows Thornless Durians After 12 Years of
Experimenting." *Mashable SE Asia*,
n.d. https://sea.mashable.com/science
/10276/indonesia-grows-thornless
-durians-after-12-years-of-experimen
ting. Accessed November 22, 2021.

"China Demand for Durian Driving Defor-
estation, Warn Environmentalists."
Malaysian Insight, February 6, 2019.
https://www.themalaysianinsight.com
/s/130934.

Chua, Beng Huat. "Taking the Street out of
Street Food." In *Food, Foodscapes and
Foodways: Culture, Community and
Consumption in Post-Colonial Singa-
pore*, edited by Lily Kong and Vineeta
Sinha, 23–40. Singapore: World Scien-
tific, 2016.

David, Cynthia. "Smells Like Hell, Tastes
Like Heaven." *Metro* (Canada),
September 18, 2007. https://www
.metro.us/smells-like-hell-tastes-like
-heaven.

Duruz, Jean. "Rich Pickings: Cultures and
Histories of Taste." Review of *The
Taste Culture Reader: Experiencing
Food and Drink*, edited by Caro-
lyn Korsmeyer, and *Taste: A Literary
History*, by Denise Gigante. *Senses
and Society* 2, no. 2 (2007): 377–83.

———. "The Taste of Retro: Nostalgia,
Sensory Landscapes and Cosmo-
politanism in Singapore." In *Food,
Foodscapes and Foodways: Culture,
Community and Consumption in
Post-Colonial Singapore*, edited by
Lily Kong and Vineeta Sinha, 133–58.
Singapore: World Scientific, 2016.

Duruz, Jean, and Gaik Cheng Khoo. *Eating
Together: Food, Space and Identity in
Malaysia and Singapore.* Lanham:
Rowman & Littlefield, 2015.

Dwyer, Chris. "Why China Loves Durian,
the Smelly Fruit Popular in Thailand,
Singapore and Malaysia but Banned
in Hotels and on Public Transport in
Many Countries Across Asia." *South
China Morning Post*, October 25,

2020. https://www.scmp.com
/magazines/style/news-trends/arti
cle/3106842/why-china-loves-durian
-smelly-fruit-popular-thailand.

Edensor, Tim. "The Culture of the Indian
Street." In *Images of the Street: Planning, Identity and Control in Public
Space*, edited by Nicholas R. Fyfe,
205–21. London: Routledge, 1998.

Family Yong. "I Love Musang King."
YouTube, November 9, 2017. Promotional video, 12:07. https://www
.youtube.com/watch?v=SeeYg
VosnVg.

Fathul Rahkman. "Mengenal Si Gundul,
Durian Unik Asal Lombok." *Monga-
bay* (Indonesia), December 14, 2019.
https://www.mongabay.co.id/2019/12
/14/mengenal-si-gundul-durian-unik
-asal-lombok.

Francis, Jolynn. "Durian Lovers Can Look
Forward to the Numbing Bliss of
Fruits with a Fifth Flavour." *The Star*,
May 25, 2015. https://www.thestar
.com.my/metro/community/2015/05
/21/scent-of-a-good-harvest-durian
-lovers-can-look-forward-to-the-num
bing-bliss-of-fruits-with-a-fifth-f.

Fruit Critic. "Chinese Import Value of Durians Grew Explosively in 2020." *Fresh
Plaza*, September 3, 2020. https://
www.freshplaza.com/article/9245931
/chinese-import-value-of-durians
-grew-explosively-in-2020.

Fuller, Thomas. "Odorless Durian Raises A
Stink." *New York Times*, March 30,
2007. https://www.nytimes.com/2007
/03/30/world/asia/30iht-durian.1
.5082196.html.

Gasik, Lindsay. "Chanthaburi Tree-Dropped
Durian Wholesaler." *Year of the
Durian* (blog), June 18, 2020. https://
www.yearofthedurian.com/2020/06
/tree-dropped-durian-thailand.html.

———. "Cut vs Tree-Fallen Durian: Race
Thai Varieties at Suan Nam Sook."
Year of the Durian (blog), April 16,
2020. https://www.yearofthedurian
.com/2020/04/cut-vs-tree-fallen
-durian-rare-thai-varieties-at-suan
-nam-sook.html.

Great Big Story. "Durian Fruit: A Smell So
Rotten, a Taste So Sweet." YouTube,

July 25, 2017. Educational video, 2:48.
https://www.youtube.com/watch?v=
UbngFAoByEo.

Han, Alan. "'Can I Tell You What We Have to
Put Up With?' Stinky Fish and Offensive Durian." *Continuum* 21, no. 3
(2007): 361–77. https://doi.org/10
.1080/10304310701460714.

"Hyped! Butter Kopi! Kopi Gu You!" *The
Great Food Guy Singapore*, November
29, 2016. https://thegfoodguysg.word
press.com/2016/11/29/kopi-gu-you/.

Jackson, Peter. "Performative Genders,
Perverse Desires: A Bio-History of
Thailand's Same-Sex and Transgen-
der Cultures." *Intersections: Gender,
History and Culture in the Asian
Context* 9 (August 2003).

"Kaya Toast and Kopi: A Guide to Singapore's Quintessential Breakfast."
Grantourismo Travels Newsletter,
n.d. https://grantourismotravels.com
/breakfast-in- singapore-kaya-toast-
and-kopi. Accessed February 2, 2021.

Kelvin. "Stanley Ho—The Man Who Made
Mao Shan Wang Famous." *99 Nine-
ty-Nine Old Trees*, April 20, 2021.
https://www.99oldtrees.com/news
/Stanley-Ho-Durian.

Koh, William. *The Top Toast: Ya Kun and the
Singapore Breakfast Tradition*. Singapore: Cengage Learning, 2010.

Kong, Lily. "From *Sushi* in Singapore to
Laksa in London: Globalising Food-
ways and the Production of Economy
and Identity." In *Food, Foodscapes and
Foodways: Culture, Community and
Consumption in Post-Colonial Singa-
pore*, edited by Lily Kong and Vineeta
Sinha, 207–41. Singapore: World
Scientific, 2016.

Korsmeyer, Carolyn. "Introduction." In *The
Taste Culture Reader: Experiencing
Food and Drink*, edited by Carolyn
Korsmeyer, 1–9. Oxford: Berg, 2005.

———. "Preface" to "Taste and Aesthetic
Discrimination." In *The Taste Culture
Reader*, edited by Carolyn Korsmeyer,
195–96. Oxford: Berg, 2005.

Lai, Ah Eng. "The *Kopitiam* in Singapore: An
Evolving Story About Cultural Diver-
sity and Cultural Politics." In *Food,
Foodscapes and Foodways: Culture,*

Community and Consumption in Post-Colonial Singapore, edited by Lily Kong and Vineeta Sinha, 103–32. Singapore: World Scientific, 2016.

———. "The *Kopitiam* in Singapore: An Evolving Story About Migration and Cultural Diversity." In *Migration and Diversity in Asian Contexts*, edited by Lai Ah Eng, Francis Leo Collins, and Brenda S. A. Yeoh, 209–332. Singapore: Institute of Southeast Asian Studies, 2012.

La Loubère, Simon de. *A New Historical Relation of the Kingdom of Siam*. 2 vols. London: F. L. Horne [Cornell Digital Collections], 1693.

Law, Lisa. "Home Cooking: Filipino Women and Geographies of the Senses in Hong Kong." *Ecumene* 8 (2001): 264–83.

Lewis, Hugh. "Urban Dimensions of the Political Economy of Nanyang Ethnicity." Lewis Micropublishing, 1989. http://www.lewismicropublishing.com/Publications/AnthropologicalEssays/UrbanDimensionsNanyangPolitical Economy.htm. Accessed June 12, 2010.

Lim, Teckwyn. "Human-Elephant Relations in Peninsular Malaysia." PhD diss., University of Nottingham Malaysia, 2018.

Lim, William S. *Asian Ethical Urbanism: A Radical Postmodern Perspective*. Singapore: World Scientific, 2005.

Lindholm, Charles, and Siv B. Lee. "You Eat What You Are: Cultivated Taste and the Pursuit of Authenticity in the Slow Food Movement." In *Culture of the Slow: Social Deceleration in an Accelerated World*, edited by Nick Osbaldiston, 52–70. New York: Palgrave Macmillan, 2013.

Love, Ken, Lindsay Gasik, and Robert E. Paull. "Durian for Hawai'i." *Fruit, Nut, and Beverage Crops*. College of Tropical Agriculture and Human Resources, University of Hawai'i at Manoa. April F_N-53 (2019): 1–22.

Low, Kelvin. "Tasting Memories, Cooking Heritage: A Sensuous Invitation to Remember." In *Food, Foodscapes and Foodways: Culture, Community and Consumption in Post-Colonial*

Singapore, edited by Lily Kong and Vineeta Sinha, 61–82. Singapore: World Scientific, 2016.

———. "Theorising Sensory Cultures in Asia: Sociohistorical Perspectives." *Asian Studies Review* 43, no. 4 (2019): 618–36.

Malaysia, Rasa. "Durian, the King of Fruits." *Rasa Malaysia: Easy Delicious Recipes* (blog). July 29, 2008; last modified October 15, 2019. https://rasamalaysia.com/durian-king-of-fruits.

Mariani, Leo. "Une odeur d'enfer: À propos du devenir universel des qualités organoleptiques d'un fruit" [Smelling the hell's pit: About the universal becoming of the organoleptic qualities of a fruit]. *Techniques and Culture* 62 (2014): 48–67.

McLagan, Jennifer. *Bitter: A Taste of the World's Most Dangerous Flavour, with Recipes*. London: Jacqui Small, 2014.

Montanari, Andrea. "The Stinky King: Western Attitudes Toward the Durian in Colonial Southeast Asia." *Food, Culture and Society* 20, no. 3 (2017): 395–414.

Nora, Pierre. "Between Memory and History: *Les Lieux de Mémoire*." *Representations* 26 (1989): 7–25.

Pollan, Michael. *The Botany of Desire: A Plant's-Eye View of the World*. London: Bloomsbury, 2001.

Reinarz, Jonathan. *Past Scents: Historical Perspectives on Smell*. Champaign: University of Illinois Press, 2014.

Roy, Daniel. "Cup of Coffee, Coffee with Condensed Milk, Toastbox, Singapore." Flickr, October 14, 2009. http://www.flickr.com/photos/backpackfoodie/4014124286.

Rushdie, Salman. "Imaginary Homelands." In *Imaginary Homelands: Essays and Criticism, 1981–1991*, 9–21. London: Granta Books, 1991.

Seremetakis, C. Nadia. "The Breast of Aphrodite." In *The Taste Culture Reader*, edited by Carolyn Korsmeyer, 297–303. Oxford: Berg, 2005.

———. "The Memory of the Senses, Part I: Marks of the Transitory." In *The Senses Still: Perception and Memory as Material Culture in Modernity*, edited by C. Nadia Seremetakis, 1–18. Chicago: The University of Chicago Press, 1996.

Small, E., and P. M. Catling. "Blossoming Treasures of Biodiversity." *Biodiversity* 6, no. 4 (2006): 33–38.

Spence, Charles. "Just How Much of What We Taste Derives from the Sense of Smell?" *Flavour* 4, no. 30 (2015): 1–10.

Suen, Wilbur. "Thai Fruits—Durian (Monthong)." Aroimakmak.com (blog), November 15, 2018. https://aroimakmak.com/thai-fruits-durian.

Sullivan, Michael. "Ooh That Smell: Designing A Stinkless Durian." *National Public Radio, Weekend Edition*, May 12, 2007. https://www.npr.org/templates/story/story.php?storyId=10016534.

Thomas, Nicholas. *Entangled Objects: Exchange, Material Culture and Colonialism in the Pacific.* Cambridge, MA: Harvard University Press, 1991.

Tim. "Shanghai Yechen First to Import Frozen Durians from Malaysia." *Produce Report*, August 26, 2019. https://www.producereport.com/article/shanghai-yechen-first-import-frozen-durians-malaysia.

Wan, Julie. "What it Takes for the Durian to Smell of Success." *Washington Post,* July 12, 2011. https://www.washingtonpost.com/lifestyle/food/what-it-takes-for-the-durian-to-smell-of-success/2011/06/14/gIQA71pjAI_story.html.

West, A. J. "Knowledge of the Durian." *Medieval Indonesia*, May 31, 2020. https://indomedieval.medium.com/knowledge-of-the-durian-39f89a6c871f.

White, Merry. *Coffee Life in Japan.* Berkeley: University of California Press, 2012.

Winichakul, Thongchai. "The Quest for 'Siwilai': A Geographical Discourse of Civilizational Thinking in the Late Nineteenth and Early Twentieth-Century Siam." *Journal of Asian Studies* 59, no. 3 (2000): 528–49.

Wong, Hong Suen. "A Taste of the Past: Historically Themed Restaurants and Social Memory in Singapore." In *Food and Foodways in Asia: Resource, Tradition and Cooking*, edited by Sidney C. H. Cheung and Tan Chee-Beng, 115–28. Abingdon: Routledge, 2007.

Yeap, Peta. *Durian, the True Pearl of the Orient.* Penang: Pepeta Sdn Bhd, 2006.

Yeo, Sierra. "Singapore Kopi Culture." *Fresh Cup Magazine*, November 23, 2020. https://www.freshcup.com/singapore-kopi-culture.

CHAPTER 5

The Aroma of a Place in the Sunshine

Breathing in Japanese History Through the
Fiction of Endō Shūsaku

Gwyn McClelland

By using a sensory transnationalist lens focused on odor and aromas, here I
will analyze the works of a fiction writer who wrote across multiple backdrops
of Japanese and non-Japanese history. In the following quote, Catholic author
Endō Shūsaku (1923–1996), despite foul smells and an ugly, "oppressive"
environment, envisages a "beautiful" redemption of the peasant populace
of rural nineteenth-century Japan.

> In the shed they used in place of a church, Petitjean said the Mass.
> Old and young, male and female, from not only from [*sic*] Nakano
> but also Ieno and Motohara, had crowded into the shed, and the
> space reeked from the smells of sweat, body odors, and their expelled
> breath. The citizens of Nagasaki thought of Urakami as a foul-smell-
> ing village caused by the stench from the animals that were raised

there. The smell had gotten worse especially of late, when the villagers began to raise goats and pigs for the foreigners who lived in
Nagasaki. As he recited the Mass, Petitjean thought of the horse
stable where Jesus had been born. This shed that functioned as a
church was similarly filled with the smells of cow dung and urine.
And yet Lord, is there another church this beautiful anywhere in the
world? . . . This shed with its oppressive air of human and animal
smells, seemed as beautiful to him as those [Roman] catacombs. It
was magnificent.[1]

As a Japanese Catholic writing from the point of view of European missionaries encountering Japan, Endō Shūsaku's fiction engages with salient issues
of translation and exchange, which in this essay, I consider from the point
of view of sensory transnationalism. Endō critiques Buddhist sensibilities of
animal (and peasant) smells as putrid. In Endō's scene, the shed is linked to
the animal manger in which Christ was laid, connecting the odor of excrement with an image of fertility. Bernard Petitjean (1829–1884), imagined
by Endō in this scene observing his poor rural Nagasaki congregation (see
fig. 5.1), is an actual historical figure who arrived in Japan as a missionary
with the Société des Missions-Étrangères de Paris (the Paris Foreign Missions
Society).[2] Petitjean oversaw the public declaration of Catholic faith of many
"Hidden Christians" during Tokugawa then Meiji persecution (and exile),
continuing his ministry after the Christians were allowed to openly practice faith from 1873.[3]

For his most popular book about the experiences of a Portuguese priest
during the early years of the Christian ban in seventeenth-century Japan,
Endō originally put to his publisher the title 日向の匂い *Hinata no Nioi* (*The
Aroma of Sunshine*), or the *Aroma of a Place in the Sunshine*.[4] The olfactory
combines with the visual in this original title, demonstrating how he uses
the senses to provide contrast and to explore psychology, religious aesthetics, and sociocultural or transnational contexts.[5] The proposed title, *Aroma
of Sunshine* was eventually rejected by Endō's publisher, who told him it had
"no appeal" and convinced him to move from his scentscape to the sound-
scape, so he used the title 沈黙 *Chinmoku* (*Silence*) (1966) instead. In this
chapter, I introduce odor and scent as discussed in Endō's fiction, returning
finally to the *Hinata no Nioi* to consider what he originally intended.

Endō Shūsaku wrote originally for an exclusively Japanese audience,
although in recent years, an increasing number of translations of his works

have become available worldwide.[6] Endō's best-selling novels are often set in historic contexts, sometimes touching upon his own experience as a Christian in a largely non-Christian country. By his use of aroma throughout his fiction, Endō evokes features of an aesthetic sensibility—dissonant aromas and scents of deathliness and life, expressed in the relationship of Christianity to the landscape—or what he calls in an (apparent) self-Orientalizing phrase, the "swamp" of Japan. Swamps are themselves caught between deathliness and life, an ecological community reeking of decay essential in itself for life, and so this metaphor hints of Endō's concern to find the transcendent in places that give off an offensive odor. In this chapter, I will draw on the work of both Julia Kristeva and Mary Douglas about boundaries between death and life, and about dirt, or filth, to support this discussion. Endō subtly critiques perceptions of impurity that impinge on socioeconomic and political class. Endō struggled to identify with a Christian "set of clothing" that clashed with his Japanese sensibility—resulting in ambiguity in his narratives, fiction writing, and reflections. By analyzing Endō's use of smell as a fictional device, I aim as a historian to investigate a range of aromas, scents, and smells in the writing of Japanese history. I will pick up on Endō's use of olfactory tropes, as he linked spiritual and transcendental themes to bodies and matter. The aromas he writes of are located in space and time and present sociocultural, psychological, and political interpretations; in this chapter, I will consider how Endō's writing could be considered as a sensory transnationalism (introduced shortly). Within Endō's oeuvre, we discern a European Orientalist perspective through a Japanese sensibility, including a sociocultural classism and a spiritualist interpretation of stench as sin.[7] Aroma and odors hint at constellations of power, suspicion, and prejudice: aspersions Endō seeks to unveil. Before discussing Endō's writing at length, it is helpful to briefly consider the influence of the olfactory within Christianity, as it influences Endō in turn.

Christianity and Scent

Scent has been a boundary-making force within Christian practices and belief through the eras, although often taken for granted. In the Torah scriptures, the scent of the food sent from heaven, *manna*, accompanied the pious to the afterlife, while sulfur originated out of the earth and represented paganism.[8] Jewish tradition, as forerunner to (and successor of) Christianity, is steeped in aromatic oils, incenses, and ointments. The Roman world of early Christianity

Fig. 5.1   Felice Beato, "View in the Native Town, Nagasaki," ca. 1865, the year Hidden Christians met Petitjean in Nagasaki. Albumen silver print, 8 11/16 × 11 7/16 in. Getty Museum Collection, partial gift from the Wilson Centre for Photography, 2007.26.207.2.

similarly drew on the senses to express religiosity.[9] Jerry Toner writes that the Roman religious sense suggested that incense was inherent to the act of sacrifice and that some fragrances indicated the presence of the supernatural, influencing the emergence of a specific olfactory culture within Christianity.[10] In this way, Christianity emerged as a culturally hybrid tradition. More recently, Andrew Kettler describes how in the seventeenth century one branch of Jesuit missionaries (while others had previously arrived in Japan) were influenced by the multisensory reverence for odors of the Indigenous North Americans. He argues Jesuit priests and Native Americans accessed a syncretic sensory experience across "aromatic middle grounds."[11] The Jesuit order withheld from a sixteenth-century Reformation tendency to "disconnect olfactory from religious conviction," Ignatius himself meditating on the evil found on earth in "the smoke, the sulfur, the filth, and the rotting things."[12] The Jesuits exerted considerable influence in the early mission to Japan, where they even established a "Christian port" in Nagasaki for a short time (fig. 5.1). The tortures of the Christians at the Unzen sulfuric vents, which occurred soon after the foreign missionaries were expelled, may have been hell for the Indigenous Christians, considering the odor of sulfur, quite apart from the scalding water and steam.[13]

The sentiment of the "stink" of sin seems to stand alongside the conception of "evil odors" in Western Christianity.[14] During the Middle Ages, Christian European ideas of fragrance as blessing, versus the stink of sin, were especially strong. The "odor of sanctity," write Classen, Howes, and Synnott, related to the idea that Christian priests were thought to smell sweet, according to the saying in 2 Corinthians 2:15, "We are the aroma of Christ to God"; "To smell God . . . was to smell of God."[15] Not only was Christ buried with aromatic spices, but Mary Magdalene (or an unnamed woman) anointed Jesus's feet with the perfume nard (of Egyptian burial chambers), such that popular Christian thought observed "two poles of divine fragrance and the sulphurous stench of the Devil."[16] Additionally, foul smells are often linked to the unclean, in Japan in varied cultural situations. Cleanliness is especially highly prized in Shintō belief. As visitors enter a Shintō shrine, they ritually wash their hands with provided bamboo containers.

By a cultural lens, I encourage the reader to imaginatively breathe in the aromas of Japanese history as interpreted in the literature of Endō, with its colonialist and cross-cultural—transnational—sensibilities. Respiration and inspiration share the Latin root "to breathe." "Breathing in Japanese history," using Endō's inspirational register, my historic lens, raises curiosity about "not what happened or was said to have happened but about what may have happened."[17] I am aware that in examining literary sensoria, there is a trap in ironically mediating olfaction by the written word and abstracting aroma. Sensory olfaction is more overwhelming, though, than, for example, the visual sense—which has occupied such a central place in much of Western scholarship. Olfaction halts a person's powers of abstraction and, rather than positioning them as masterful, leaves protagonists almost subjugated by the environment.[18] As a result, it is instructive to reexamine Endō's fascination with landscape, environs, and the swamp. Aromas and smells disrupt, engage, and force physical reactions in those who experience them. There is an imaginative power in olfaction when a writer refers to a pungent scene, invoking the memory of the reader and even a bodily response.

Having briefly introduced Endō, his influences, and his use of olfaction as literary device, I elaborate upon a methodology for exploring his sensoria. There is a pressing need for more studies that analyze sensoria in Asian contexts.[19] According to sensory scholar Kelvin Low, sensory transnationalism observes how "colonialists and explorers tend to operate on the basis of assuming sensory pollution from and transgressive behavior among local populations."[20] As commonly understood in migration or sensory studies, a lens of transnationalism assists in understanding cross-border social phenomena.[21] Low writes that a sensory transnationalism encompasses colonialist, migratory, and cross-cultural interfaces. It turns colonialist or explorer-biased assumptions of sensory pollution and transgressive behavior of locals on its head, by examining how the local population understands or "discerns" both colonial and sensory impacts.[22] Endō's descriptions, especially from the point of view of European protagonists, allow us an intriguing view of Eurocentrism, while he simultaneously unsettles assumptions about pollution and transgressions of his Japanese readership. Through transnationalism, this lens allows us to consider Asia as a "product of interaction with other regions."[23] Religious beliefs, class dynamics, and power relations are mediated by the senses, and especially olfaction. Within Endō's fiction, sensory encounters raise questions of geography and offer an opportunity to theorize about intercultural and interclassist phenomena. Endō is concerned with the located-ness of smell in the landscape, the relationship of people to natural processes, the cooking, eating, and expelling of foods and animal products. Thus, by the lens of sensory flows and intercrossing, Low encourages researchers to reimagine Asia as category, and the work of Endō, picking up on European encroachment and movements, draws us vibrantly into this reimagining. What do sensory interconnections suggest about the themes of colonialism and migration? By beginning with the Japanese writer, we may attend to particular "Indigenous, local, or regional ideas and concepts."[24]

To support the survey in this chapter, I reviewed a number of Endō's well-known novels, including 白い人、黄色い人 shiroi hito / kiiroi hito (White Man / Yellow Man) (1960), 沈黙 Chinmoku (Silence) (1966), 女の一生: キク の場合 onna no isshō: Kiku no baai (Kiku's Prayer: A Novel) (1982), 女の一 生: サチ子の場合 onna no isshō: Sachiko no baai Sachiko (1986), and 深い 河 fukai kawa (Deep River) (1993; 1996) for the author's use of "smell."[25] These novels are rich in their exploration of meeting places, convergencies, and points of cultural hybridity in the Japanese landscape.

There is a tendency to stereotype Endo as a Grahame Greene of the East, given that he was heavily influenced by foreign literature. However, Mark Williams writes that Endō's writing fits within the twentieth-century Japanese shōsetsu genre, a "literary form of the confession," confessions of the true self, that presented the deep inner life of his protagonists.[26] Endō, like

others in his peer group, was influenced by a push to write about the "self."
He was further affected by the postwar environment by a "splintered perspective." Van Gessel explains:

> Japanese works involve an expanded, often splintered, range of
> perspective and point of view; questioning of the narrator's reliability
> and authority to speak by his own alter ego; and a new, invigorat-
> ing dosage of irony. These stories are told both in the voice of the
> narrator, who relates his own personal experience in much the same
> manner as the creators of shishōsetsu [subform of the shōsetsu]
> dominated the realm of fiction before the war, and in the voice of
> the narrator's dopelgänger—his "spirit double"—who infuses the
> text with critical commentary or provides an ironic view of the
> narrated events.[27]

Thus, Endō's literature shows a strong determination to deeply probe the
psychological state of his characters.[28] Endō employs olfaction to communicate perceptions, prejudices, and finally the emergence of the subconscious
self in his writing. Aroma forces reaction and thus allows oneself to observe
or reflect upon prejudices, boundaries, and, for Endō, the transcendent.

The olfactory tendency to overwhelm is described by Endō as his protagonists' inadvertent bodily reaction to stench or "evil" smells. Philosopher Julia
Kristeva writes of visceral reactions to odors, adding that anything bordering
on deathliness is what we thrust aside in order to live: "A wound with blood
and pus, or the sickly, acrid smell of sweat, of decay, does not *signify* death.
In the presence of signified death—a flat encephalograph, for instance—I
would understand, react, or accept. No, as in true theater, without makeup
or masks, refuse and corpses *show me* what I permanently thrust aside in
order to live. These body fluids, this defilement, this shit are what life with-
stands, hardly and with difficulty, on the part of death. There, I am at the
border of my condition as a living being."[29]

In the Japanese context as well, death is a particular marker or boundary of impurity, kept at arm's length, and not transcended, but avoided.
There is an intrinsic cultural hybridity to consider, whereby in discussing
Endō's fiction, the Buddhist-Shintō-Christian concerns and sensibilities are
all significant. Shintō concepts of impurity may be traced to the eighth-century documents the Kojiki and Nihonshoki, which construe contact with the
dead through pollutions as itself "dangerous" and "deathly."[30] Shintō purity

codes historically emphasized the importance of cleanliness and the avoidance of pollution and defilement, associated with death, leading to discrimination against those who handled the deceased and who disposed of dead animals.[31] People who encountered the dying or dead would be exposed to the most serious form of contamination in medieval Japanese society.

Kristeva cites olfaction as material evidence of "abjection," what occurs when the boundary of oneself is under threat of invasion. To take an olfactory example of sensory transnationalism that we might understand as an example of Kristeva's abjection from Endō's writing, the main protagonist in the book *Silence*, the Portuguese priest, Rodrigues, experiences an involuntary reaction to odor in a chapel jammed with peasant Christians. Rodrigues writes in a letter: "The crumbling farm house that I use for a chapel is jammed tight with their bodies, and so they confess their sins, their mouths close to my ear and emitting a stench that almost makes me vomit."[32] We may consider three possible interpretations of Rodrigues's sense of smell and his involuntary bodily reaction, all of which have a psychological and symbolic underpinning. A recent arrival in Japan, the fictional Rodrigues holds a European Orientalist gaze (well known to Endō from his time in France) and a sociocultural classism, disparaging about the peasants themselves. Finally, as a priestly character, he also likely has a body-spirit interpretation of stench symbolizing sin.

Rodrigues gags and almost vomits in reaction—in Kristeva's terms, this reaction is a form of "abjection." He is conscious of the "sinful" confessing, their stinky breath emanating from them as they whisper to the priest. Endō's writing engages with the potentiality of evil and good in his characters, their bodies emblematic and affective.

Endō's personal history and psychological development holds olfactory clues as to his development as a writer. In the following section, I briefly introduce the influence of smell on his own memories, of his exchange journey as a young student, before he became known as a novelist. Whereas Endō's characters usually migrate from Europe to Japan, he himself experienced the reverse.

A Stinking Ship

In the immediate postwar period, the author Endō had already experienced considerable rejection within Japan, due to his belief in the Catholic "enemy religion."[33] At twenty-seven years old, on June 5, 1950, Endō traveled from

Yokohama, Japan, by ship to Lyon, France, to study the main focus of his university research, the writings of French Catholic authors. Endō recalled the heat and stench he was forced to endure while traveling with a group of Japanese students, traveling in their fourth-class berth in the gallies of the ship *Marseille*.[34] People often remember past indignities by strong or negative odors, as our memory is stimulated by smell. The smell in Endō's memory represented the oppression of the Japanese students by the ship's crew in the postwar decade and ongoing suspicions held about their "true" motives. This journey for Endō reinforced "difference" and the extension of barriers between East and West after the Pacific War and as a result of the recent occupation of Japan at the time.[35] He traveled to France and lived there for three years before an ignominious return to Japan due to illness.

Shortly after his trip to France in 1955, Endō wrote the novella *kiiroi hito* (*Yellow Man*) as a twin to *shiroi hito* (*White Man*). *White Man,* based on Endō's study in Lyon, France, is the story of the gradual and dramatic decision of a young Frenchman to collaborate with the Nazis against the French Resistance. Endō frequently returns to the theme of betrayal and weakness, and an autobiographical view of his own weaknesses almost comes into view in his writing. *Yellow Man* is a novella in the form of a letter, which is written by a Japanese man who is no longer a Christian to a disgraced French missionary. The pair of novels at first glance delineate a dichotomy from the point of view of the West and the East, but scholar of literature Mark Williams argues that they are rather a starting point for Endō's "literature of reconciliation" between the self and the unconscious self. Rather than essentializing Japan from the "West," Endō instead offers a literature of humanity, acknowledging the potential for evil and for good within each person.[36]

When the Japanese first encountered Portuguese missionaries and traders in the 1500s, some of the locals were offended by their smell. Endō reportedly recalled the disgust felt by Japanese vegetarians when they first encountered the "carnivours [sic] peoples of the West." They labeled the smell *bata kusai* (stinks of butter).[37] Endō purportedly spoke of an odor of cheese particular to foreigners. Smell can operate as boundary maker, illuminating the "other," and Occidentalist or Orientalist stereotypes have often drawn on this sense, although the first quote in this chapter disrupts this view. Memory of olfactory difference was evoked in the city of Nagasaki, which originated as a Jesuit outpost, through to recent times. The city planner and historian Shimauchi Hachiro described smell, or *nioi*, as recently as 1951 as part of the international culture of Nagasaki, including in his description of this culture the

Fig. 5.2   Painting of Japanese and Dutch trade at Dejima, between 1800 and 1825. Paint on silk. British Museum, 1881, 1210,0.2761. Photo © The Trustees of the British Museum.

French-built Oura Cathedral, two "Chinese" Buddhist temples, the Dutch Dejima Island, the Chinese compound, the Twenty-Six Martyrs' Museum, and the Glover residence (Dejima Island is depicted in fig. 5.2).[38] "Othering" through smell stands to be pursued as a political strategy.

From the European standpoint, in welcoming the English publishing of Japanese scholar Okakuro Kakuzō's (1863–1913) *Book of Tea* (1906), the authors of an English broadsheet, "The Gentlewoman," wrote, "How many of us Westerners when 'drinking the liquid amber within the porcelain' touch the 'sweet reticence of Confucius, the piquancy of Loates [Laotse *sic*] and the ethereal aroma of Sakyamuni himself?'"[39]

The broadsheet and the book evoke an Orientalist imagination about an aroma that is not easy to define. Okakuro was one of the early Pan-Asianists during the Meiji and Taishō eras who is remembered for promoting a spiritual unity of Asia. Thus, in the *Book of Tea*, Okakuro's motives were to defend Japan against modern thinking and "Western" culture by the employment of an ethno-nationalist trope.[40] Fragrances are mixed with religious exoticism in this quote from Okakuro, who is keen to show the religious undertones of the tea ceremony, a superior ceremony (he suggests) to Western tendencies toward alcoholism, just as the "Eastern" is perceived as offering a source of potential enlightenment via the aroma of Buddhism. From the English exoticizing perspective, the review markets an imagined sweet aroma from the "Spice Islands" and the colonies of the East.

Classist Odors

Endō uses odor to unsettle the readers' assumptions about Japan. By writing in the view of non-Japanese characters, Endō is allowed more freedom in his critique of Japanese society. *Silence* records the trip of protagonist Rodrigues to Japan in 1639 to find out whether a priest named Ferreira has actually apostatized (given up faith). Rodrigues is captured and is forced to observe the torture of fellow Christians to encourage him to apostatize. The Christians of the seventeenth century are, like their forebears, peasants and farmworkers, among the lower classes.

For Endō and his immediate Japanese audience of readers, any connection of smell to "filth" might be read as societal critique. The derogatory name of outcastes in the Tokugawa period was literally filth, or エタ *eta*, and in the early 1970s (four hundredth anniversary of the opening of Nagasaki Harbor) a map was found in Nagasaki city that included this word, written approximately in the location where a modern-day 部落民 *burakumin* outcaste community lived until the atomic bombing of 1945.[41] Can the dirty be redeemed from this position? Can the filthy be freed from the oppression they suffer? Endō portrayed Petitjean, the French missionary in the first quote in this chapter, suggesting a redemptive and sacred site in a shed, despite pervasive smells. Rodrigues, the Portuguese priest and outlaw, on the other hand, is turned off by the similar foul odors he encounters. For Rodrigues, the peasants' distinct smell is due to the "filth" in which they live and due to their "poor" diet of fish and of soured vegetables. We already know, given the setting of the book *Chinmoku (Silence)*, that after 1639, when Rodrigues arrived in Japan, the Christians experienced exclusion and persecutions lasting for two hundred and fifty years, until at least 1873.

In Western scholarship, Mary Douglas (1921–2007) was influential in challenging concepts of dirt and pollution (see also Toulson in this volume). She writes that conventional "dirt-avoidance" can be set aside due to friendship but that dirt might be considered as "matter out of place."[42] Dirt for Douglas is symbolic rather than inherent, linking with symbolic systems of religious and sociocultural purity. In systems of religious purity, she suggested that uncleanness and dirt represent what should be excluded to maintain a pattern. In Endō's fiction, too, the odors and aromas both expose prejudices and signal redemptory or transcendental possibility.

To analyze the concept of filth in Japan, it is important to understand that the Shintō and Buddhist concepts are as integral as the Christian, and throughout the persecution period, the Christians took on a hybrid faith, often combining Shintō, Buddhist, and Hidden Christian calendars, or integrating with Buddhism, sometimes with a Buddhist Kannon to cover as the Virgin Mary.[43] In the Japanese context, death and deathliness symbolize impurity and are boundary markers, as per both Kristeva and Douglas. Jayne Sun Kim writes in a Columbia University dissertation of two varieties of defilement in Japanese society, which she calls "touch defilement" and "transgression defilement."[44] Touch defilement might include situations and contexts around death, pregnancy, childbirth, and menstruation, animal birth and death, foods, and accidental fire. Transgression defilement is related to outcaste groups, crime, and religious transgression, or the occurrence of illness, said to be due to sins of the past. Odor and smells, adding to Kim's discussion, would accompany both forms of defilement and add to prejudice leveled against the outcaste groups.

Aroma is, of course, only one of the senses Endō draws on throughout his works. The novel *Silence* is constructed around themes of death, oppressiveness, and contrasting liveliness, drawing on multiple, synesthetic senses. Endō, through his character's voice, describes an utter blackness that envelopes Rodrigues, as he travels on a boat to the island. "All around me is the black sea; it is impossible to tell where the blackness of the night begins. I cannot see whether or not there are islands around me. The only thing that tells me I am on the sea is the heavy breathing of the young man who rows the boat behind me . . . now I was all alone in the black sea of the night and must take upon myself the cold and the darkness and everything else."[45]

Blackness sharpens Rodrigues's other senses, including hearing, as he attempts to evade the Japanese authorities. The landscape is itself integral to the plot, including the black sea and islands. Arriving on an island after this lonely trip, most likely on the Gotō archipelago about one hundred kilometers from the mainland, he comes to a village where he is once again assailed by an evil smell. The odor physically overwhelms him, and he has an involuntary bodily reaction approaching abjection: "Into my nostrils the wind blew an awful stench which almost made me vomit. It was like rotten fish. But when I set foot in the village, I found myself surrounded by a fearful, eerie silence. Not a single person was there."[46]

Finally meeting the villagers, Rodrigues cannot communicate, although he is aware that they are Christian or at least Hidden Christian believers. Soon, though, shogunal officials arrest Rodrigues and the villagers, and a village woman gives Rodrigues a small cucumber. The cucumber is not sweet

Fig. 5.3   Yanagawa Shigenobu I, "Scenting a Kimono with Incense." Color woodblock print, 8 5/6 × 7 1/4 in. Art Institute Chicago, Gift of Helen C. Gunsaulus, 1954.691.

to taste, given the inhospitable conditions. Endō contrasts the evil smell from the cucumber with the sacralized name of the woman, making the Portuguese priest think again about his conception of the villagers. For the Japanese reader too, the non-Japanese name would indicate a cultural hybridity. "When he bit it, his mouth was filled with its green stench. . . . 'Your name?' he asked. 'Monica.' Her answer was somewhat bashful. . . . What missionary had given the name of Augustine's mother to this woman whose body was reeking with the stench of fish?"[47] "A smiling little plump samurai . . . came slowly down the cliff as he spoke. . . . As he passed there was a dry swish of his cloak. His clothes gave forth a sweet perfume"[48] (see fig. 5.3).

The pleasing smells of government officials signify Endō's societal or moral critique, questioning whether we should accept pleasant aromas as evidence of righteousness. He challenges "purity codes" in Japan—the sense of smell in the villages envisage the ugly and the impure. Endō's contrasting of the peasants' bodies and the Christian names they have been given questions a normative condemning of the poor and odorous as impure.

Endō's writing spans a wide period of Japanese history from the beginning of the Kirishitan (Christian) ban to its end. In *Kiku's Prayer*, we move from the early sixteenth century to the late nineteenth, in the same region of Japan near Nagasaki. In the late nineteenth century, there was a controversy over the Emperor Meiji's rescinding of the long-held ban on red meat. Ordinary people only gradually began to eat meats, and a largely vegetarian diet had been common for many, as it was associated with Buddhist belief. As a marker of transgressive defilement, the smell of leather was considered offensive and was strongly associated with outcaste groups.[49] Thus, when Endō describes Urakami, a northern suburb of Nagasaki, in the nineteenth century from the point of view of a French priest as a "foul-smelling" village (in a quote from *Kiku's Prayer*), the mention of animal smells has a particular connotation. It was the outcaste groups, by the late nineteenth century known as *burakumin*, who traditionally dealt with animal slaughter and leather goods, so these smells that Petitjean mentions would have been both offensive and effective boundary markers in the religious and sociocultural context. They marked these peasants as people to stay away from, quite apart from their religious practices. It is possible that, at the time, the animals were raised for the appetites of the foreigners who lived in Nagasaki (having arrived after the unequal treaties of the 1850s) as well as for trade in leather. Many of the Christians who returned from exile in the 1870s became butchers, whereas a small outcaste community on the northern side of Nagasaki had, prior to the Meiji era, been the only ones involved in this occupation.[50]

In Search of the "Aroma of Life"

Endō's sensory transnationalism widens its scope to South Asia in *Deep River* (1996), the novel he wrote shortly before he died. It is the story of a group of Japanese travelers on a spiritual journey to India, the birthplace of both Buddhism and Hinduism. Rather than European protagonists viewing Japan, in this novel, the Japanese characters enter into the metanarratives of

Buddhism and Hinduism. The novel could be imagined as a subtle response to the writings of Okakuro Kakuzō (*The Book of Tea*), disrupting a self-referential Oriental essentialism. Okakuro claimed of course that in the tea ceremony one might touch the "sweet reticence of Confucius, the piquancy of Laotes, and the ethereal aroma of Sukyamuni himself." The physicality of odor appealed to in this statement provides a method of transportation through the tea ceremony to a sacred space (of Japan). In his novel, Endō critiques stereotypes of the poor and their smells. One traveler on the Indian tour, Kiguchi, falls ill in Varanasi, India, a place where people go to die, and Mitsuko offers to stay to look after him, missing an opportunity for local sightseeing at the origin place of the Buddha. By deciding to stay with Kiguchi, Mitsuko asserts she does not seek the aroma of Sakyamuni. She says, "Pristine places like Buddha-Gaya where Sakyamuni attained enlightenment really don't suit my fancy. I feel much more at home amid the vile smells of this city. I'm actually grateful you'll let me stay on here."[51]

Enlightenment, for Endō, is not in the sweetly scented places but rather should be sought beyond the boundaries of the accepted or acceptable. Later, Mitsuko finds the other protagonist in a whorehouse in a dingy section of the city, which smells worse than the rest of Varanasi. Consistently, Endō insists that enlightenment and the sacred may invert societal impressions and prejudices, which is observable via transnational sensibilities.

In terms of landscape, the novel *Deep River* reveals further Endō's concern with environmental metaphor. Endō had previously described the concept of Japan as a swamp, or alternatively, the image of the swamp as human consciousness.[52] Netland suggests that Endō was likely influenced by the work of philosopher Watsuji Tetsurō (1889–1960), who wrote on both Western and Eastern philosophy. Influenced by Heidegger, Watsuji's *Climate and Culture* suggests that human culture may be classified into three main climate zones: North Africa, the Middle East, and Central Asia (desert); Europe and the Mediterranean (meadow); and Asia (monsoon).[53] Whereas the harsh desert conditions meant that humans in this region struggled with the elements, the meadow region was associated with an Enlightenment sentiment of human-centered objectivism about the environment. The "monsoon" climate of Asia, on the other hand, led to a human sense of "resignation," Watsuji suggested, due to the destructive and unpredictable aspects of the forces of nature. Perhaps it was at least partly Watsuji's influence that led to Endō's characterization of the "swamp" of Japan.

Within the novel *Deep River*, interspersed in his description of the grainy and pungent smells of Varanasi, Endō writes of an "Aroma of Life" in the forests, perhaps similar to the aroma of a place in the sunshine envisaged in *Silence*. The Australian scientific agency the Commonwealth Scientific and Industrial Research Organisation invented a new word, petrichor, to describe the scent of oil released into the air before rain. We may well be reminded that the smell of the swamp, as in the rainforest, decay, and humus—the dirt and grime—welcome new life. The Japanese protagonist, Numada, observes and deeply breathes in the air of the trees around him:

> He heard the rustle of leaves on a linden tree. The flapping of insect wings near his ear. Those sounds served to deepen the silence of the forest. Something quickly swung from one coconut tree to another, and when he turned his eyes and inhaled the sultry, unrefined aroma, *like the fermented smell of sake brewing that emerged from the earth and the trees. The unadorned aroma of life.* That life flowed back and forth between the trees and the chirping of the birds and the wind that slowly set the leaves fluttering.[54] (emphasis original, quoted from Mase-Hasegawa)

Endō embraces a moving, living ecosystem and, with the smell of fermenting sake, evokes an aroma, the petrichor(!) of life. He alludes to the sacred monkey, swinging from one coconut tree to another, an insect flapping past and an unrefined aroma, a literally intoxicating smell. In Japan, the aroma of sunshine in summer entails a smell of humidity, as summer is also wet season, contributing the heavy smell of the soil.

Conclusion

Returning to Endō's beloved novel *Silence*, what is the aroma of a place in the sunshine that he sought to highlight? Did Endō intend the aroma of sunshine in this place to be an allusion to a powerful symbol of Japan, the rising sun? I suggest, rather than an image of Japan, that by examining the memorable conclusion, we may understand his intentions. Just prior to the climax of the novel, Endō writes about his protagonist, Rodrigues, the priest. "The first rays of the dawn appear. The light shines on his long neck stretched out like a chicken and upon his bony shoulders." Rodrigues tramples on the *fumie*, an image of Christ, which will prove his apostasy, and "dawn broke. In the distance the cock crew." A few pages later, Endō continues, "There was little rain that summer. . . . Wherever he went, the air was heavy with the stench of fertilizer." As opposed to the dryness envisaged in this moment of betrayal, is it the relief of petrichor, an anticipation of the rain that Endō envisages as the aroma of a place in the sunshine? The cock crowing alludes biblically to Peter who, like Rodrigues, betrayed Christ. Yet Christ forgave him, in looking ahead to that dry moment. The aroma of a place of sunshine heralds hope despite everything.

Scents, foul, and fertile, paint descriptive pictures in Endō's fiction. In this chapter, I have described varied elements of a sensory transnationalism evident in Endō's fiction, especially how he uses the olfactory sense as both a contrasting tool and as a transnational or culturally hybridic method of unsettling sociocultural norms and historical purity codes. Scent symbolically connects matter across Asia and globally, as part of Endō's reconciliatory work, demonstrating connections between human, animal, nature, and land to the spiritual in Endō's fiction. The historical environment he reenvisions as a swamp, which shows a psychology of humanity, the unconscious self, and his protagonists' yearning—for a place that transcends East and West, darkness, oppression, and fear—for a fragrant place in the dawning sunshine where they may breathe in intoxicating and delicious aromas and find a place of healing.

Notes

1. Father Bernard Petitjean in Endō's imagination, Endō, *Kiku's Prayer*, 98.

2. McClelland, "Foreign Missionaries."

3. The Meiji era in Japan ran from 1868 to 1912, after the Tokugawa Shogunate was overthrown.

4. Gessel, "Hearing God in Silence," 150. Van Gessel, who has translated some of Endō's work, writes that his original title might have been rather *mahiru no nioi* (the scent of midday). Gessel explains that although in a video produced in 1992 the original title is cited as *hinata no nioi*, Endō's widow wrote his original title was *mahiru no nioi*.

5. Nowadays, in Sotome, a region north of Nagasaki where "Hidden Christians" once lived and location of the Shusaku Endō Literature Museum, some traders have commercialized a "rest-place" located

between the Ono Catholic church and alongside some small shops on the western coastline of Kyushu, calling the small park the *Hinata no Nioi* after the original title of the Endō book (http://www.kanko-sotome .com/taberu/taberu08).

6. Endō was awarded the Akutagawa Prize in 1955, the Tanizaki Prize in 1966, the Order of St. Sylvester in 1971, and the Order of Culture in 1995. In my own research, I have focused on historical Nagasaki studies. McClelland, *Dangerous Memory in Nagasaki*.

7. For more on odor as sin, see, for example, Shemesh's work on body odor and morality in Shemesh, "Scent of the Righteous," 165–82. Shemesh writes that in Christian, Muslim, and Bahai traditions, those who were holy were represented as smelling good. In Jewish discourse, smell

could distinguish between the good and
the corrupt. A similar trope is found in
Christian literature. Harvey describes an
early Christian martyrdom of Polycarp in
155AD, "And he was within it not as burning flesh, but rather as bread being baked, or
as gold and silver being purified in a smelt-
ing furnace. And from it we perceived such a
delicious fragrance as though it were smoking incense or some other costly perfume."
Harvey, *Scenting Salvation*, 12. She also
notes that Theophrastus wrote, "Putridity
however is a general term, applied, one may
say, to anything which is subject to decay:
For anything which is decomposing has an
evil odor." Harvey, *Scenting Salvation*, 31.
For discussion of olfaction and distinctions
of class, see Low, *Scent and Scent-Sibilities*,
chapter 5; Reinarz, *Past Scents*, 145–76.

8. Kettler, "'Ravishing Odors of Paradise,'"
832.

9. Toner, *Smell and the Ancient Senses*,
158.

10. Ibid., 159.

11. Kettler, "'Ravishing Odors of Paradise,'"
830.

12. Ibid., 834.

13. Unzen is a volcano, located on the
Shimabara peninsula south of Nagasaki, and
the tortures carried out are mentioned, for
example, in Brockey, "Books of Martyrs,"
206–8.

14. Classen, Howes, and Synnott, *Aroma*,
54.

15. Toner, *Smell and the Ancient Senses*,
159.

16. Ibid., 163.

17. Walters, *Archives of the Black Atlantic*,
1.

18. For another example where the lens
of olfaction is used to explore literature, see
Phillips, "Nose-Gaping."

19. Low, "Theorising Sensory Cultures,"
631.

20. Ibid., 628.

21. Boccagni, "Rethinking Transnational
Studies," 117–32.

22. Low, "Theorising Sensory Cultures,"
628.

23. Wang, "Idea of Asia and Its Ambigu-
ities," 989.

24. Low quotes Alatas, "Captive Mind and
Creative Development," 691–700; Alatas,

*Alternative Discourses in Asian Social
Science.*

25. Endō, *Kiku's Prayer*; Endō, *Silence*;
Endō, *Deep River*; Endō, "White Man, Yellow
Man"; Endō, *Sachiko*.

26. Williams, *Endō Shūsaku*, 5.

27. Gessel, "Voice of the Doppelgänger," 199.

28. Williams, *Endō Shūsaku*, 27.

29. Kristeva, *Powers of Horror*, 3.

30. See Namihira's discussion of the
concept of pollution, 汚れkegare. Namihira,
"Pollution,"65.

31. Reber, "Buraku Mondai in Japan," 303.

32. *Silence* quoted in Inoue, "Reclaiming
the Universal," 77.

33. Williams, *Endō Shūsaku*, 59.

34. Ibid., 58–59.

35. Perhaps this contributes to Endō's
strong consciousness of the irony that the
Japanese empire project had been halted by
"Christian cultures" themselves set on colonizing the planet, populating, dominating,
using, and converting the world. Keller, "Lost
Fragrance," 366. A strong critique is evident
in Endō's books of the non-Japanese priest
characters who populate them.

36. See, for example, Mathy, who argues
Endō did perceive an essential divide between
East and West: Mathy, "Endo Shūsaku,"
58–74. Williams discusses Endō's reconciliatory literature in Williams, *Endō Shūsaku*.

37. Le Breton cites Birolli in this quote of
Endō's. Le Breton, *Sensing the World*, 165.

38. Diehl, *Resurrecting Nagasaki*, 35.

39. Okakuro, *Book of Tea*, 2.

40. Porcu, *Pure Land Buddhism*, 33.

41. McClelland and Chapman, "Silences,"
382–400.

42. Douglas, *Purity and Danger*, 7; 36.

43. McClelland, "Mother of Sorrows as
Hibakusha," 111–32. E.g., Buddhist holy day
Aki no Bon, San Jiwan Sama no Hi (*Kakure*
event), and *Yuki no Santa Maria* (Christian)
events listed on the same calendar. Whelan,
"Japan's Vanishing Minority," 448.

44. Kim, "History of Filth."

45. Endō, *Silence*, 106–7.

46. Ibid., 110.

47. Ibid., 137.

48. Ibid., 138–39.

49. Not only in Japan. See also Shivani
Kapoor's chapter in this volume and Hankins,
"Ecology of Sensibility."

50. Otsuki, "Reinventing Nagasaki,"
395–415; McClelland and Chapman,
"Silences," 382–400.
  51. Hanson, "Conflict and Confusion."

52. Netland, "From Cultural Alterity," 30.
53. Watsuji, *Fudo*.
54. Endō, *Deep River*, 331.

Bibliography

Alatas, S. F. *Alternative Discourses in Asian
    Social Science: Responses to Eurocen-
    trism*. New Delhi: Sage, 2006.
Alatas, S. H. "The Captive Mind and Creative
    Development." *International Social
    Science Journal* 24, no. 1 (1974):
    691–700.
Boccagni, Paolo. "Rethinking Transnational
    Studies: Transnational Ties and the
    Transnationalism of Everyday Life."
    European Journal of Social Theory 15,
    no. 1 (2012): 117–32.
Bradley, Mark. *Smell and the Ancient Senses*.
    London: Routledge, 2014.
Breton, David Le. *Sensing the World: An
    Anthropology of the Senses*. Oxford:
    Bloomsbury Academic, 2017.
Brockey, Liam Matthew. "Books of Martyrs:
    Example and Imitation in Europe and
    Japan, 1597–1650." *Catholic Histor-
    ical Review* 103, no. 2 (Spring 2017):
    206–8.
Classen, Constance, David Howes, and
    Anthony Synnott. *Aroma: The
    Cultural History of Smell*. London:
    Routledge, 1994.
Diehl, Chad Richard. *Resurrecting Nagasaki:
    Reconstruction and the Formation of
    Atomic Narratives*. Ithaca: Cornell
    University Press, 2018.
Douglas, Mary. *Purity and Danger: An Anal-
    ysis of Concepts of Pollution and
    Taboo*. London: Taylor & Francis,
    2002.
Endō, Shūsaku. 遠藤周作. *Deep River*.
    Translated by Van C. Gessel. New
    York: New Directions, 1996
———. *Kiku's Prayer: A Novel*. New York:
    Columbia University Press, 2012.
———. *Sachiko*. Translated by Van C. Gessel.
    New York: Columbia University Press,
    2020.
———. *Silence*. Translated by William John-
    son. New York: Taplinger, 1980.

———. *White Man, Yellow Man*. Translated
    by Teruyo Shimizu. Mahwah, MJ:
    Paulist Press, 2014.
Gessel, Van C. "Hearing God in Silence: The
    Fiction of Endō Shūsaku." *Christian-
    ity and Literature* 48, no. 2 (1999):
    149–64.
———. "The Voice of the Doppelganger."
    Japan Quarterly 38, no. 2 (1991):
    198–213.
Hankins, Joseph. "An Ecology of Sensibil-
    ity: The Politics of Scents and Stigma
    in Japan." *Anthropological Theory* 13,
    nos. 1–2 (2013): 49–66.
Hanson, Alan S. "Conflict and Confusion:
    Bewildered Travel in the Fiction of
    Shusaku Endo." Master's thesis,
    Georgetown University, 2009. https://
    repository.library.georgetown.edu
    /handle/10822/553328.
Harvey, Susan Ashbrook. *Scenting Salva-
    tion: Ancient Christianity and the
    Olfactory Imagination*. Fulcrum.Org.
    Berkeley: University of California
    Press, 2015.
Hui, Wang. "The Idea of Asia and Its Ambi-
    guities." *Journal of Asian Studies* 69,
    no. 4 (2010): 985–89.
Inoue, Masamichi. "Reclaiming the Univer-
    sal: Intercultural Subjectivity in the
    Life and Work of Endo Shusaku."
    Southeast Review of Asian Studies 34
    (2012): 153–70.
Keller, Catherine. "The Lost Fragrance: Prot-
    estantism and the Nature of What
    Matters." *Journal of the American
    Academy of Religion* 65, no. 2 (1997):
    355–70.
Kettler, Andrew. "'Ravishing Odors of
    Paradise': Jesuits, Olfaction, and
    Seventeenth-Century North Amer-
    ica." *Journal of American Studies* 50,
    no. 4 (2016): 827–52.

Kim, Jayne. "A History of Filth: Defilement Discourse in Medieval Japan." PhD diss., Columbia University, 2004.

Kristeva, Julia. *Powers of Horror: An Essay on Abjection.* New York: Columbia University Press, 1984.

Le Breton, David. *Sensing the World: An Anthropology of the Senses.* London: Routledge, 2017.

Low, Kelvin E. Y. *Scent and Scent-Sibilities: Smell and Everyday Life Experiences.* Newcastle upon Tyne: Cambridge Scholars, 2009.

———. "Theorising Sensory Cultures in Asia: Sociohistorical Perspectives." *Asian Studies Review* 43, no. 4 (2019): 618–36.

Mase-Hasegawa, Emi. *Christ in Japanese Culture: Theological Themes in Shusaku Endo's Literary Works.* Leiden: Brill, 2008.

Mathy, Francis. "Endo Shusaku: White Man, Yellow Man." *Comparative Literature* 19, no. 1 (1967): 58–74.

McClelland, Gwyn. *Dangerous Memory in Nagasaki: Prayers, Protests and Catholic Survivor Narratives.* New York: Routledge, 2019.

———. "Foreign Missionaries and Indigenous Communities in Nineteenth Century: Japan." In *The Palgrave Handbook of the Catholic Church in East Asia,* edited by Cindy Yik-yi Chu and Beatrice Leung, 1–36. Singapore: Palgrave MacMillan, 2021.

———. "The Mother of Sorrows as Hibakusha." In *Representations of the Blessed Virgin Mary in World Literature and Art,* edited by Elena V. Shabliy, 111–32. Lanham: Lexington Books, 2017.

McClelland, Gwyn, and David Chapman. "Silences: The Catholics, the Untouchables and the Nagasaki Atomic Bomb." *Asian Studies Review* 44, no. 3 (2020): 382–400.

Namihira, Emiko. "Pollution in the Folk Belief System." *Current Anthropology* 28, no. 4 (1987): 65–74.

Netland, John T. "From Cultural Alterity to the Habitations of Grace: The Evolving Moral Topography of Endo's Mudswamp Trope." *Christianity and Literature* 59, no. 1 (2009): 27–48.

Okakura, Kakuzō. 岡倉覚三. *The Book of Tea* 茶の本. New York: Duffield, 1906.

Otsuki, Tomoe. "Reinventing Nagasaki: The Christianization of Nagasaki and the Revival of an Imperial Legacy in Postwar Japan." *Inter-Asia Cultural Studies* 17, no. 3 (2016): 395–415.

Phillips, Mike. "Nose-Gaping: The Smells of Mason and Dixon." *Orbit: A Journal of American Literature* 7, no. 1 (2019): 1–16.

Porcu, Elisabetta. *Pure Land Buddhism in Modern Japanese Culture.* Leiden: Brill, 2008.

Reber, Emily A. S. "Buraku Mondai in Japan: Historical and Modern Perspectives and Directions for the Future from the Perspective of an American Researcher." *Dowa Mondai Kenkyu* 20 (1998): 45–62.

Reinarz, Jonathan. "Uncommon Scents: Class and Smell." In *Past Scents, Historical Perspectives on Smell,* 145–76. Champaign: University of Illinois Press, 2014.

Shemesh, Abraham Ofir. "The Scent of the Righteous vs. the Scent of the Wicked: Body Odor as a Social Indicator of Morality in Rabbinic Literature." *Review of Rabbinic Judaism* 23, no. 2 (2020): 165–82.

Toner, Jerry. "Smell and Christianity." In *Smell and the Ancient Senses,* edited by Mark Bradley, 158–70. London: Routledge, 2014.

Walters, Wendy W. *Archives of the Black Atlantic: Reading Between Literature and History.* Routledge Research in Atlantic Studies. New York: Routledge, 2018.

Watsuji, Tetsurō. 和辻哲郎. 風土 人間学的 考察 *Fuudo: Ningengakuteki kousatsu.* Tokyo: Iwanami Shoten, 1935.

Whelan, Christal. "Japan's Vanishing Minority: The 'Kakure Kirishitan' of the Goto Islands." *Japan Quarterly* 41, no. 4 (1994): 434–49.

Williams, Mark B. *Endō Shūsaku: A Literature of Reconciliation.* London: Taylor & Francis, 1999.

CHAPTER 6

Words That Smell

Caste and Odors in Hindi Dalit Autobiographies

Shivani Kapoor

Caste, Writing, and Senses

In the opening paragraphs of Dr. Tulsi Ram's autobiography, *Murdahiya*, we encounter a sentence which starts "My grandfather, who was called Joothan. . . ."[1] *Joothan*, a Hindi word, refers to leftover or half-eaten food.[2] It also refers to the practice, followed across India, of giving away leftover food to people from lower-caste communities. This practice derives from the discriminating and humiliating principles of caste, which bind people in a "graded hierarchy" according to the caste group into which they were born.[3] Tulsi Ram's autobiography, *Murdahiya*, introduces us to his grandfather Joothan, who belonged to the Chamar caste in eastern Uttar Pradesh and used to work as a bonded laborer in the fields of Brahmin landlords—an occupation that was passed on to Tulsi Ram's father as well.[4] The name "Joothan," possibly a metonym given to the grandfather by the upper-castes, signifies his lowly and degraded status, much like half-eaten food. It also signifies the caste-marked feudal relationship between those who throw away food and those forced to consume it. The name also draws our attention to the ways in which the organization of the senses and sensory experience are crucial in the practice and structuring of the caste system. Leftover food, or half-eaten food, invokes a strong sense of disgust. It assails the visual, olfactory, and gustatory senses by signifying something that was discarded or could be rotten or putrefying. Further, leftover food carries with it the strong association of being contaminated with another's saliva.[5] Joothan's name thus reiterates his permanently polluted state at every utterance. It is significant that another Dalit[6] writer, Om Prakash Valmiki, also agrees to name his autobiography *Joothan* at the suggestion of a fellow writer and editor.[7]

The caste system, with its fundamental reliance on maintaining norms of purity and pollution, is an exercise in careful negotiation of sensory perception and experience. Caste produces a discourse where names and their spellings, clothes (their material, their color, and their absence), the odors and taste of food and of bodies, the dialects and intonation of language, the height of the home's boundary wall, and the nature of life rituals are indicative of caste status. The "graded hierarchies" of the caste system thus produce performative selves expected to arrange their sensoria, bodies, and environments according to their position in the caste hierarchy.

In caste-stratified societies, Gopal Guru argues, due to the "compulsions" of modernity, untouchability as "a practice and as consciousness" may no longer appear on the "surface of social interaction" and has been forced to "slide" to the "bottom of the hierarchical mind." Hence, to understand how caste functions, Guru argues one needs to use "archaeology as a method."[8] I take forward this suggestion to argue in this chapter that one way to understand the deep layers of caste would be to take in its odors. The politics of smell constitutes, in a significant manner, the politics of caste. The practice and experience of caste is smeared with the odors of bodies, spaces, and objects, which, when breathed in, reveal the intricate ways in which the powers of caste operate. Surajpal Chauhan, in his autobiography *Tiraskrit*, writes about the dexterity that his caste community has in dealing with pigs. Chauhan recalls one such instance when his uncle Gulfan, who possessed great skills in slaughtering, was working on recently caught pig to distribute the meat within the community. As Gulfan was dismembering the pig, he flung its urinary bladder at a group of children nearby, secretly signaling Chauhan to catch it. As Chauhan caught the coveted bladder, the urine within it fell all over his body. Later, his mother cleaned the bladder, and for the next few days, Chauhan played with the bladder as a balloon. Later, he converted it into a small drum. Chauhan writes, "The bladder would stink when I would bring it close to my mouth to fill it with air. But I was not disgusted by that stench. However, the thing is that poverty forced us to have such a destiny."[9] Chauhan's narrative and the stench of the pig's bladder that it conveys is deeply indicative of the ways in which practices of caste force certain communities into the margins of sociality, dignity, and resources. This narrative also provides an insight into how caste structures and produces sensorial experience for the person experiencing them firsthand as well as for the reader. It also provides crucial clues about how Dalit communities have negotiated this sensorial experience, especially in the case of disgust and humiliation.

The sensory nature of the language of literature in general and autobiographies in particular, I thus argue, presents a vast archive of the odors of caste. Dalit autobiographical literature is a "rich sociological text" that "opens up an intellectual and emotional corridor into the social reality of dalits."[10] These texts are thus more than simply self-writing (as autobiographies are often characterized) or "testimonios" to the social injustice and humiliation inflicted upon Dalits.[11] These texts, I argue, are intensely political forms of writing that argue for creating a space for hitherto marginalized voices in the public sphere and in history. These texts in fact announce "the emergence of a Dalit personhood as a figure of suffering" and demanding due recognition and resignification for this self.[12] Because these are texts of protest and resignification, most Dalit autobiographical literature also adopts distinct literary and aesthetic tropes, often in direct confrontation with Brahmanical ideas of language and propriety.[13] As such, these texts are often written on more affective registers compared to upper-caste texts, showing the humiliation, injustice, and disgust that Dalit selves have been subjected to. Complicating this argument, however, works of scholars such as Laura Brueck and Sarah Beth also show how Dalit autobiographical narratives often fall into conventional modes of dealing with issues of class and gender, similar to the upper-caste narratives.[14]

Reading has primarily been thought of as an audiovisual process. However, I argue that reading needs to be thought of as an affective and sensorial act, a synesthetic activity that conjoins, however momentarily, the worlds of the reader and the writer. Smells also have a synesthetic quality that allows them to merge with other senses. Within the caste discourse, the sense of smell is often thought of as a "contact sense" much like touch.[15] If smells indeed touch us, then it can be argued that odors fundamentally alter our internal states. Reading a Dalit text then effectively means inhaling the odors of the Dalit world and immersing oneself into the sensuousness presented by the author. This could then also mean that Dalit texts have the potential to pollute, modify, and resignify the selves and bodies of the reader. This is where the most subversive potential of the odors of Dalit text lies.

Foregrounding sensory registers of caste, this chapter asks two questions: First, what do the odors of caste, conveyed through writing, mean for our understanding of caste? Second, what does it mean to smell caste through these writings? The chapter begins by examining how odors constitute caste and how they are represented in writings on caste. The discussion then moves to the reproduction of this olfactory sensorium in autobiographical literature and the consumption of these smells by the reader. The stench of blood, raw meat, tanned skins, and fecal matter is translated into words and becomes a part of the reader's ontology, invoking repulsion, disgust, embarrassment, and sometimes guilt. The chapter thus examines the relationship between caste and odors by locating these in the act of writing and consumption of Dalit literature. In doing so, the chapter asks what the political significance of a sensory reading of Dalit literature is. Does it affect the way in which we understand caste and Dalit politics?

Dalit autobiographical literature is a significant moment of assertion in Dalit movement and politics. This moment is defined not just by the act of writing but also by the fact that this writing is meant for the society at large to take cognizance of the historical and social injustices faced by the Dalit community and their demands for redress. Dalit autobiographical literature is thus a discursive act. Senses, which are not just our windows to the world but also produce and categorize the experience of this world for us, reiterate the discursive connections between the readers' and the writer's worlds. The self, as Waskul, Vannini, and Wilson have argued, "is not only a knowing subject and the object of symbolic (and largely linguistic) knowledge but also and more precisely a feeling and sensing subject and the object of somatic experience."[16] A sensory overlay on this reading and writing seeks to understand this sensing subject of caste. This discussion returns the debate on caste to the terrain of the body and not just that of the Dalit autobiographer, but since these are circulatory texts, the bodies of everyone who comes in contact with or who constitute these texts is involved in a discursive performance and production of sensations. In effect, the chapter draws attention to the discursive nature of not just writing and reading but also of caste, sense of smell, and odors.

One way to examine the sensory nature of Dalit writing is by description, using these accounts to enter the complex web of caste interactions and to map various kinds of odors, their meanings, and their boundaries. The second method, which will be preferred here, is to use odors as an analytical category. This means to not just focus on the physical odors and their descriptions but also to examine the nonodorous through the lens of smell—for instance, do words smell?

Writing Life: Memory, Senses, and Politics

In an evocative moment in Valmiki's autobiography, he narrates an incident from 1984 when a Brahmin schoolteacher asked students to tear out the pages of a lesson on B. R. Ambedkar from their books.[17] Valmiki, deeply influenced by this event, became a part of the protests that followed and subsequently wrote a poem, "Vidrup Chehra" ("Crooked Face") on the incident. In Valmiki's words, "At that moment I experienced my belonging to the Dalit movement intensely."[18] This incident brings to focus two related issues. First, under caste rules, the lower castes are not allowed to gain knowledge of religious texts such as the Vedas. This resulted in Dalits's exclusion from formal education in many parts of the country by the discrimination practiced by upper-caste teachers and administration. Even though these actions have been declared illegal by the Indian Constitution and the Scheduled Caste and Scheduled Tribes Act (Prevention of Atrocities) of 1989, ongoing denial of education and other basic rights has continued to occur. Valmiki himself writes about his experience in the government school in the 1950s: "Although the doors of the government schools had begun to open for untouchables, the mentality of the ordinary people had not changed much. I had to sit away from the others in the class. . . . I was not allowed to sit on a chair or a bench. I had to sit on the bare floor; I was not allowed even to sit on the mat. Sometimes I would have to sit way behind everybody, right near the door. From there, the letters on the board seemed faded."[19]

Guru rightly points out that in educational institutions the "stigmatized other" is produced through "social boycott."[20] The exclusion of Ambedkar's anticaste ideas from the classroom and the discrimination faced by Valmiki because of their caste status are examples of this "social boycott," aimed at erasure of memory and history, and perpetuated by the upper-caste and

Brahminical establishment on society. Ambedkar and his ideas represent the odor of caste that may be quite intolerable for some upper-castes. Second, Valmiki's autobiographical writing brings these ideas into the public and illuminates the disgust, repulsion, and oppression caused by this erasure. This kind of writing also forces the reader to reckon with the struggle involved in forging the Dalit self through writing and reading in the face of blatant denial of knowledge to Dalits by the caste discourse.

Writers like Valmiki compare autobiographical writing to wrenching out parts of one's life, reliving pain and disgust to present an account of oneself.[21] Others write about the perils of implicating the whole community through writing about an individual life.[22] Perhaps one of the strongest statements on writing of this kind about life has been that it is like digging oneself out of a burial ground, where memories of caste and its oppression have been buried for a long time, alongside those who suffered it.[23] The following section will build upon the acts of tearing and digging to examine the debates and the contestations involved in writing about life in the Dalit world. This section will also examine the role of senses in writing and reading Dalit writing.

Autobiographical writing in Hindi grew as a genre from around the 1990s, influenced by the growth and circulation of Dalit literature in Marathi.[24] The first well-known autobiography in Hindi seems to be Mohandas Naimishraya's *Apne Apne Pinjare*, published in 1995. Valmiki's autobiography, *Jhoothan*, came out in 1997, after being first published as an autobiographical narrative *Ek Dalit ke Aatmakatha* in 1995 in the book *Harijan se Dalit*. These two texts are largely regarded as the first in the field of Hindi Dalit autobiographies, and they generated a great deal of discussion on the form, content, and language of Dalit writing in Hindi. They also inaugurated a wave of Dalit autobiographies throughout the next two decades.

By writing and circulating Dalit texts, individuals and communities make an assertive claim to Dalit identity in a context when the discussion on the humiliation and injustice of caste in the public sphere is limited at best. Anupama Rao suggests that caste subalterns transform key political categories, including rights, equality, and citizenship, through recourse to constitutionalism and the use of the universal adult franchise.[25] Similarly, one could propose that caste subalterns also transform the genre of writing, literature, and autobiography by their acts of "digging out." Their acts of writing immediately implicate others, and, therefore, these are not just instances of the subaltern speaking, or speaking differently, but also a forced transformation on society. Sharmila Rege has rightly argued that Dalit life narratives cannot be accused of bringing an undesired past into the present, for they are one of the most direct and accessible ways by which the silences and misrepresentation of Dalits has been countered.[26] This is why Dalit writing is a political act.

The act of choosing, and consequently forgetting, parts of one's life and memories to write as a public text is an exercise in politics. Recalling and reproducing one's life in the public sphere or choosing not to reveal these details are ways in which people "understand the past and make claims about their versions of the past."[27] This is complicated by the fact that "memory is an inescapably intersubjective act" and "acts of personal remembering are fundamentally social and collective."[28] Writing about one's life always implicates the "other" and often also one's own community.[29] This can be compared to the intersubjective and discursive act of smelling and interpreting odors. Senses, particularly smell, have an intrinsic relationship with memory. "Sensory memory is a form of storage," argues Nadia Seremetakis, where "the memory of one sense is stored in the other."[30] Paul Stoller terms smells as "the strongest catalyst of memories" that "cannot be silenced."[31] Classen, Howes, and Synnott have argued that "the perception of smell, thus, consists not only of the sensation of the odors themselves, but of the experiences and emotions associated with them."[32] The odors described in Dalit autobiographies are equally important in terms of understanding the politics of remembering and forgetting. Sensory perception is not merely a biological process but instead is a social and political phenomenon that actively produces the world around us. Odors are present all around us and have an influence on how we inhabit space, create memories, evaluate people and places, and interact with our environment. The carriers of smells—bodies and objects— are political actors constructed through their location in power/knowledge. The politics of odor derives from aesthetic, moral, and social power, which inheres in their description and classification. The power or knowledge to name an odor as good or bad, as disgusting or pleasant is ultimately an exercise in politics (see also McClelland in this volume). Within the discourse of caste, the power of pollution makes the issue of odors more urgent. Why do certain odors pollute? Can an odor "pollute" one's caste status?

Describing an instance of interpellation of odors and memories, Naimishraya writes in his autobiography about a meeting with a Muslim girl from his neighborhood whom he was attracted to while she was making dung cakes.[33] The girl, he writes, was often smeared in cow dung because of her household duties, and Naimishraya recalls how he found the smell of dung mixed with the odor of her body extremely desirous. In this instance, the odors are assigned contextual meanings, especially through the trope of memory. While in the popular discourse, cow dung is thought of as smelling bad, it has an import-ant place in social life. Dried cow dung cakes are a commonly used household fuel in many parts of India. Cow dung is considered as having purifying and medicinal properties within the Hindu religious and caste discourse. In the autobiography mentioned, however, cow dung becomes a signifier of desire and memory between a Dalit-Muslim couple.[34] Odors thus enable not just descrip-tions of materials, spaces, and bodies, but their recollection and association in memory and writing can also provide analytical tropes for understanding the ways in which caste operates and is challenged.

Ultimately, one must return to the "sociological richness" of these texts, which invokes sense memories sometimes even in the absence of material triggers. M. S. S. Pandian thus rightly proposes that those narrative forms such as autobiographies, which Guru characterizes as "raw empiricism" or what social science theory describes as "emotional, descriptive-empirical and polemical," can in most instances produce "morally and politically enabling knowledge(s) about Dalits and other subaltern groups."[35] Not bound by evidentiary rules of social science, the privileged notions of teleological time and claims to objectivity and authorial neutrality, these narrative forms produce enabling redescriptions of lifeworlds and facilitate the reimagina-tion of the political.

The next section exemplifies some of these writings in detail in order to understand how the smells of caste are represented in writing and what they mean for our understanding of caste. I will consider these texts along four registers—public identities and spaces, occupational identities, naming, and acts of resistance.

The Smells of Caste

Writing about smells challenges their "absence from history writing"[36] and further, "olfaction serves to construct the subject."[37] Yet it is notoriously difficult to write about smells. Smells are often represented through other sense words and concepts. There is also always the question of being able to represent smells through words. "To write of smell," writes Alison Booth, "is like drawing a fruit-scented highlighter over the lines of representa-tion."[38] Yet writing about smells is a revelatory exercise in spite of these challenges. The subject constructed through olfactory descriptions represents carefully composed sensory descriptions of memory, politics, and knowledge. Danuta Fjellestad has argued that in literature, smell, taste, and touch may not always be "sensorily available" and are always "linguistically mediated."[39] The nonolfactory and the multisensory nature of smells are thus an interesting characteristic of these texts. In this section, I will examine the smells of caste identified in Dalit autobiographical writing under four registers— public spaces and identities, occupational identities, naming, and resistance. Mohandas Naimishraya provides an olfactory mapping of the city of Meerut in his autobiography *Apne Apne Pinjare*. He writes:

> The Muslim neighbourhoods were rife with the fiery smell of kababs [meat]. Mornings in the Hindu localities brought the odors of jalebi [sweets] and kachori [savory], while the evenings would be filled with the smells of balushyahi and imarti [sweets]. But our areas would be naked . . . flattened of all sense of smells, maybe odorless but then maybe a peculiar sense of malodor would hang over the locality. Every house was filled with leather in various forms and the heavy malodorous air would give away the fact that somewhere nearby there exists a chamarwada.[40]

Naimishraya's smell mapping of the city overlaps its caste and religious boundaries. The passage also indicates ways in which the olfactory character of spaces determine their caste status and how certain odors like that of leather hides and tanning mark the lower-caste spaces, "as both a space apart and a space to pollute."[41] This revelatory potential of odors when combined with the signification that odors carry makes them powerful agents of classification and hierarchization.[42] Hans Rindisbacher has argued that in the European context, as public spaces became more sanitized, smells retreated to passages in books, which became more sensuous than actual spaces.[43] This process was more complicated in the case of caste. Under the influence of colonial modernity and the postcolonial developmental state, public space was sought to be ridden of caste-based identities while, at the same time, Brahmanical sensibilities were normalized as the default.

For instance, Valmiki writes about the behavior of the upper-castes in his village:

> If we ever went out wearing neat and clean clothes, we had to hear their taunts that pierced deep inside, like poisoned arrows. If we

went to school in neat and clean clothes, our classmates said, "*Abey, Chuhre ka*, he has come dressed in new clothes."⁴⁴ If we went wearing old and shabby clothes, then they said, "*Abey, Chuhre ke*, get away from me, you stink."

This was our no-win situation. We were humiliated whichever way we dressed.⁴⁵

Similarly, Surajpal Chauhan, in another Dalit autobiography, writes about coming back to his village from the city. On the way, he asked an old upper-caste man for water. The man asks Chauhan who he is visiting in the village, thereby eliciting his caste identity. On realizing that Chauhan belongs to the "untouchable" family in the village, the older man says, "When those born of Bhangis and Chamars come back from the cities wearing new clean clothes, we cannot even identify whether they are Bhangi or not."⁴⁶

Both Valmiki and Chauhan challenge the myth of a "modern" nation-state and an egalitarian public sphere by pointing out how bodies and spaces were marked as "lowly" and "smelly."

In postcolonial India, caste was viewed as the remnants of a rural feudal order that still held some power and significance in village economies and was studied in benign categories like the jajmani system. As a result, it was understood that antimodern practices such as untouchability would simply wither away from the impact of development. Simultaneously, legal and policy measures created a public sphere devoid of untouchability, and this was by default understood to be a public sphere without caste. The decades following independence would, however, prove that the obituary of caste was far from written, and in fact it would adapt itself to not just modernity and democracy but to the nation-state itself. The "transcoding" of caste in urban contexts only attempts to flatten the visual markers of caste.⁴⁷ This chapter argues that while urban and modern contexts may provide this visual anonymity from the oppression of caste identities, other sensory markers, such as odors of the body, flavors of food, and accent of speech, have continued to give away caste and cause the extenuation of oppressive environments.

Attempting to dispel the myth of the absence of caste in the modern public sphere, Valmiki comments on the identification of caste through uniforms issued to municipal sanitation workers. Lacking resources to buy woolen clothes, Valmiki manages to procure a "khaki jersey from a municipal employee."⁴⁸ Although the jersey he got is dyed green, his college mates still call him a "sweeper."⁴⁹ Both Chauhan's civil "city" clothes and Valmiki's "khaki jersey" do not conceal their caste identities, hinting at the larger failure of the modern public space and the state to dispel caste hegemony. Dalit literature and politics has simultaneously engaged with the emancipatory potential offered by modernity and the Indian nation-state while also engaging in a deep critique of "triumphant nationalism,"[50] "privileged modernity,"[51] and "civilizational claims of Indian nation-making."[52]

The Brahmanical order, which came to stand in as the mainstream public order, was certainly not deodorized, but while its smells were accepted in the public sphere, other "undesirable" affects were pushed to the margins. Naimishraya writes, "The crisp texture of the starched white *dhoti-kurta* [traditional male garments] of the priest, the click-clack of his wooden slippers, the sounds of chants coming from his mouth," identified him as an upper-caste member.[53] Given the encoding of senses through caste, the sonic and haptic effects of the priest's body create the illusion of a body that does smell good. In contrast to the Brahmanical odors, the *chamarwada* is thus made to stand out as malodorous. Sanitization and deodorization of space and language constitute each other, not just making a space of caste but also a language of caste. In some measure, the Dalit literature used as a lens in this chapter challenges the normalization of Brahmanical sensibilities by writing about the repressed and elided odorous contexts.

However, as mentioned before, nonolfactory triggers can at times also trigger a sense of smell. Aniket Jaaware[54] and Sunder Sarrukai[55] write about the nonphysical nature of touch. In a slightly different but related formulation, Laura Marks talks about haptic visuality—the ability of film images to "touch" the viewer and to convey smell and taste. (See also Tang on Hong Kong cinema in this volume.)[56] Written words thus powerfully convey sensory stimuli such as olfactory sensations, as is evident in the "Joothan" or the sense of repulsion felt at seeing a "sweeper's uniform." Names, occupations, and language themselves become important olfactory markers of caste bodies.

The politics of caste and naming, including "Joothan," is discussed at length in these autobiographies. Chauhan writes about the names of his family members, "However pleasant sounding our names might be, the upper-castes in the village had made it a practice to distort them. Bhup Singh became Bhopa, Swarup Singh was called Sarupa, Radha Devi as Radhiya and Kiran became Kinno . . . my father Rohan Lal was called Rona. When these upper-castes cannot even tolerate our names, how will they like us?"[57] Disfiguring names forces an undesirable aspersion on the person. Being interpellated with negative, demeaning names is a denial of coevalness and of personhood.

Ambedkar, commenting on Gandhi's efforts to engage with the question of caste and untouchability, writes a scathing critique of the latter's ideas. Here we could imagine that the name "Untouchability" evokes a bad smell: "Mr. Gandhi felt that an organization which will devote itself exclusively to the problem of the Untouchables was necessary. Accordingly, there was established . . . the All-India Anti-Untouchability League. The name, Gandhi thought, did not smell well. Therefore . . . it was given a new name—The Servants of the Untouchables Society. That name again was not as sweet as Mr. Gandhi wished it to be. He changed and called it the Harjan Sevak Sangh."[58]

Ambedkar was probably referring to a metaphorical smell of "Untouchability," which did not bode as well for Gandhi's ideas as did the smell of "Harijan" (children of God). In changing the name from "Untouchable" to "Harijan," Gandhi removed the smell of untouchability from the public sphere, but in the end, this made no difference to the social and political position of the untouchables. Thus, Guru, in critiquing the idea of "Harijan" writes, "It was artificially imposed on the untouchables by Gandhi and those upper-caste people who could not genuinely integrate them within their social consciousness despite its divine association. Overall, the category of Harijan lacks a discursive capacity."[59] It is perhaps the restoration of this discursive capacity and the production of resistance to the caste order that Guru refers to when he writes about the Dalit resignification of *joothan* as "poison bread" that denies "the tormentor a complete sense of domination."[60] Guru is referring to the many instances of Dalit resistance where the threat of pollution has been exercised against the upper-castes.

Two short stories provide us further instances of these resistances. In *Sadhandh*, Arjun Sawediya writes about a sensory relationship between two Dalit communities—the Chamars and the Bhangis/Mehtars, who live next to each other in *tin ka nagla* in Agra.[61] The Bhangis occupy a mound in the colony, marked by the stench of a leather tannery (see McClelland in this volume). The Chamars, the more socially dominant Dalit caste among the two, who work at the tannery, live a little further down the mound, away from the sights and smells of hides. A religious occasion brings the two communities together inter-dining, and the situation explodes when the Bhangis refuse to pick up leftover food and plates—work assigned to them under the caste order—claiming that they are equal participants in the event. Several days pass as the whole place begins to stink of rotten food. When Chamar elders ask a young Mehtar woman to pick up the filth because it is impossible to live with the stench, she replies, "Who knows about smell better than us, but now we will not do this work."[62] Her reference to the malodorous work her community is forced to do and the stench of leather hides among which they are forced to live, challenges the imposition of the caste norms by the Chamar elders. The young woman juxtaposes two malodorous contexts with each other to complicate caste norms.

Writing Smell, Reading Caste

"The most discriminating nose must admit all odors," writes Booth while writing about the smell of literary narratives. The important question within my own research was to ask whether the readers of the autobiographies, especially the upper-caste reader, smell caste when reading these narratives. I argue that Dalit literature forces readers to alter their sense of self—from an individualized atomized self to one that is porous, mixing with the self of the text. What does this do to our notions of the self and the body? Aniket Jaaware, in his writing on Dalit literature, states provocatively that one can eat the Dalit—and consume Dalit literature.[63] The consumption of such writing provides an inward gaze for Dalit readers, as it allows their assertion of marginality and community formation. Non-Dalit readers, according to Jaaware, are relieved of the burden of caste and touch, as literature is consumed, celebrated as revolutionary, and thus digested and contained as "Dalit literature." Therefore, according to Jaaware, non-Dalits manage to eat the Dalit without ever eating with the Dalit. It is only through this act of "metonymy"—of substituting touch for words—Jaaware argues, that the non-Dalits can bear to touch the Dalit through the Dalit's words.[64]

Other formulations further complicate the idea of readership of Dalit literature. Guru argues that the Dalit middle class may find these texts as a source of embarrassment because they "summon an undesirable past."[65] On the other hand, Guru argues, these autobiographies may invoke "guilt in the minds of the upper-castes by recording the social wrongs done to Dalits by their ancestors."[66] Arun Prabha Mukherjee, the English translator of Valmiki's autobiography writes, "Although I had been introduced to Marathi Dalit literature in translation before I read Joothan, its impact was much higher on the Richter scale of my consciousness because it was speaking of my corner of India, in my first language, Hindi, in a way that no other text had ever spoken to me."[67] The text fundamentally alters Mukherjee's sense of self and becomes a part of his knowledge system through a familiar language and context.

Conclusion

The "scent of the narrative" is a powerful trope from which to unravel the issues of power and hierarchy in any system of gradation.[68] "To write of smell is to couple the body with a history of discourse that has colonized that sense," argues Booth.[69] Caste, with its location on the physical and the social body, can be written and read through these scents, which often also operate through synesthesia. While these odors do depend on the reader to be decoded and understood, Dalit writing shows how the odors of caste speak on their own very loud, defiant, and messy terms. They provide a resistance to a neat and circumscribed "progressive emplotment" of Dalit worlds and in doing so challenge the Brahminical hegemonic sensorium.[70] Dalit texts act as powerful narratives where sensuous knowledge and affects are used in an embodied fashion to produce and resignify caste-marked selves. This embodied and sensorial nature of writing draws the reader into the complex histories, bodies, and memories of the Dalit world. More importantly, odors transcend boundaries and may even at times threaten to alter the readers' sense of their caste selves. This is an important outcome of the continuing widespread circulation and discussion of Dalit literature and its odors.

Notes

1. Tulsi Ram, *Murdahiya*, 9.
2. All translations from Hindi are my own, except for Om Prakash Valmiki's autobiography, Joothan, where Arun Prabha Mukherjee's translation has been used.
3. Ambedkar, *Annihilation of Caste*, 234.
4. Chamars are a Dalit caste in Uttar Pradesh and other parts of north India. Under the caste system, they have been "associated with impure activities such as leatherwork and the removing of dead animals." Chamars also work as "landless agricultural and manual labourers." Ciotti, "Chamar," 900.
5. Douglas, *Purity and Danger*, 34.
6. Dalit, meaning "broken down" is a self-referential term adopted by large sections of the former Untouchables. The

word was first used by B. R. Ambedkar in his newspaper *Bahishkruit Bharat*. He defined "Dalit-hood" as "a kind of life condition which characterizes the exploitation, suppression and marginalization of Dalits by the social, economic, cultural and political domination of the upper caste Brahminical order." The Dalit Panther movement in the 1970s popularised the use of "Dalit" as a "revolutionary category" for its ability to signify oppression and "recover the emancipatory potential of the historical past of Dalit culture." Guru, "Politics," 15.
7. Valmiki, *Joothan*, xiv.
8. Guru and Sarrukai, *Cracked Mirror*, 203. Untouchability is one of the important practices of caste, where lower-caste

bodies are regarded as "polluting" for those higher than them. This manifests as physical and social distancing, prohibition on physical and social contact, inter-dining, and intercaste intimate relationships. There have been extensive cases of violent punishments and retributions for the lower caste on the ostensible violation of these boundaries. There have been debates on the relationship between caste and untouchability. Most famously, M. K. Gandhi was in favor of abolishing untouchability but retaining the caste system as integral to the Hindu social fabric. In strong opposition to this position, B. R. Ambedkar argued for a complete annihilation of caste itself as the only way for emancipating the untouchable groups.

9. Chauhan, "Tiraskrit," 26–27.

10. Guru, "Review of Joothan."

11. Nayar, "Bama's Karukku." The term "testimonio," as Ana Forcinitio describes, is "used in Latin American Cultural and Literary Studies to refer to a narration marked by the urgency to make public a situation of oppression or injustice and/or of resistance against that same condition (and therefore a narrative that accounts for the construction of collective subjects and emphasizes agency). It is also used to refer to a narration that reveals the urgency to bear witness to an event or series of events perpetrated with the aim of eliminating a community or a group." As such, the term has also been used to refer to Dalit autobiographical writing, which also takes up the task of calling out injustices.

12. Ganguly, "Pain, Personhood and the Collective," 431.

13. See Limbale, *Towards an Aesthetic of Dalit Literature.*

14. Brueck, "Narrating Dalit Womanhood," 25–37; Beth, "Hindi Dalit Autobiography."

15. McHugh, *Sandalwood and Carrion,* 6.

16. Waskul, Vannini, and Wilson, "Aroma of Recollection," 7.

17. B. R. Ambedkar was one of the foremost anticaste thinkers and political leaders of India. He was the chair of the Drafting Committee of the Indian Constitution. For more details, see Rodrigues, *Essential Writings of Ambedkar.*

18. Valmiki, *Jhootan,* 129.

19. Ibid., 3.

20. Guru, "Tragic Exit."

21. Valmiki, *Jhootan,* xiv.

22. Chauhan, *Tiraskrit,* 7.

23. Ram, *Murdahiya,* 9.

24. Beth, "Hindi Dalit Autobiography," 547. Between 1952 and 1954, the serialized autobiography of Hazari had appeared in *Hindustan* with the caption "*Ek Harijan Ki Ram Kahani*"; it was subsequently translated in English under the heading "An Outcaste Indian."

25. Rao, *Caste Question.*

26. Rege, *Writing Caste / Writing Gender,* 13.

27. Smith and Watson, *Reading Autobiography,* 20.

28. Ibid., 20–21.

29. On the collective nature of Dalit writing, see Ganguly, "Pain, Personhood and the Collective"; Nayar, "Bama's Karukku"; Satyanarayana, "Experience and Dalit Theory."

30. Seremetakis, "Memory of the Senses," 4.

31. Stoller, *Sensuous Scholarship,* 85.

32. Classen, Howes, and Synnott, *Aroma.*

33. Naimishraya, *Apne Apne Pinjare,* 115.

34. Although Islam does not have caste in its scriptural tradition, in South Asia due to conversions and the assimilation of Islam in the wider society, Hindu caste norms and practices have become adapted within parts of the Muslim community.

35. Pandian, "Writing Ordinary Lives," 34.

36. Jenner, "Follow Your Nose?," 337.

37. Booth, "Scent," 3.

38. Ibid, 3.

39. Fjellestad, "Towards an Aesthetics of Smell," 642.

40. Naimishraya, *Apne Apne,* 11–12. A 'chamarwada' is the locality where Chamars, an outcaste community that works with leather, live; for an example of a similar community in Japan, see McClelland in the previous chapter.

41. Lee, "Odor and Order," 475.

42. For more on the relationship of odors, caste, and hierarchical spaces, see Kapoor, "Violence of Odors."

43. Rindisbacher, *Smell of Books,* 28.

44. Meaning, "born of a Chuhra." Chuhras, also called Bhangis and Mehtars, are a Dalit caste in parts of north India, especially Uttar Pradesh and Punjab. Under the caste system,

they have been forced to work as sweepers and manual scavengers. Some sections of this caste have claimed the "Valmiki" identity, which seeks to resignify the humiliation and discrimination carried in the term "Chuhra" or "Bhangi."

45. Valmiki, *Joothan*, 4.
46. Chauhan, *Tiraskrit*, 32.
47. I borrow the idea of "transcoding" from Pandian, "One Step Outside Modernity."
48. Valmiki, *Joothan*, 88.
49. Ibid., 88.
50. Gajarawala, "Some Time," 576.
51. Ibid., 576.
52. Ganguly, "Pain, Personhood and the Collective," 431.
53. Naimishraya, *Apne Apne*, 29.
54. Jaaware, *Practicing Caste*.

55. Sarukkai, "Phenomenology of Untouchability."
56. Marks, *Skin of the Film*.
57. Chauhan, *Tiraskrit*, 41.
58. Ambedkar, *Untouchables*.
59. Guru, "Politics of Naming," 16.
60. Guru, "Review."
61. Sawediya, "Sadhandh."
62. Ibid., 75.
63. Jaaware, "Eating."
64. Ibid., 281.
65. Guru, "Review."
66. Ibid.
67. Valmiki, *Joothan*, x.
68. Booth, "Scent," 17.
69. Ibid., 6.
70. Ibid.

Bibliography

Ambedkar, B. R. *Annihilation of Caste: The Annotated Critical Edition*. New Delhi: Navayana, 2014.
———. *The Untouchables*. New Delhi: Siddhartha Books, 2008.
Beth, Sarah. "Hindi Dalit Autobiography: An Exploration of Identity." *Modern Asian Studies* 41, no. 3 (2007): 545–74.
Booth, Alison. "The Scent of a Narrative: Rank Discourse in 'Flush' and 'Written on the Body.'" *Narrative* 8, no. 1 (2000): 3–22.
Brueck, Laura. "Narrating Dalit Womanhood and the Aesthetics of Autobiography." *Journal of Commonwealth Literature* 54, no. 1 (2019): 25–37.
Chauhan, Surajpal. *Tiraskrit*. Ghaziabad: Anubhav Prakashan, 2002.
Ciotti, Manuela. "'In the Past We Were a Bit "Chamar"': Education as a Self-and Community Engineering Process in Northern India." *Journal of the Royal Anthropological Institute* 12, no. 4 (2006): 899–916.
Classen, Constance, David Howes, and Anthony Synnott. *Aroma: The Cultural History of Smell*. London: Routledge, 1994.
Corbin, A. *The Foul and the Fragrant: Odor and the French Social Imagination*.

Cambridge, MA: Harvard University Press, 1986.
Douglas, Mary. *Purity and Danger: An Analysis of Concepts of Pollution and Taboo*. New York: Routledge, 2001.
Fjlellestad, Danuta. "Towards an Aesthetics of Smell, or, the Foul and the Fragrant in Contemporary Literature." *Cauce* 24 (2001): 637–65.
Gajarawala, Toral Jatin. "Some Time Between Revisionist and Revolutionary: Unreading History in Dalit Literature." *PMLA* 126, no. 3 (2011): 575–91.
Ganguly, Debjani. "Pain, Personhood and the Collective: Dalit Life Narratives." *Asian Studies Review* 33, no. 4 (2009): 429–42.
Guru, Gopal. "How Egalitarian Are the Social Sciences in India?" *Economic and Political Weekly* 37, no. 50 (2002): 5003–9.
———. "The Politics of Naming." *Seminar* 471 (1998): 14–18.
———. "Review of Joothan. A Dalit's Life." *Seminar* 530 (2003).
———. "A Tragic Exit from Social Death." *Outlook*, February 1, 2016. https://www.outlookindia.com/magazine/story/a-tragic-exit-from-social-death/296480.

```

Guru, Guru, and Sundar Sarrukai. *The Cracked Mirror: An Indian Debate on Experience and Theory*. New Delhi: Oxford University Press, 2012.

Jaaware, Aniket. "Eating, and Eating with, the Dalit: A Re-consideration Touching upon Marathi Poetry." In *Indian Poetry: Modernism and After*, edited by K. Satchidanandan, 262–93. New Delhi: Sahitya Akademi, 2001.

———. *Practicing Caste: On Touching and Not Touching*. New York: Fordham University Press, 2018.

Jenner, Mark S. R. "Follow Your Nose? Smell, Smelling, and Their Histories." *American Historical Review* 116, no. 2 (2011): 335–51.

Kapoor, Shivani. "The Violence of Odors: Sensory Politics of Caste in a Leather Tannery." *Senses and Society* 16, no. 2 (2021): 164–76.

Lee, Joel. "Odor and Order: How Caste Is Inscribed in Space and Sensoria." *Comparative Studies of South Asia, Africa and the Middle East* 37, no. 3 (2017): 470–90.

Limbale, Sharankumar. *Towards an Aesthetic of Dalit Literature: History, Controversies and Considerations*. Translated by Alok Mukherjee. Hyderabad: Orient Longman, 2004.

Marks, Laura. *The Skin of the Film: Intercultural Cinema, Embodiment and the Senses*. Durham: Duke University Press, 2000.

McHugh, James. *Sandalwood and Carrion: Smell in Indian Religion and Culture*. Oxford: Oxford University Press, 2012.

Naimishraya, Mohandas. *Apne Apne Pinjare: Part I*. New Delhi: Vani Prakashan, 2009.

Nayar, Pramod K. "Bama's Karukku: Dalit Autobiography as Testimonio." *Journal of Commonwealth Literature* 41, no. 2 (2006): 83–100.

Pandian, M. S. S. "Writing Ordinary Lives." *Economic and Political Weekly*, September 20, 2008, 34–40.

Rao, Anupama. *The Caste Question: Dalits And the Politics of Modern India*. Ranikhet: Permanent Black, 2009.

Rege, Sharmila. *Writing Caste / Writing Gender: Reading Dalit Women's Testimonios*. New Delhi: Zubaan, 2006.

Rindisbacher, Hans J. *The Smell of Books: A Cultural-Historical Study of Olfactory Perception in Literature*. Ann Arbor: University of Michigan Press, 1992.

Rodrigues, Valerian. *The Essential Writings of B. R. Ambedkar*. Delhi: Oxford University Press, 2014.

Sarukkai, Sunder. "Phenomenology of Untouchability." *Economic and Political Weekly* 44, no. 37 (2009): 39–48.

Satyanarayana, K. "Experience and Dalit Theory." *Comparative Studies of South Asia, Africa and the Middle East* 33, no. 3 (2013): 398–402.

Sawediya, Arjun. "Sadhandh." *Dalit Asmita* 1, nos. 4–5 (July–December 2011): 75–78.

Seremetakis, C. Nadia. "The Memory of the Senses: Historical Perception, Commensal Exchange and Modernity." *Visual Anthropology Review* 9, no. 2 (1993): 2–18.

Smith, Sidonie, and Watson, Julia. *Reading Autobiography: A Guide for Interpreting Life Narratives*. Minneapolis: University of Minnesota Press, 2001.

Stoller, Paul. *Sensuous Scholarship*. Philadelphia: University of Pennsylvania Press, 1997.

Tulsi Ram. *Murdhiya*. New Delhi: Rajkamal Prakashan, 2010.

Valmiki, Omprakash. *Joothan: A Dalit's Life*. Translated by Arun Prabha Mukherjee. New York: Columbia University Press, 2003.

Waskul, Dennis D., Phillip Vannini, and Janelle Wilson. "The Aroma of Recollection: Olfaction, Nostalgia, and the Shaping of the Sensuous Self." *Senses and Society* 4, no. 1 (2009): 5–22.
```

CHAPTER 7

Love Is in the Air

A Study of Johnnie To's *Blind Detective*

Aubrey Tang

This chapter investigates the changed sensory model of post-1997 Hong Kong society to discover Hong Kong's repressed political unconscious after colonial rule.[1] I will draw on the 2013 thriller-comedy *Blind Detective*, by commercial film director Johnnie To, to explore the disruption of seeing, a hegemonic sensory modality in modern society, by olfaction, a sensory modality that is repressed in the modern West.[2] This chapter discovers a new perceptual direction of the postcolonial city that deviates from the general financialization pattern of developed economies. As used in the film, this sensory turn reflects Hong Kong's postcolonial trajectory gone awry. Such a historical trajectory challenges many common assumptions of contemporary history, including classical postcolonial theory, postmodernism, and studies of Chinese postsocialism. A significant epistemological shift to smelling and tasting has taken place in *Blind Detective*, powerfully revealing an affect of despair and rage.

To get a clear picture of this sensory turn in To's cinema, I will contrast *Blind Detective* with the 2018 Hollywood blockbuster *Crazy Rich Asians* as a counterexample. Referencing Jacques Rancière's Marxist aesthetic theory, this chapter observes that To's non-ocularcentric modalities demonstrate a more democratic and egalitarian aesthetic than contemporary American cinema of diversity and inclusion does. To investigate To's democratic treatment of the senses, I will explain how Raymond Williams's and Brian Massumi's notions of "structures of experience" and affect can help connect the nonocular, olfactory sensations in *Blind Detective* with the affect in post-1997 Hong Kong. As for the intimate and persistent natures of olfactory perception, they will inform an understanding of post-1997 Hong Kong people's collective feelings as not only ideological constructions—as most studies formulate—but also in nonrational, nonideological terms—that is, prepersonal, ingrained consciousness developed in the sensory body, which is resistant to being judged as politically correct or incorrect. Employing an interdisciplinary approach that will reference Marxist aesthetics, affect theories, and sensory neuroscience research, this study offers a phenomenological analysis of the film.

To imagine the divergence from contemporary historical patterns, one must first consider what the city was expected to become: Hong Kong has been historically imagined as a cosmopolitan city. In the 1980s, prior to its 1997 transfer of sovereignty from the United Kingdom (UK) to the People's Republic of China (PRC), Hong Kong was idealized on the global stage as an experiment in modernity and democracy aimed at the PRC, which was considered a developing country at the time. On the contrary, already transforming from a manufacturing economy to a service economy, Hong Kong in the 1980s was hailed as a twentieth-century metropole, the "pearl of the Orient," at a time when the PRC was still picking up the manufacturing industry where the closed Hong Kong factories had left off. The then colony was expected to help modernize the PRC and transform it into an economy like Japan or Hong Kong itself.[3] While Hong Kong did help tremendously with modernizing the PRC in the 1980s and 1990s, there has been a considerable decline of the city's affective life since the transition in 1997, which we watch unfold in *Blind Detective*.

A Democratic Sensory Culture

Blind Detective (2013) is a farcical detective comedy about a legendary former detective, Johnston (played by Andy Lau), who has lost his eyesight after staring at a suspect for eight days. The film chronicles four cases that John-ston solves: (1) he discovers the attacker who randomly pours sulfuric acid on passersby, (2) he reveals the true killer of a missing funeral-home worker, who was mistaken as the killer of another worker, (3) he identifies the serial killer who is a taxi driver and has murdered ten girls, and (4) he finds Minnie, a teenage girl who has been missing for over ten years in Hong Kong.

The film begins with an indiscriminate-attack case Johnston solves with his sense of smell. The camera shows a black screen, and the audience hears sounds of radio news broadcasts and taxi dispatchers, followed by sirens, traffic, and acoustic traffic signals for the visually impaired. Twenty seconds into the film, still on a black screen, we hear someone opening and closing a car door while sniffing noisily. We then see the feet of a well-dressed man and of various passersby next to the tip of a folding cane. At this point, we realize that what we have just seen is a point-of-view shot from the perspec-tive of a blind man—hence the black screen—as he exits a taxi into a busy Hong Kong street at night. An omniscient camera then shows us a police car and LED screens of a news broadcast on multiple sides of a tall build-ing. The broadcast reports that there has been a third case of sulfuric acid being randomly poured from above and that the total number of injuries from these cases has reached one hundred. Since there are no witnesses to any of the incidents, the police are offering a US$900,000 reward. As the story unfolds, we learn that former detective Johnston is here to investigate the case and that monetary rewards for solving cold cases have become his only source of income after he went blind. Johnston keeps sniffing around and eventually follows a middle-aged man who appears sweaty, unclean, and distressed. The distressed man keeps calling his wife and leaving her voice mails because she never picks up. One moment, he is yelling on the phone that he knows about her extramarital affair and telling her to go back to her hometown (*laojia* 老家, a term usually used to refer to one's hometown in mainland China); the next moment, he is begging her to come home even though she is cheating on him with a young truck driver. Led by this disgrun-tled husband's foul body odor, Johnston follows him to a supermarket and notices him picking up a bottle of liquid. Johnston picks up another bottle of the same product and asks a sighted woman what it is. She tells him it is sulfuric acid—and just like that, the blind detective has found the "acid attacker" and cracked the case.

Blind Detective's venture into olfactory knowledge underlines the unin-telligibility of Hong Kong's affective life, which is no longer narratable in spoken and conventional film languages—the city is so mad that one has to smell it to understand it. The focus on a blind detective's olfactory capacity in *Blind Detective* delivers a strong message about post-1997 Hong Kong's modernity, suggesting that the city's affective life can no longer be understood by seeing or with words. Odors also lack precise language for being named and explained. Studies have shown that children can master different smells without knowing their names: "For example, when confronted with a range of odours from hazardous household products, children gave the correct name to only 15% of them but accurately rated their edibility in 79% of cases."[4] Odors are difficult to represent with words and are perceptually more accessible than words. Olfaction is, by nature, the most ineluctable form of perception. According to literature on the development of olfactory perception in humans, "olfaction is an unavoidable and ubiquitous source of perceptual experience from the earliest steps of mammalian development. Olfaction is unavoidable because, in all mammals, nasal chemosensors develop functionally in advance of other sensory systems (with the exception of somesthesic/kinesthesic sensors), and are thus in a position of neurologically-imposed readiness to 'feed' the brain before the functional inception of hearing and vision, and to bind with their inputs when these latter sensory systems set on."[5]

Even the sense of hearing plays only a secondary role in Johnston's investigation. The detective is able to learn of the suspect's marriage crisis through hearing, but it is the man's foul body odor that ultimately directs him to identify this deeply upset and troubled man as the instigator of the crime. Of course, although marriage problems are universally common, they are not typically associated with or manifested by odors. In the language of film, stories about troubled marriages are usually told with words, sounds, or visual images, such as music or cold colors being associated with sadness, anger, and so forth.

To get an idea of the city's delirious psychological condition, one need only consider the period between 2008 and 2011 when numerous (sulfuric) "acid attacks" took place in the city, perpetrated by different individuals and resulting in over 130 injuries. Many of those cases remain unsolved. The motivations behind these indiscriminate attacks are unknown, but they clearly show that the psychological health of the population had deteriorated. *Blind Detective* appeals to this shared feeling of distress with its story of lost love. As the story unfolds, the cause of the acid attacker's antisocial behavior is revealed to be his marriage problems, which alludes to a larger crisis in

Hong Kong, where the number of divorces had quadrupled during the two decades prior to 2013. According to the Hong Kong Census, the number of divorce decrees granted in 2013 was nearly four times the number granted in 1991, rising from 6,295 to 22,271, with the overall divorce rate rising from 1.1 per 1,000 people in 1991 to 3.1 per 1,000 in 2013.[6] The upset husband's voice-mail message about his wife's hometown underlines common problems among China-Hong Kong couples in cross-border marriages—for example, power differentials, cultural differences, and so on.[7] With the hot-button issue of cross-border marriage remaining unsettled in mainstream Hong Kong media, the PRC media, global media, and academic scholarship, *Blind Detective* portrays this marital distress as a stench that can literally be smelled without seeing or talking about it.[8]

This notion of perceiving Hong Kong, or "smelling" it, through the detective character's body may explain the relationship between the protagonist's name and the city's cultural and historic identity. "Johnston" is the name of a major road in Wan Chai, Hong Kong Island, built as part of the colonial government's Praya East Reclamation Scheme in the early 1920s. The road was named after A. R. Johnston, who served as British Deputy Superintendent of Trade roughly around the time of the First Opium War and later became Hong Kong's first government administrator prior to the 1842 appointment of Sir Henry Pottinger as the colony's governor.[9] In other words, A. R. Johnston was one of the first British officials in Hong Kong, having examined, documented, governed, and developed Hong Kong Island before the colony of Hong Kong came into existence.[10] The name "Johnston" essentially connotes the origin of today's Hong Kong. If Johnston the blind detective personifies Hong Kong, then his senses refer to the perception of Hong Kong, his investigation of love relationships refers to the reality of Hong Kong's affective life, and his consciousness is Hong Kong's cultural consciousness. And because his keen understanding of the city comes from an odor specifically associated with the city's contemporary crisis of marital relationships, post-1997 Hong Kong's smell is a socially symbolic manifestation, similar to the way (textual) narrative is thought of as a socially symbolic act in Jameson's theory about the repressed political unconscious of society—except, in this case, in the form of odorous molecules.

Although olfaction is not a systematically repressed sensation in Hong Kong's modernity, its epistemological value certainly is. Critics have established the primacy of sight over smell within the sensorial hierarchy of the modern West, and modern Hong Kong society is similarly affected by this tendency.[11] The disruption of ocularcentric hegemony in Johnnie To's film, I argue, enacts a sensorial subversion through film aesthetics. Rancière's theory about aesthetics and politics is helpful for explaining this subversion. In his essay "The Distribution of the Sensible," Rancière politicizes the domination of the sensible in terms of democracy. He defines the sensible as "the manner in which a relation between a shared common [*un commun partagé*] and the distribution of exclusive parts is determined in sensory experience."[12] For the purposes of this discussion, we can assume for the moment that "the sensible" is what one is made to perceive within an ocularcentric hegemony—that is, most spectacles in modern society. Rancière argues that a truly egalitarian, genuinely democratic politics takes place through aesthetic endeavors that can disrupt "the system of self-evident facts of sense perception"[13] and that to resist the existing regime of the sensible—to redistribute the sensible—requires disrupting the way the world is perceived.[14] Following Rancière, a democratic sensory culture must make way for a different model of perception, a different distribution of spectacles as well as of other objects currently deemed insensible, but it must not seek to replace a dominant spectacle with a less dominant one, which would fail to change the mode of address.

As reasonable as it may sound, this idea about democratic equality is almost completely opposed to most widely accepted democratic practices today. Before we continue to examine the successful example in *Blind Detective*, we should first look at one of today's democratic failures: the film *Crazy Rich Asians*, which attempts to offer a clear picture of an ocularcentric film presenting a positive representation of a people—but falls flat. Debates about equity, diversity, and inclusion in all aspects of American public life have continuously evoked the underrepresentation of minority groups. In response to the expectation of diversity in film, *Crazy Rich Asians* was therefore hailed as a milestone in Asian representation.[15] The film became an "Asian" brand. Not only is the designation of "Asian" itself problematic, but the very notion of classifying visibly kindred Asian bodies as a (racial) identity in *Crazy Rich Asians* is arguably quite vulgar.[16] The film's narrative is constructed from the perspective of the heroine, Rachel, an American-born woman of Chinese heritage and a poster child of the American dream: raised by a single Chinese immigrant mother, she has found success as the youngest professor to be hired at New York University. She travels with her mysterious boyfriend to Singapore, where she encounters scores of local women who are presented as inferior to her. Catering to American audiences, the film constructs a deep moral divide between women from America and women from Asia. The

American Asian woman is highly educated, hard-working, driven, intelligent, sincere, modest, truthful, monogamous, and indifferent to wealth, while women from Asia are classist, unambitious, controlling, jealous, materialistic, fake, sneaky, nosy, promiscuous, and appearance-obsessed.[17] Ironically, if Rachel's character had been a Western Caucasian female, the film's Orientalism might have been more easily discernible. Nonetheless, because race—a construction heavily based on visual taxonomy as a legacy of Western colonialism—has been historically cast and stressed as the central organizing principle of perception in American society, the film's Orientalism went unnoticed in popular discourse, since all the female figures in the story are visually registered as Asian.[18]

This distribution of Asian bodies into an identity is an example of what Rancière refers to as "the order of distribution of bodies into functions corresponding to their 'nature.'"[19] Bodies labeled "Asian" are organized to function according to a contrived "nature," that of race, within the logic of American society. In *Crazy Rich Asians*, race is therefore visually constituted with bodies of recognizable East Asian heritage.[20] Although the American protagonist and the characters from Asia might sound and act differently, they are all part of the film's Asian representation in the popular imaginary. "[Groups are] tied to specific modes of doing, to places in which these occupations are exercised, and to modes of being corresponding to these occupations and these places."[21] This schematic way of classifying bodies determines what is sensible in society—the visible racial attributes. Rancière calls this classification method into question because it is the opposite of democracy.[22] He warns that it misleads us by imposing limits on our perceptive understanding of the world. In other words, it buries the truly underrepresented in a scandalously inequitable social institution—such as Hollywood.

Against Hollywood's tendency to privilege vision in the portrayal of race, To's cinema demonstrates an epistemological defense of smell and taste for portraying a people. Through the detective's smelling and tasting, *Blind Detective* offers up a sensual on-screen body as the corporeal locus for experiencing the affective crisis and coping mechanisms of post-1997 Hong Kong.[23] One of the cases Johnston solves is the 1997 disappearance of a preadolescent girl, Minnie. As a young child, Minnie's mother killed her father and preserved his body in salt because he had cheated on her. Minnie was subsequently adopted by her grandmother. Soon after, in elementary school, she found her grandmother deep-frying the body of her boyfriend who had refused to divorce his wife and marry her. Johnston must now find this now twenty-eight-year-old woman who was raised by a pair of women who killed for love. Accompanied by his apprentice Ho (played by Sammi Cheng), he goes to Granny's apartment, where they find a neighbor frantically moving his furniture and belongings to the hallway. When Ho calls out for Granny, we hear a woman's voice singing off-key but do not see her. Johnston then leads Ho to the neighbor's closet. When Ho opens the closet door, a pungent odor is released. It is Granny's perfume. The singing voice is coming from her cell phone's ringtone—Granny is hiding in the closet because she is in love with the neighbor and wants to follow him to his new home.

As the closet scene suggests, perfume is the metaphor for love, indicating that love in post-1997 Hong Kong is more breathable than visible or audible. To acknowledge the city's romantic excess, as compared to Granny's obsessive love, the scene features an unconventional sensorial array. Sight is the most useless of the senses, since none of the characters see Granny. Sound—her out-of-key singing—only informs the detective of her delirious presence but does not allow him to find her. It is the aroma of romance, in all its vulgar excess, that gives the detective full knowledge of her presence. When he discovers her in the closet, he complains, "The perfume is intoxicating!" The word he uses to describe the intensity of the perfume, "劫" (intoxicating), is an adjective often used for strong alcoholic drinks and is exclusive to spoken Cantonese. Colloquial Cantonese speakers from Hong Kong also use it to describe other objects as intense, difficult to handle, or unmanageable. This literary choice further indicates that the intense love being named is unique to Hong Kong.

The Structure of Hieroglyphic Experience

What does this intoxicating love indicate about post-1997 Hong Kong culture? One might first note that *Blind Detective* refers to a pair of murders that shocked the city during the 1990s. In 1993, a vendor of barbecued meat murdered her two-timing boyfriend's wife and deep-fried her body in the presence of her ten-year-old granddaughter. She then made the child dispose of some of the remains.[24] In 1999, a young mother murdered her boyfriend, chopped up his body, and cured it with salt in a metal trunk—while their three-year-old daughter watched.[25] These incidents alarmed the city, not only because of their gruesomeness but also because they were serious crimes of passion committed by ordinary people and thereby reflected the city's crumbling affective life since the early 1990s.

The recurring affect of 2013 Hong Kong's collective psychology, as alluded to in *Blind Detective*, is that of every intense, unrequited love relationship: despair, resentment, revenge, disgust, and so on. These feelings are inscribed in the film's images, which function in Hong Kong's postcolonial economy much like hieroglyphs did in ancient Egypt—and in fact the notion of filmic signs functioning like hieroglyphs is a common trope in cinema criticism. Hieroglyphic images do not portray historical reality but signal contemporaneous affect. The "hieroglyphs" in *Blind Detective* await their decoding by the detective (i.e., by the virtual body of the audience). Diverging from the many critics who see the hieroglyphs as visual (and mental) images, Williams formulates his notion of "structures of feeling" in terms of (potentially multisensorial) social experience. One of his definitions of structures of feeling is "structures of experience," though there are no past events prior to such experience. The experience itself *is* the actual historical event in the present, not an emotional reaction to the past. It does not follow a chronological time of the past but instead opens its own sensory history in the form of "affective elements, . . . thought as felt and feelings as thoughts."[26] These feelings "cannot . . . be reduced to established belief systems, institutions, or explicit general relationships." They inform us what cannot be told via "recognizable systematic elements," such as any articulated, established political ideologies.[27] It does not matter during which historical period the referenced crimes actually happened in Hong Kong. What matters is the historical period of the film's reception—after 2013—because hieroglyphic images are always allegorical; they are supposed to be symbolic, not realistic.

In this sense, *Blind Detective*'s hieroglyphic images of intense, excessive, and ultimately derailed love effectively evokes the post-1997 Hong Kong affect of despair and rage. These images allude to the people's new structure of experience (registered via perception but less through vision than through nonvisual modalities) of "the true social present."[28] This structure reveals the city's culture of hurt, despair, anger, resentment, vengeance, and disgust. While most Hong Kong residents in the post-1997 era have not killed their lovers like the two troubled lovers in *Blind Detective*, many of them have likely experienced this combination of debilitating affect, regardless of its causes, which then forms a new recognizable structure of experience in Williams's terms.

While in Williams's theory affect is mostly synonymous with feeling,[29] for Massumi, affect has more to do with *effect*. Drawing on Baruch Spinoza, he conceives affect as the capacity of a corporeal or mental body to affect other bodies and be affected by them.[30] Because his notion of the affective body is both corporeal and mental, Massumi perceives the cognitive body almost as a corporeal medium of transmission (he uses the word "transition").[31] Affect is transmissive, contagious, and prepersonal.[32] As epitomized in *Blind Detective*, the city's contagious feelings of despair, resentment, revenge, disgust, and so on are shared among post-1997 Hong Kong bodies. These bodies affect one another, whether intensifying or diminishing the feelings in question, thereby constituting a local economy of affect. The exchanged feelings do not come from any particular personal source because affect is prepersonal. This does not mean that the personal experience of residents does not evoke emotions or that there is some sort of a mesmerizing spell making everyone sad and angry for no reason. Personal experience causes emotions, but as Massumi explains, emotions are not affect. "An emotion is a subjective content, the sociolinguistic fixing of the quality of an experience which is from that point onward defined as personal."[33] Emotions are predictable and prescriptive. They can be qualified in terms of the coherent, concrete factors behind them. In *Blind Detective*, the sadness of the brokenhearted husband and Granny, who have been respectively cheated on and abandoned, is an emotion. Affect, however, cannot be qualified. "It is not ownable or recognizable and is thus resistant to critique."[34] The sadness in the film that characterizes the entire city and its bodies for unknown reasons is affect. It is unqualifiable. Its causes are impossible to pin down. There is no right or wrong about this sadness—it just "is." It disturbs causal reasoning and requires a different mode of analysis to be grappled with. Therefore, the issue at hand becomes the impossibility of explaining post-1997 Hong Kong with traditional methods of analysis, such as political debates: in the first decade of the 2000s and in the 2010s, sociological and historical debates had been ubiquitous in almost all aspects of life in Hong Kong, yet few of them helped the people reach a consensus about the current political reality.

The Politics of Smell in Post-1997 Hong Kong

Doing away with overly rational reasoning, giving up on ideological polarization, and attending to affect and sensations might therefore bring us one step closer to a different understanding of the collective feelings of post-1997 Hong Kong people. This is where olfactory sensations come in. Smell is an important gateway to post-1997 Hong Kong's affective consciousness. The special connection between affect and olfaction in the case of Hong Kong has something to do with particular spatial and cognitive factors. In an over-crowded urban environment such as Hong Kong, olfaction is considered harder to negotiate than other sensory experiences.[35] Compared to rural or suburban life, living and working in skyscrapers frequently entails difficult negotiations with regard to one's "nose space." In New York, for instance, "apartment-dwellers believe . . . that tainted air is an unavoidable price of living on top of one's neighbors."[36] Sharing the air is simply an obligatory compromise for people in small spaces and tight quarters. Smell, like other sensations, is particularly present and insistent in an accelerated culture of human and material exchange like that of Hong Kong. In *Blind Detective*, the use of olfactory expression becomes an effective aesthetic means for illustrating the affect of despair and rage in post-1997 Hong Kong, as in the disgruntled husband's foul body odor and the desperate Granny's pungent perfume.

In *Blind Detective*, smell becomes a sense that indicates various kinds of intense love—the lost love of the jilted husband, Granny's unrequited love, but also true love. The film features a love triangle between Johnston, Ho, and ballroom dancer Ding Ding (played by Gao Yuen-yuen). Ho and Ding Ding are polar opposites. Ho is a tomboyish, plain Hong Kong woman, while Ding Ding is a feminine, beautiful PRC woman. Ho is in love with John-ston. Johnston is in love with Ding Ding. Ding Ding is in love with someone else. Johnston's character develops from his infatuation with Ding Ding to his shared interests with Ho—largely food. His love for Ding Ding is based on looks. It is shallow and baseless. His perception of Ho is heartfelt and grounded. It changes as the two embark on a journey of sharing many ecstatic dining experiences—red wine, steak, seafood, Mandarin dishes, *teppanyaki* (Japanese grills), Macau pastries, instant ramen, fruit desserts, and more. He falls in love with the woman who knows how to appreciate his favorite foods—especially Hong Kong's quintessential street-cart food.

Johnston's discovery of true love through dining reveals the intimate nature of olfaction from eating. Like deep love, olfaction from eating is an intimate sensation. It moves us from within. Not all smelling involves tasting, but most tasting involves smelling, except when one loses the sense of smell, as can happen with age or due to illness. One's perception of food is almost always a mixture of both smell and taste. "[Food] tastes different when you are sick and stuffed up."[37] The detective's perception of food is constituted by both olfactory and gustatory sensations, but smelling happens differently in his body. The olfaction of food does not only include what one smells before one eats but also what one smells *when* one eats. "[Molecules] are also released from food by the action of mastication and swallowing, making their way by the interior passages to the olfactory receptors through the back of the mouth and throat: retronasal smelling."[38] Like an affect with multiple converging feelings, smell is a complex, powerful, and highly integrated sense. It not only refers to what the nose does; the gustatory sensations via the taste buds and the somatosensations (like burning or cooling) via the epithelium that lines the upper respiratory tract all interact with and constitute olfaction as well.[39] In turn, the nose informs one as to whether the mouth should take in or avoid external substances.[40] Although most sensory experiences are multisensorial in some way, the synesthesia of olfaction-taste is exceptionally important among them.

Johnston's journey to love through food also demonstrates the persistent nature of olfactory experiences. His unexplainable attraction to the unique and vibrant foods available in Hong Kong reveals a lasting memory of the city. Much like affect is an enduring discursive process, olfactory memory is a persistent type of memory. "[Odor]-based representations are better remembered and for longer than vision- and word-based representations."[41] They stick around longer than other sensory memories, leaving a lingering impression. Since the sense of smell offers the most persistent memory among all the senses, one's (dis)likes of foods carry a powerful and uncompromising memory of one's culture.[42] This explains why Ding Ding, a nonlocal woman, reacts with disgust when she smells fried pork intestines in the film—some eaters of this food who are unaccustomed to the taste complain that this infamous street food smells and tastes like feces. Nevertheless, as the old saying goes, one person's trash is another person's treasure. In an earlier scene, we see Johnston chowing down with relish at the same street cart. Tastes are a corporeal memory of one's past.

Ultimately, the intimate and persistent nature of olfactory memory helps explain part of the foundation of a Hong Kong consciousness. Since 1997, the Hong Kong Special Administrative Region government has implemented countless policies to try to integrate Hong Kong society into PRC society. However, although Hong Kong and the PRC have long become intertwined in many aspects of life, the local consciousness remains distinct and strong. Most studies explain the phenomenon by using traditional methods of analysis, such as political and historical debates, which focus on different belief systems and institutions. Little scholarly attention has been paid to the nonrational, nonideological dimensions of the mind and body of Hong

Kong people, such as affect and sensations. Nonetheless, neuroscientists remind us of the obscured preconditions of sensory experience. One's sense of smell and taste develops even before birth. "In all placental mammals, the foetuses are bathed in an odorous amniotic fluid (which is also likely to give rise to tastes)."[43] These senses are so ingrained in the body's consciousness that they can in some ways be considered prepersonal. In addition, the body is a growing organism. Its sensory receptors, which are cells that detect chemicals, temperature, and stimuli, are changing at every moment. If the body itself is limited by the biological and environmental conditions of its sensory systems, then the political accountability of its sensations is hard to determine. Nothing is achieved by blaming the human body for harboring "incorrect sensations," which is unproductive and fails to address the real problems concerning the senses. Essentially, all sensations are critical objects, historical artifacts (although nonpreservable). They are inscriptions of individual and collective feelings awaiting a restorative examination of diverse experiences, not cultural practices to be devalued.

This is not to romanticize sensations but to stress the importance of finding new ways to understand the sentient (and collective) body. For instance, new understandings of the senses may untangle some of the deadlocked discussions about feelings in post-1997 Hong Kong. In the local discourse, there was never much consensus on what postcolonial subjects were feeling. However, a year after the release of Blind Detective, when frustrations and rage exploded into the protests of the Umbrella Revolution,[44] state or state-influenced media and public intellectuals continued to insist on a questionable notion of public opinion to gauge reactions to the unrest. It was not only state media outlets that claimed the general public's disapproval of the democratic movement using questionable poll numbers;[45] in global discourse, Western public intellectuals such as Martin Jacques also propagated the idea that half of Hong Kong's population "support China's proposals on universal suffrage, either because they think they are a step forward or because they take the pragmatic view that they will happen anyway." Jacques insisted that the rage of the other dissenting "half" of the Hong Kong population was due to jealousy toward wealthy PRC tourists and immigrants, attributing the outbreak of the Umbrella Revolution to the drastic increase in visibility of the PRC people and other signs of the PRC rule after 1997.[46] Not only was it slightly odd for an ostensibly Marxist intellectual to celebrate consumerism and economic disparity, but Jacques also insisted on assessing the situation by privileging sight and competition in the modern age.

As previously explained, popular discourse in post-1997 Hong Kong has undergone a sensory turn from sight to other sensory modalities, signaling a diminished importance for seeing. This shift can be seen in *Blind Detective*'s contrast between the PRC dancer Ding Ding's identification with visuality and the plain policewoman Ho's identification with other sensory modalities. The camera films Ding Ding using natural lighting, close-ups, slow motion, and an extradiegetic love song, whereas Ho is filmed with low-key lighting and medium shots that de-emphasize her association with the visual gaze. Ding Ding wears tight, feminine clothing and dances; Ho wears loose, masculine attire, eats, and constantly gets wounded. Ding Ding speaks Cantonese with an accent, suggesting her association with the PRC. Ho's mode of communication is more olfactory and haptic than visual. The contrast between the two women already informs us of two completely different types of perception, that of a postsocialist Chinese subject and that of a postcolonial Hong Kong subject.

For the postsocialist Chinese subject, seeing is a powerful sense for intensifying psychological competitiveness. This association between power and sight is exemplified in Shakespeare's *Othello*, which can be read as a parable of the role of sight in displaying and viewing wealth and power—as emphasized by Jacques in his eagerness to focus on a visible, powerful PRC presence in Hong Kong.[47] Othello is a self-made man who is jealous of an imagined rival, his wife's adulterer, who in fact does not exist. Othello grows increasingly jealous (of no one) when he is unable to find visible proof of his wife's adultery—the more he sees, the more convinced he becomes of what he does not see. He "craves confirmation of suspicion to end the agony aroused by what he cannot really see."[48] Instigated by his manipulative friend Iago, Othello ends up mistakenly murdering his wife. Similarly, in the political unconscious of Hong Kong, the more the self-made competitive body—the PRC—sees its own wealth and power, the more it craves visible confirmation of its rival Hong Kong's lesser wealth and power, yet this "lesser" Hong Kong does not exist. Nevertheless, when this craving is met with an absence of competition—since there is no mutually subscribed rivalry of equals between the PRC and Hong Kong—the competitive, ocular-driven body feels anguish. Instigated by the PRC state media and manipulative opportunists, the idea that "they are just jealous of me" becomes a propaganda strategy designed to alienate sovereign bodies (of the PRC and Hong Kong), all starting with the PRC's incessant and growing need—like that of most modern political entities—for visual confirmation of its competitiveness.

Conclusion

Post-1997 Hong Kong saw a redistribution of the sensible that resulted in a heartbroken, delirious affective life for its bodies. Despite the city's historical background of British colonialism and Chinese socialism, this affective aspect of its collective experience eludes the framework of most classical postcolonial theory and studies of postsocialism. As discussed with regard to the despair and rage in *Blind Detective*, the city's affective experience also contradicts a distinct feature of postmodernism: the waning of affect.[49] As for affect theory itself, the increased interest in affect in the humanities and social sciences starting in the early to mid-1990s was more a shift of research method than a focus on a shared, identifiable historical pattern. Consequently, Hong Kong remains an unpredictable, elusive object of study.

In response to this problem, this chapter has focused on the multisensory on-screen expressions in *Blind Detective* of otherwise imperceptible feelings about the city, calling attention to the insights that can be gained by examining sensorial registers—such as smell—that have been largely disregarded in critical discourse. Such a shift from the ocular to the nonocular senses further explains the different modes of perception in postsocialist Chinese postcolonial Hong Kong that has led to the misunderstanding of Hong Kong being imagined first as an asset and then as a rival to the PRC. To consider Hong Kong's idiosyncratic historical situation and the complexity of its affective life effectively, a different lens—or better, a different sensing body—is required. A year after the release of *Blind Detective*, many asked how the second largest social movement in Hong Kong's history, the seventy-nine-day sit-in protest that paralyzed the city, could have happened in light of the infamously politically apathetic, work-obsessed, and acquiescent population. By de-emphasizing ideological debates, this chapter has analyzed the situation in Hong Kong by looking for signs from bodies rather than focusing only on belief systems and institutions.

Notes

1. Jameson, *Political Unconscious*, ix–7, 18–20.

2. We must not confuse this shift from vision to smell (often combined with taste) with Hong Kong's return to a premodern, primordial, or "natural" Chinese culture. It would be erroneous to consider post-1997 Hong Kong cinema's interest in smell and other nonocular and non-phonocentric senses as indicating an essential characteristic of Eastern, Chinese, or Indigenous culture, which is in itself an Orientalist construction. Levin, *Modernity*; Classen, Howes, and Synnott, *Aroma*.

3. "Much to Look Forward to"; Choi, "External Ties"; Lowe, "So Much Can Change."

4. Ibid., 37.

5. Schaal and Durand, "Role of Olfaction," 29.

6. Census, "Marriage and Divorce Trends."

7. Centre for Suicide, *Study on The Phenomenon of Divorce*, 50–51.

8. Pong et al., "Blurring Boundaries?"

9. Wordie, *Streets*, 112–13.

10. Johnston, "Note on the Island of Hong-Kong"; Tsang, *Modern History of Hong Kong*, 18.

11. Classen, Howes, and Synnott, *Aroma*; Levin, *Modernity*.

12. Rancière, *Dissensus*, 36.

13. Rancière, *Politics of Aesthetics*, 12.

14. Ibid., 14.

15. Ho "*Crazy Rich Asians* Is Going."

16. Lo, "There Is No Such Thing"; Sakai, *Translation and Subjectivity*.

17. See also Wong, "Crazy, Rich, When Asian."

18. Fanon, *Black Skin, White Masks*, 109.

19. Rancière, *Disagreement*, 101.

20. Whether race is visually constituted is a controversial topic. Generally speaking, if we accept the postcolonial, phenomeno-logical, and anthropological recognition of the privileging of sight (Fanon, *Black Skin, White Masks*, 109; Levin, *Modernity*; Hans, *Phenomenon of Life*; Classen, *Worlds of Sense*, 5–7), then race is a consid-erably ocularcentric construction, especially during the age of visual media. However, it should be noted that some scholars object to this idea. For instance, Mark M. Smith calls into question the focus on the visual percep-tion of race, pointing out that "the preference for 'seeing' race is as much a social construc-tion as 'race itself'" and calling for the restoration of other senses for understand-ing Black stereotypes and their ramifications (*How Race Is Made*, 2–4). Similar ideas can be found in Constance Classen, David Howes, and Anthony Synnott's defense of academic studies of smell as well as studies on the olfactory constructions of ethnic groups (*Aroma*, 5, 165–69, 172–75).

21. Rancière, *Dissensus*, 36.

22. Rancière, *Politics of Aesthetics*, 36.

23. Johnston, "Note on the Island of Hong-Kong."

24. Tam and Leung, "Human Remains Found in Tai Po."

25. Lau, "Girl, 3, Witnessed Parents."

26. Williams, *Marxism and Literature*, 132.

27. Ibid., 133.

28. Ibid., 132.

29. Ibid., 132–33.

30. Massumi, *Parables for the Virtual*, 15.

31. Ibid., 15.

32. Massumi, "Notes on the Translation and Acknowledgments," xvi.

33. Massumi, *Parables for the Virtual*, 28.

34. Ibid.

35. Classen, Howes, and Synnott, *Aroma*, 34.

36. Rogers, "What's That Smell?"

37. Saab, *Seeing, Hearing, and Smelling*, 68–69.

38. Bell and Parr, "Olfaction and Taste," 1054.

39. Schaal and Durand, "Role of Olfaction," 31.

40. Ibid., 34.

41. Ibid., 36.

42. Ibid.; Classen, Howes, and Synnott, *Aroma*, 2–4.

43. Schaal and Durand, "Role of Olfaction," 29.

44. The global news media, including CNN, BBC, Reuters, Agence France-Presse, and Associated Press, used this term (Umbrella Revolution or Umbrella Movement) in their coverage of the 2014 Hong Kong sit-in protest, rather than naming it as an outgrowth of the Occupy Central Movement (as part of the global Occupy Move-ment), which was organized in 2013 by two university professors, Benny Tai and Chan Kin-man, and a priest, Rev. Chu Yiu-ming. Because the high school and university students of the Umbrella protests autono-mously assumed leadership as early as the first day of the movement, it is inaccurate to regard this historical event as "Occupy Central" (占中), which is the term used by government mouthpieces, such as *Renmin Ribao* (People's Daily), which published a total of forty-two articles about this move-ment in 2014. Technically speaking, Occupy Central never took place, although its

original engineers joined in the Umbrella Revolution.

45. "Jieshu 'Zhanzhong' Shi Renxin Suoxiang; Yin, "Liangtian 65 Wan Xianggang."

46. Jacques, "China Is Hong Kong's Future," 33.

47. Ibid.

48. Bell, "Othello's Jealousy," 120–21.

49. As Timothy Mitchell explains, the assumed succession of different stages of (primarily European) modernity is debatable, especially when it comes to the non-West ("Stage of Modernity," 1–6). Not only is it Eurocentric to assume the already performed history of (Western-style) modernity as the norm ("Stage of Modernity," 2), but this assumption ignores the many idiosyncratic factors that contribute to non-Western modernity. A case in point is postcolonial Hong Kong. Jameson, *Postmodernism, or the Cultural Logic of Late Capitalism*, 9–15.

Bibliography

Bell, Graham, and Wendy V. Parr. "Olfaction and Taste in the Food and Beverage Industries." In *Handbook of Olfaction and Gustation*, edited by Richard L. Doty, 1051–66. Hoboken: John Wiley & Sons, 2015.

Bell, Millicent. "Othello's Jealousy." *Yale Review* 85, no. 2 (1997): 120–36.

Census and Statistics Department, Hong Kong Special Administrative Region. "Marriage and Divorce Trends in Hong Kong, 1991 to 2013." *Hong Kong Monthly Digest of Statistics* (2015). https://www.statistics.gov.hk /pub/B71501FA2015XXXXB0100.pdf.

Centre for Suicide Research and Prevention, The University of Hong Kong. *A Study on The Phenomenon of Divorce in Hong Kong Final Report* (2014). https://www.legco.gov.hk/yr13-14 /english/panels/ws/papers/ws0609cb2 -2288-1-e.pdf.

Choi, Barry. "External Ties: China Link Works in Hongkong's Favour." *South China Morning Post*, April 11, 1982, 92.

Classen, Constance. *Worlds of Sense: Exploring the Senses in History and across Cultures*. New York: Routledge, 1993.

Classen, Constance, David Howes, and Anthony Synnott. *Aroma: The Cultural History of Smell*. London: Routledge, 1994.

Fanon, Frantz. *Black Skin, White Masks*. Translated by Charles Lam Markmann. New York: Grove, 1986.

Hans, Jonas. *The Phenomenon of Life: Toward a Philosophical Biology*. Evanston, IL: Northwestern University Press, 2001.

Ho, Karen K. "*Crazy Rich Asians* Is Going to Change Hollywood: It's About Time." *Time*, August 15, 2018. https://time .com/longform/crazy-rich-asians.

Jacques, Martin. "China Is Hong Kong's Future—Not Its Enemy." *Guardian*, October 1, 2014. https://www .theguardian.com/commentisfree /2014/sep/30/china-hong-kong -future-protesters-cry-democracy.

Jameson, Fredric. *The Political Unconscious: Narrative as a Socially Symbolic Act*. London: Routledge, 1983.

———. *Postmodernism, or the Cultural Logic of Late Capitalism*. Durham, NC: Duke University Press, 1991.

"Jieshu 'Zhanzhong' Shi Renxin Suoxiang 结束"占中"是人心所向 [Ending "Occupy Central" Is The Will of the People]." *Renmin Ribao* (People's Daily), December 13, 2014.

Johnston, A. R. "Note on the Island of Hong-Kong." *Journal of the Royal Geographical Society of London* 14 (1844): 112–17.

Lau, Angel. "Girl, 3, Witnessed Parents Locked in Deadly Struggle." *South China Morning Post*, March 1, 2000.

Levin, David Michael, ed. *Modernity and the Hegemony of Vision*. Berkeley: University of California Press, 1993.

Lo, Kwai-Cheung. "There Is No Such Thing as Asia: Racial Particularities in the 'Asian' Films of Hong Kong and Japan." *Modern Chinese Literature and Culture* 17, no. 1 (2005): 133–58.

Lowe, Bill. "So Much Can Change in 14 Years in Both China and Hong Kong:

Education for Life." *South China Morning Post*, October 12, 1983.

Massumi, Brian. "Notes on the Translation and Acknowledgments." In *A Thousand Plateaus: Capitalism and Schizophrenia*, translated by Brian Massumi, xvi–xix. Minneapolis: University of Minnesota Press, 2005.

———. *Parables for the Virtual: Movement, Affects, Sensation*. Durham, NC: Duke University Press, 2002.

Mitchell, Timothy. "The Stage of Modernity." In *Question of Modernity*, edited by Timothy Mitchell, 1–34. Minneapolis: University of Minnesota Press, 2000.

"Much to Look Forward To." *South China Morning Post*, January 21, 1984.

Pong, Suet-ling, David Post, Dongshu Ou, and Maggie Fok. "Blurring Boundaries? Immigration and Exogamous Marriages in Hong Kong." *Population and Development Review* 40, no. 4 (2014): 629–52.

Rancière, Jacques. *Disagreement: Politics and Philosophy*. Translated by Julie Rose. Minneapolis: University of Minnesota Press, 1999.

———. *Dissensus: On Politics and Aesthetics*. Translated by Steven Corcoran. London: Continuum, 2010.

———. *The Politics of Aesthetics: The Distribution of the Sensible*. Translated by Gabriel Rockhill. London: Continuum, 2007.

Rogers, Teri Karush. "What's That Smell?" *The New York Times*, August 6, 2006. https://www.nytimes.com/2006/08/06/realestate/06cov.html.

Saab, Carl Y. *Seeing, Hearing, and Smelling the World*. New York: Chelsea House, 2007.

Sakai, Naoki. *Translation and Subjectivity: On Japan and Cultural Nationalism*. Minneapolis: The University of Minnesota Press, 1997.

Schaal, Benoist, and Karine Durand. "The Role of Olfaction in Human Multisensory Development." In *Multisensory Development*, edited by Andrew J. Bremner, David J. Lewkowicz, and Charles Spence, 29–62. Oxford: Oxford University Press, 2012.

Tam, Bonny, and Jimmy Leung. "Human Remains Found in Tai Po." *South China Morning Post*, July 9, 1993.

Tsang, Steve. *A Modern of History of Hong Kong*. London: I. B. Tauris, 2007.

Williams, Raymond. *Marxism and Literature*. Oxford: Oxford University Press, 1977.

Wong, Siang-Ting. "Crazy, Rich, When Asian: Yellowface Ambivalence and Mockery in Crazy Rich Asians." *Journal of International and Intercultural Communication* (2020): 117–52. doi: 10.1080/17513057.2020.1857426.

Wordie, Jason. *Streets: Exploring Hong Kong Island*. Hong Kong: Hong Kong University Press, 2002.

Yin, Shi-chang 尹世昌. "Liangtian 65 Wan Xianggang Shimin Qianming Fan 'Zhanzhong' 两天 65 万香港市民签名反'占中' [650,000 Anti-Occupy Citizens Signed Expressing Disapproval in Two Days]." *Renmin Ribao* (People's Daily), October 27, 2014.

PART III

BODIES—LIFE, WORK, DEATH

CHAPTER 8

Pregnancy, Childbirth, and the Smell of Vulnerability in Lombok, Indonesia

Saki Tanada

In the first two years of living in Japan, my husband, Uji, often claimed that I stank when I came home from work. With disgust, he complains in Sasak and Indonesian, "You stink *bakeq* [a variety of spirit]! So many *bakeq* have followed you. You should have thrown them out on the way home." Uji claims that his head and body "*rasa*" (a Sasak term referring to "feel," "sense," and "taste") are heavy, as he simultaneously feels my exhaustion and that these symptoms are caused by the spirits, which I do not smell, clinging to my shoulders. He peels garlic (*langsuna*), whispers the Arabic phrase of prayer, cuts the clove in half with his nails, breathes onto the cut clove of garlic, rubs the lower half of the clove on my *semanget* (a central point on the upper forehead), temples, back of ears, palms, heels, and foot soles. Then he reminds me as always, "Don't forget to say in your heart '*bismillah*' while you are out, wherever you are."

Carrying prayer words into the sufferer's body with breath and the protective scent of garlic is one of the ordinary healing treatments among the Indigenous Sasak people of Lombok Island, central Indonesia. Uji and I first met in 2016 during the third time I was conducting my anthropological fieldwork in his home village of Reragi (pseudonym) in the eastern region of the island. He worked at the textile store run by my host mother Inaq Nir, who is a second cousin of his grandmother. We soon became friends and started spending time together, as he frequently assisted me to get around and meet people in the village, and as we spoke and shared experiences of losing parents early. We got married in October 2018, the final year of my doctoral field research, and consequently moved to my hometown in Japan, where we have lived until the present.

My doctoral research primarily focused on the notions of the maternal body and the fetal, newborn, and infant personhood embedded in the ordinary care practices of pregnancy and childbirth among the Sasak Muslims. During my field research from 2014 to 2018, I repeatedly found people sharing stories of social-sensory experiences, of interacting with beings other than humans as they suffer from and cope with the emotional and physical pains or a sense of disgust in daily family lives.[1] Uji's aforementioned allusions to *bakeq* are typical of many I encountered in Reragi. Immaterial but touchable, mostly unseen but sometimes smelly and audible, the presence of *bakeq* spirits permeates everyday life in the village, including activities such as going to the morning market, returning from work, and visiting friends.

Sensations including olfaction, revealing vulnerability toward the ubiquitous presence of agentive beings, are embodied among people in many regions of Indonesia and beyond. As Woodward puts it (about the Islamic context), "While some healing techniques, including reciting passages from the Qur'an and belief in the healing power of barakah (blessing) of saints and descendants of the Prophet Muhammad are universal or at least nearly so, others are unique to particular cultures."[2] In Indonesia, due to the scent and taste, fresh garlic, shallots, betel leaves, and flowers are used to chase the spirits away.

Among the Sasak Muslims in Lombok, one of the most common healing practices is the use of formulas called *jampi*, in which potent words and materials are combined and applied to the sufferer—as we have seen in Uji's treatment of my exhaustion. *Jampi* formulas, with various words and materials, are widely performed by both Indigenous healers and ordinary people in Lombok, often casually combining prayer (*doa*) in Arabic and mantras (*puji-puji*) in Sasak. While the Sasak Muslims in Reragi village recognize words of prayer do not require tangibles (*nyata*), they expect the efficacy to be strengthened, like the Sasak mantras, when carried into the sufferer's body by tangibles such as breath, water, fragrance, and other materials as a medium for both pushing out and closing the paths for other beings to enter (*tama*) the person through a point of the forehead, mouth, or skin.[3]

According to Telle, the Sasak people in the 1990s already recognized many ritual practices "less as a deviation from Islam's straight path and more as the beginnings of Sasak understandings of Islam."[4] In Reragi, such tendencies align in terms of current healing practices among Reragi villagers.

In an in-depth interview with one of the religious teachers in the village, I asked about the relationships between cultures and religion in questioning the efficacy of *jampi*. As he preaches, "It is not the water that has the power to heal the illness. It is just a mediation (*wasilah*) of our prayer to Allah." As he put it, "The rituals and traditions from ancestors that we have now are the ones that accord with the religious teachings, and the contradicting ones are already gone." In daily life, however, I observed no such conversations problematizing the tradition versus religion or *jampi* versus prayer. To my understanding, the so-called traditional customs, their conflict with modern institutions and their ideologies, and the processes of marginalization are almost dismissed from everyday social life in Reragi—if not deliberately assigned to the past and the history of grandparents and ancestors, as is necessary when the two are juxtaposed.

Further, as Telle argues in her case study of the Sasak people's treatment of their residence and as my research attests, the Sasak people experience vulnerability in their intersubjective relationships with things surrounding them, and thus their conceptions of sociality involve materiality.[5] As Telle puts it, "Rather than operating with a stark dualism between subjects and objects, of people on the one hand and inanimate things on the other, Sasak conceptions are somewhat more fluid. . . . In such a world, people are continuously affected by their reciprocal engagement with the various beings, more or less person-like or thing-like, with which they come into contact."[6] It is such a context of social-sensory relationships where Reragi villagers find themselves vulnerable to *bakeq* and their acute olfaction, so they practice various healing treatments, including Uji's allusions to *bakeq* and his *jampi* counteracting their presence. As we will see in this chapter, while the ubiquitous presence of *bakeq* is supposed to bring various misfortunes, this omnipresence paradoxically serves pregnant women and new mothers, who are considered most vulnerable to spiritual offense, to cope and survive in the aftermath of illnesses and losses through learning how to sense or feel one's own vulnerability and defend themselves against spirits. Drawing on an episode of stillbirth that a mother and her family members claimed to be the result of an encounter with *bakeq*, this case study explores the resilient way in which people in Lombok acknowledge the presence of *bakeq* and relate themselves to the broader social-sensory assemblage of people and things, counteracting modern medical objectification and segregation of birthing bodies.

Pregnancy and childbirth are ethnographically and theoretically rich stages of human vulnerability for social, religious, medical, and other varied perspectives, but it is a time of life that deserves far greater attention from sensory scholars. For instance, the transformation of olfactory and taste sensibilities is one of the most common experiences in pregnancy among women across the world. For many women, pregnancy changes how they smell and taste, and that also applies to their male partners among the Sasak people, who attribute *ngidam* (pregnancy sickness and craving) to both expectant mothers (*inaq ebon*) and prospective fathers (*amaq ebon*).[7] While pregnancy sickness and cravings will require more investigation by sensory scholars, my case study reexamines the notion of vulnerability and its lived realities in pregnancy and childbirth by exploring the social-sensory context where birthing women find themselves.

In Asia, anthropologists have increasingly and critically observed maternal and infant health in taking up the call to contribute to improving the undesirable reproductive health conditions for local women. Lombok, with the poorest recorded health statistics in all of Indonesia in the 1990s, has been a particularly resourceful vein for studies of women's health. Scholars have found in Lombok the health disadvantages that people suffered during this dramatic life change and the relative underdevelopment of medical landscapes. Findings include the high rate of maternal mortality caused by physical and psychological inaccessibility to proper healthcare and knowledge,[8] and an evident stigma, shame, isolation, and morbidity surrounding premarital sex and abortion.[9] Among these, Hunter observes severe discontinuities and tensions that emerge between the village social relations and the state-oriented modern medical settings.[10]

Significant in their own right, medical anthropological studies on childbirth in postcolonial Asia derive from the urgent need to contribute to improving the health and welfare of people they study. Consequently, scholarly interest is focused on making developmentalist evaluations. Empirical accounts underpinning nonexpert sense and methods of healing and precaution in the context of everyday life have been scarce unless found in direct links to critical medical concerns. Hence, although previous studies present critical sets of sociomedical realities, I suggest that the discussion on people's lived experiences surrounding childbirth will be limiting insofar as it further entrenches the notion of vulnerability as predicated on medical interventions.

As Alter points out critically, "The politics of culture—manifest in both nationalism and transnationalism—has made it virtually impossible to talk about Asian medicine as anything but medicine, and medical knowledge as anything other than science."[11] To critique the authority of the disciplinary category itself, as Alter puts, one must map out "a route of escape from a whole series of false or problematic dichotomies that have plagued the analysis of health, healing, and the body in Asia."[12] To this end, I revisit in this chapter the body and childbirth, diverting from a critical medical context, and instead exploring how people sense and make sense of their vulnerability in relationships with their social, material, and spiritual surroundings.

In doing so, I employ the notion of "spiritual landscapes" to illustrate the ongoing ways people in Reragi interact with *bakeq* and engage in varied healing and protection strategies in their daily lives.[13] Allerton argues that the notion of spiritual landscapes can be adopted as "a way to sidestep the problematic Christian heritage of our anthropological concepts"[14] and to suggest that sacred sites and ancestor worship imply "an attitude of reverence and contemplation."[15] According to Allerton, spiritual landscapes are "not necessarily one that we would recognize as 'religious' . . . . People may engage with spiritual landscapes in ritual activities, but also in a more pragmatic fashion in the course of everyday life. Moreover, even when a converted population abandons older ritual forms, many taken-for-granted notions regarding spirits and their places may be retained."[16] As we will see in the next section, an exploration of the quotidian contexts of taking care of smells of vulnerability against *bakeq* allows us a glimpse into the spiritual landscapes in Lombok.

My field research involved semistructured interviews in Sasak and Indonesian languages with fifty women, in-depth interviews with six Indigenous healers with various expertise, three Indigenous midwife-healers, three clinic midwives, two hospital nurses, and one Islamic religious teacher, as well as participant observation in numerous occasions of childbirth, illness, death, and religious events. In the meantime, the primary ethnographic stories in this chapter mostly belong to a small number of people who are closely related to me, including my huband Uji's mentions of *bakeq* and a story of stillbirth by a young village mother Ais, who is a younger sister-in-law of Uji's older sister-in-law Nana. I also drew on my interviews with Nana regarding her own experiences of pregnancy loss and with my host sister (Inaq Nir's daughter) Ani on her difficult birth.

This chapter proceeds as follows. First, I describe how the local notion of agencies other than humans in Reragi aligns with or controverts established understandings of religious and spiritual landscapes in anthropology. The main section is devoted to an ethnographically rich account of pregnancy loss, in which Ais and her family-in-law considered the possibility of *bakeq* with keen olfactory sense attacking and killing the child. Finally, I illustrate how people communicate birthing women's vulnerability in terms of *bakeq* and their olfaction. As I argue, vernacular relationships to spiritual surroundings entail the ways to counter modern medicine's objectification of the human body and exteriorization of illnesses from social relationships. Simultaneously, the case discussed illuminates that admitted divergence in how people smell and sense their surroundings paradoxically generate or regenerate shared understandings of the spiritual landscapes, enabling synesthetic experiences of coping and healing. While previous olfactory studies discuss prominently instinctive, pervasive, and undeniable qualities of smell, I suggest that the ways people keep up with the peculiarity and irreplaceability of smell and sense illuminate an equally important aspect of lived realities in society.[17]

Bakeq and the World of "Onion Skins"

Recalling his childhood in Lombok, Uji mentioned that adults often scolded him when they found him around rice fields, saying, "Don't play there! Later it will bump into you!" He asked who was going to bump into him, and he received the same stock phrase as an answer: "The one who owns the land, of course." According to Uji, "the landowner" (*isin paer*) refers to anyone that belongs to the place. In a rice field, for instance, they include the human landowner, frogs, and water striders, but in this context as well the *bakeq* living and guarding that place.

The Sasak term *bakeq* refers to a large category of various spirits, sometimes synonymous with Satan in Islam and other times not. My informants in Reragi commonly describe the world as constitutive of tangible, human territory, and the intangible (*endek nyata*) realm of other beings, the adhesion of which is "tight like the onion skins" (*tipis mangkun kulit bawang*). The spirit world—*Alam gaib* in Arabic, *Alam jin* in Indonesian—is spoken of in almost equivalent terms as *Alam bakeq* (*bakeq* world) in Reragi. Oral reports and dialogues show that health concerns in everyday life in Reragi are deeply embedded in relationships to beings other than humans, including the ones with *ilmu*,[18] material things, the dead, and *bakeq*.

Various illness episodes are the result of being pranked by a variety of spirits; these sicknesses include the illnesses of *ketemuq* or, in other words, being called by the dead persons. Further, people are concerned about the illnesses of *pepedaman* or being affected by tangible beings in objects that they did not treat properly with respect. These include specific kinds of power-ful things such as an ancestral healing cloth (*pedam reragian*) for being stepped on, as well as more ordinary things such as earrings for being lost and ignored. Concern also extends to the human body, including the fetus (*pedam adik*) for being unnoticed or neglected by their elder siblings, placenta (*pedam ariq-ariq*) for being disturbed after burial. People in Reragi sense and relate to *bakeq*—among the diverse beings other than humans—by various sensations, illnesses, and misfortunes.

Bakeq are ubiquitous and in all places, and each of them has a different personality. The good, peaceful personalities of *bakeq* are reticent (*penedok*), a favorable characteristic also attributed to human personalities among the Sasak. On the other hand, there are undesirable, offensive *bakeq*, which are associated with noisiness (*biur*) and restlessness (*noak*). People in Reragi feel affected by *bakeq*, as the "body feels sick" (*ndek mik idap*), their "mind feels distracted" (*ndek keruan rasak*), or they are affected by occasional signs of belches that keep erupting. People in Reragi on a daily basis recog-nize the presence of *bakeq* by guessing (*badek*), feeling (*rasak*), or smelling (*ngidok*) them. More likely, they find out the closeness of *bakeq* by being made uncomfortable (*keriru*) with the occasional sign of horripilation (*seso-rotan*) and shudderings (*ger-ger*). Uji claims to have acute olfaction (*keras ngidok*) and reports that *bakeq* stinks like rotten garlic, while the good spir-its smell like flowers, although the descriptions vary among my informants. The smell of *bakeq* is only momentarily sensed, as it "passes by" (*liwat*) and is not contained or held to things.

Unexpected encounters with *bakeq* are articulated with abundant sensory terms, including being called (*ketemuq*), whispered (*sedut*), followed (*turut*), slapped (*tepes*), and pushed (*sembokang*). The concerns toward *bakeq* are asso-ciated with heat (*beneng*) dangerous to a person's coolness (*mel*), which is essential to health.[19] Numerous episodes of the failure to avoid *bakeq* can be cited, including the occasions of an ear being "burned black" (*motong*) by being whispered to and an unborn child being burned to death, as we will see later in this chapter. One woman reports the experience of *bakeq* taking her fetus taken away and making her abdomen shrink; she was later cured as the *bakeq* was chased away, and the baby was returned by a healer called *belian*.[20] People in Reragi associate various illnesses and accidents with offenses of the *bakeq* in the aftermath of events rather than as a category of diagnosable illness.

People in Reragi consider that one may reduce the risk of encounter-ing *bakeq* by keeping an appropriate distance from them. One of the most

Fig. 8.1   Burning sugar incense at a family gathering before a funeral, September 28, 2016. Photo: Saki Tanada.

common gestures of daily precaution against *bakeq* is sharp spitting (*betusik*) on the ground, by which people express salutation toward *bakeq* in a superior manner to excuse their presence in the *bakeq*'s place and to implicitly order them not to disturb them. Spitting or imitative spitting is common, especially before entering and leaving houses, as well as when entering an apparent residence of *bakeq*. Other gestures for keeping distance from *bakeq* include saying "*bismillah*," as Uji reminds me, or whispering prayer phrases (*doa*) aimed to chase jinn away, reading the Sasak mantra (*puji-puji*), or both simultaneously. On other occasions, as I have witnessed, it is a custom for people to cook meals outside the house throughout the night for a family gathering (*gawe*), for events such as the naming ritual of a child, or for weddings and funerals. They prepare incense (*dupa*) and a small amount of food for *bakeq*, who will be attracted by the smell of the food (fig. 8.1). When families and relatives gather to cook the rice and stews overnight after sacrificing, cutting, and dividing animals with cutlery, they typically choose a few men or women to be in charge of cooking and simultaneously guard the food against *bakeq* by enforcing particular *ilmu* that help keep them away.

Bakeq intake food by inhaling with their nose (*idong*). Their sense of "smell" involves not only smell of physical substances but also scents of emotional vulnerability, which makes birthing women and their children an easy victim of offenses by the spirits.

With their acute olfaction, *bakeq*'s favorite food is considered to be blood (*darak*), and to this end, the villagers suspect that menstruating or postpartum women, newborn children, and the placenta (*ariq-ariq*)—as they "stink blood" (*ngeru*)—are easily smelled and offended by *bakeq*. On the day of exorcising a child (a ritual called *molang malik*), typically held within a few months after birth, it is a norm in the village that men apply *aik kembang* or water filled with a sweet fragrance of flowers and leaves on the forehead of the child; they do so after they send their wishes for the child at the end of the ritual of naming and hair cutting (*ngurisang*) (fig. 8.2). Similarly, the placenta is usually buried immediately after child delivery (fig. 8.3). The placenta is typically wrapped in white cloth, placed in dehusked coconut shells, and buried underground with wet soil, and a bamboo branch is inserted as a breathing pipe. Then the pile of soil is decorated with aromatic plants such as betel leaves, dried tobacco, and flower petals, and the candle is lit to secure the placenta from being smelled by *bakeq* and people who have *ilmu teselaq* (cannibalistic sorcery). A newborn child and placenta are considered as siblings (*adik-kakak*) whose susceptibilities to harm are in sync. Failure to protect the placenta is considered to cause the previously mentioned illnesses of *pedam*, or being called.

Further, *bakeq* are typically considered as landowners of ghostly (*simbit*) places marked by dark, wet, or deserted (*sepi*) qualities, including vacant houses, shady streams, rice fields, and rainforests. As *bakeq* prefer being in "deserted" (*sepi*) places, they also prefer to approach and sometimes enter human bodies when people feel "lonely" (*sepi*) or when they are "absent-minded" (*girang momot*). Reragi villagers typically attribute such emotional conditions to newly married women (*penganten baru*), who are thought to feel isolated from their natal homes since marriage, and pregnant women; who are thought to have diminished concentration, as we will see specifically in the next section.

As things in the intangible world work in opposition from those in the tangible world, the twilight (*sendikala*) here is the early morning there and vice versa, and the twilight in the tangible world is the time when *bakeq* are most actively out of their own residences. Pregnant women and the carriers

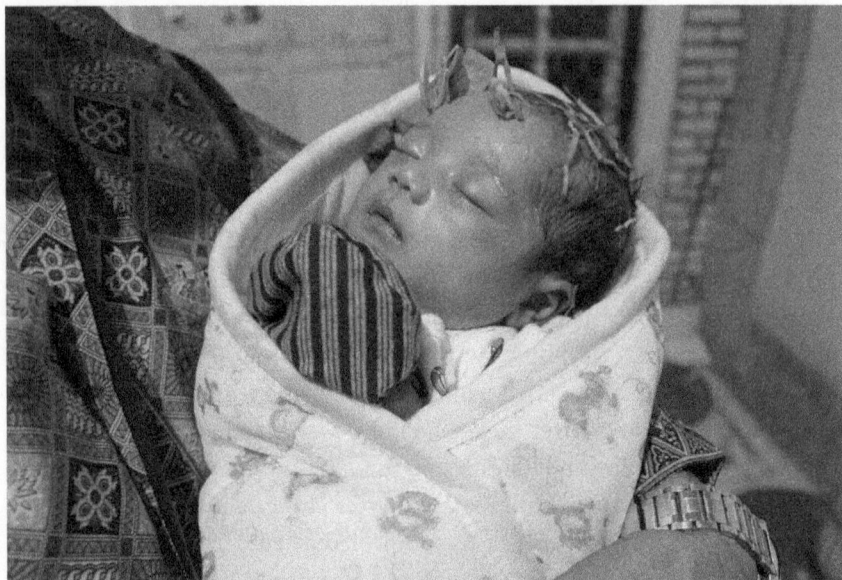

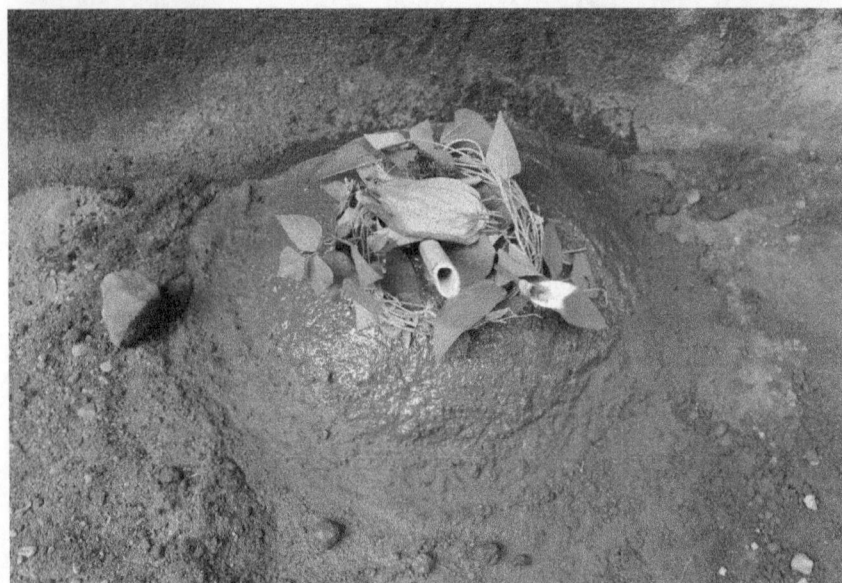

Fig. 8.2   A scene from the ritual of exorcising a child, August 1, 2015. Photo: Saki Tanada.

Fig. 8.3   Newly made mount of the placenta burial, July 15, 2015. Photo: Saki Tanada.

of babies are expected to take precautions such as staying inside the house around the time of twilight. They are typically encouraged by their older family members to stay inside the house around the time of sunset prayer to reduce the risk of meeting *bakeq*, although they often fail to do so, as we will see. In daily activities such as going to the morning market or visiting houses of relatives and friends, people typically tie a clove of fresh garlic on the child's clothing or bring it in a pocket so that its fragrance discourages *bakeq*'s approach.

While diverse social configurations of the smell of blood are witnessed in and beyond Asia, including problematic restrictions and menstruating women and girls, Reragi villagers' treatment of the smell of vulnerability of birthing women and their children as described here is interesting because they consider it is not only humans but also *bakeq* who smell their surroundings. According to my informants, what smells foul (*mambu*) in the tangible world, including human excrement, women's menstrual blood, and the placenta, is a pleasant fragrance (*senger*) to *bakeq*. Vice versa, what smells good to ordinary people, such as fresh garlic and flowers, is considered a foul odor to them.

With hybrid practices of prayer, mantra, and materiality, the ongoing concern for healing and protection is an important part of both everyday lives, such as assisting children to stop crying, and the most vulnerable times of childbirth, illnesses, and death. As Telle puts it, "People are continually affected by their reciprocal engagement with the various beings, more or less person-like or thing-like, with which they come into contact."[21] The various ways in which Reragi villagers treat things with intense scent to counteract the smell of the human body against *bakeq* substantiate the notion of spiritual landscapes in Southeast Asia, where people do not necessarily regard their interaction with beings other than humans as unusual or supernatural. Rather, their relationships are embedded in mundane routines and material surroundings as a part of the quotidian in life. As we will see in the next section, their ordinary treatments enable peoples' resilient way of relating to the world in the face of change, aspects of which have been largely overlooked by previous studies of childbirth in postcolonial Asia.

Stillbirth and the Slap of *Bakeq*

As Hunter points out in her study of shifting birth settings in the 1990s in East Lombok, for the majority of residents, clinical settings have been the place where "the social context is replaced by a biomedical, cartographic and objective reality in which persons become things."[22] In Southeast Asia, local birth settings have been transformed dramatically under the influence of Western medicine, national and international health policies, and the broader factors of social and economic changes. Under pressure from international health organizations and foreign aid donors, governments in Asia have promoted the medicalization of childbirth to replace traditional practices in a premise that appraises, almost without any doubts, biomedical procedures as superior.[23] As Samuel puts it, discourses of modernity and development "figure the traditional birth attendant as ignorant, dirty, and dangerous, and present clinic or hospital birth as both safer and associated with modernity."[24]

Since the early 2000s, the East Lombok Regency has implemented a program encouraging traditional midwife-healers to take their patients to clinics by promising them a payment for each recommendation that the healers give to the clinics. In the following decade, clinical birth rapidly replaced home birth in Reragi. However, as I conducted my research in the region, I observed several unrecorded midwife-healers continuing their limited treatments in various ways. At their homes, midwife-healers gave pregnant women massages, in which they said they moved the uterus in the right position or made the congested veins fluid to ease abdominal pains; families of birthing mothers brought bottles of water to seek a healing formula from these healers; and the healers also received other patients with various needs related or unrelated to maternal health.

Simultaneously, as people became accustomed to health facilities over time and as clinical and hospital birth became more common in and around Reragi village in the first decade of the twenty-first century, most of my informants in their twenties and thirties turned out to be among the last generation of children born at home. This means that they grew up being used to medical services and seek healthcare programs as a matter of course. For these women, home birth mostly belongs to childhood memories of watching the birth of younger siblings, family members, and neighbors. They grew up taking both medicines from clinics and drugstores as well as healing formulas and protective materials from family members and healers in the neighborhood. During my fieldwork, I witnessed people casually seek both biomedicine and traditional healing as a norm. That shows an overall dramatic contrast to a general anxiety and confusion in the area in the

1990s, when Hay observed that a fear of incompatibility between the two medicines prevented proper treatments and led to fatal consequences.[25]

Despite the spread of clinic and hospital birth, however, pregnancy loss is not a rare occasion in Reragi. In my semistructured interviews with fifty women in Reragi village, I recorded fourteen cases of miscarriage (*nyelok*) and two cases of stillbirth (*lahir mate*) from eleven informants, among which three women experienced miscarriage twice. The following ethnography draws on the pregnancy loss experienced by Ais, my distant relative.[26]

On February 16, 2018, Ais had a stillbirth of her first child. I heard the news on that day from Inaq Nir, my host mother, and the aunt of Ais's mother-in-law. Ais got married to her husband in March 2017 at the age of nineteen after spending a couple years weaving and sewing professionally after graduating from high school. Four months later, her husband had two days of a heavy headache and food craving, which her mother-in-law guessed were symptoms of pregnancy sickness. Ais waited and found her menstruation was delayed, so she took a pregnancy test at home and went to a clinic in the neighboring village where she had a blood test.

Ais reflects that during her pregnancy she experienced nausea, dizziness, tiredness, loss of energy, and food cravings for fruits such as custard apples and pears. From around the third and fourth months of pregnancy, Ais also found herself often sick with fever, headaches, coughs, and a running nose, which she thinks was just fatigue. According to Ais, both the first time she went to the midwife's clinic and the second time she decided to go there to consult her symptoms, the staff prescribed internal medicine, telling her no more than what she already knew—you should rest a lot and never carry anything heavy.

At times she felt sick, and as Ais recalls, she rested for several hours until the pains would go away. When the pains did not ease, her sister-in-law Nana and mother-in-law often guessed she might have been called (*ketemuq*). On several occasions when she experienced headaches, Ais or her family went to their neighbor to identify who was calling, whether it could be the dead or *bakeq*, and she received *jampi* on her head. In the seventh month, her mother-in-law invited orphaned children from the asylum and hosted an event of having them read *Yaseen* (the thirty-sixth passage of the Qur'an) to wish for a healthy birth, which costs less than holding the traditional pregnancy bath (*mandiq besembet*).[27] Ais and her husband also went to an obstetrician in the nearby city in the third and eighth months to check the baby's health and gender by ultrasound. The obstetrician said that the baby was healthy and was due on March 20, 2018.

However, as Ais recalls, "Pains suddenly came," in the middle of the night in February. Her husband immediately took her to the midwife's clinic by motorcycle. Nana and her mother followed them by motorcycle. Ais reflects that the clinic midwife effectively communicated to alleviate shock by telling her the child was "not healthy" (*kurang sehat*) rather than telling her immediately that she was dead. This is a common method of gentle communication in Lombok to keep a shocking event secret when possible until the person who needs to be told the truth is confirmed to be in a safe place and time. As she recalls, Ais repeatedly asked whether she could give birth, to which the midwife replied, "'Yes, possible, if she is born . . . tonight . . . the baby won't be so healthy. If the baby is born two weeks later, if Allah wills it [*Insha'Allah*], the baby would be healthy." Ais continues, "The reality is that we gave birth that night, so yeah, Allah willed another way, like that." Ais added that she did not know whether the child was unhealthy (*kurang sehat*) before birth because it was her first pregnancy. She had noticed that the baby had not moved for three days before the stillbirth, but there was a sudden movement inside as if something was sticking out in the abdomen that night before the pains had come. Ais talked with her husband: "Wow, what's going on?" "Maybe it's her hand!" As Ais put it:

> AIS, speaking fast: [We] thought the baby was healthy, but it turned out not. At the time of the ultrasound before, "*Woo, the baby is healthy [and] active!*" [The doctor] said like that, "*amniotic fluid is good!*"
> UJI, encouraging her to elaborate: Haven't [you] carried heavy things?
> AIS, answering immediately: No, I haven't! I wasn't brave.
> UJI, pausing: Um . . .
> AIS: [The death of the child was] waiting to happen . . .
> UJI: Yeah, [it] wasn't our fortune yet!
> AIS: [It] wasn't our fortune yet!
> AUTHOR, joining hesitantly: Not [blessed] yet?
> AIS, responding to the author: Not blessed yet! Not yet trusted by Allah!

In a tea break after around an hour of listening and observing, I asked Ais if the clinic midwife explained the cause of stillbirth. Feeling the awkwardness of the question myself, I stammered that I had heard that it was not because of the mother that the child was born deceased. Turning to our dialogue:

AUTHOR, hesitantly: Has the midwife, wh-wh-what, explained the cause?

AIS: [It] wasn't explained . . . wasn't explained . . .

AUTHOR, still hesitantly: I ha-ha-have heard from a midwife that it is not because of the mother, if the child, a-a, is born . . .

AIS, taking over: Deceased.

AUTHOR: Deceased. It is not because of the mother.

AIS, taking over: No, no . . . Many times people say, well, in Sasak language, it's "*tepes bakeq*" [the slap of *bakeq*].

AUTHOR: Is that what your family says?

AIS: Yes, more likely people say so. The thing is that, when she [the child] came out, the skin color was like that, like burned? Like blackish, like that . . .

UJI: The slap of *bakeq* . . . Maybe burned . . . because this child . . . that baby died in the abdomen, right? Of course burned, for sure.

AIS: Yeah, right . . . more likely people say so.

UJI: Yeah, maybe depends on beliefs.

AIS: And [it] depends on beliefs.

AUTHOR: Well, do you believe [that] as well?

AIS, making a half-smile: [I] believe here, don't believe there. Both, yeah, [I] don't know!

By remarking on the possibility that stillbirth was the outcome of being slapped by *bakeq*, as "people's words" (*dengan muni*) in a generic sense, Ais sugercoated that those comments were made by her mother-in-law and sister-in-law "reminding" (*perengetin*) Ais that she was often out of the house around sunset. As I mentioned previously, people consider themselves vulnerable outside around twilight, and typically older family members tend to advise pregnant women and postpartum women to stay home particularly to avoid meeting *bakeq*. As Ais states, she regardless missed her natal home and often visited her parents during pregnancy until the night, being "fussy" (*nyelek*) and often disobeying her in-laws even when she was reminded not to go out. As Ais claims, "[I did] not feel at home, wanted [to be] at [my] mother's house because [I was] also lonely here, you know. Over there are nieces and nephews, sisters, many. Like that, there were friends. Look, if here, there are no, just mother[-in-law], sister-in-law, and husband only, like that. So [I was] lonely. [I] felt lonely, so wanted time off, hanging out at mother's house."

From this recollection, we find that her social state of being a young newlywed and her emotional state of "loneliness" entail relating herself to the assemblage of people and the environment. This exemplifies the ways in which social-sensory experiences of vulnerability—the smell of the emotionally isolated and unguarded self—is embodied among the Sasak Muslims in Reragi in connection to the spiritual landscapes of "onion skins." I suggest that ethnographies should take into account such processes of the embodiment of such social-sensory vulnerability, which has been largely dismissed by the previous studies of childbirth in postcolonial Asia, to witness the lived realities of people in the subject of studies. As we will see in the next section, an analytical focus on social-sensory vulnerability enables us to rethink of olfactory experiences as work in progress. This adds a significant point of discussion as we rethink of Asia while challenging the persistent premise in previous approaches to the perception that regards "cultural sensibilities" inherent to people and places.

Learning the Smell of Vulnerability

As I mentioned previously, Telle investigated the smell and disgust provoked by a neighborhood theft in central Lombok, arguing for the significance of olfaction in the Sasak conceptions of the world. As Telle puts it, "The border-transcending quality of smell is both a resource and a problem for the Sasak, who accord odor considerable importance in sensing, and making sense, of the world."[28] Telle argues further, "Of all the senses that orient and connect people to the world, the Sasak give smelling a central place since odor is perceived to give access to what is inner and intrinsic yet hidden from view. Whereas sight gives access to surfaces, smell puts people in sensuous contact with interiors."[29]

While such studies on olfaction in Lombok offer rare insight into the less represented arena of smell and its border-transcending qualities, I am skeptical of the generalization that privileges Sasak olfaction over other senses. Indeed, a lack of accounts of diversity in the ways people in the society engage with senses in personal experiences may not only diminish people's lived realities but also evoke false essentialist imaginations that "cultural sensibilities" are inherent to the society. To understand the matter of olfaction, the body, and vulnerability as lived realities, we must carefully disentangle anthropological interest in the senses from speculation on cultural otherness, which is often predominant.

Ais is only half-committed in an acceptance that it must have been because of *bakeq*, which she had not concerned herself about much before the loss. Such ambivalence toward *bakeq* is also echoed by many other young mothers' indeterminate feelings toward the efficacy of healing formulas, which they suggest "sometimes" (*separo ja*), "maybe" (*sang*) make sense. During my fieldwork, I also heard and witnessed them missing and visiting their natal homes, disobeying their mothers-in-law, and breaking pregnancy taboos. For instance, Ani, my host sister and a hospital nurse, denies the validity of Indigenous pregnancy food restrictions and her mother-in-law's complaints about her breaking the taboos, which her mother-in-law claims induced a difficult birth of her first child. As Ani claims, "Mythos! [Don't] eat squids, wear the towel, sit down in the doorway. So many! So many myths here!" On the other hand, Ani also assertively sought massage therapies and and took *jampi* from healers to reduce abdominal pains during pregnancy. While I asked Ani whether she trusted in her natal mother's frequent allusions to *bakeq*, the dead, and the materiality in dealing with occasions of the child's illnesses and crying, Ani frankly answered "sometimes yes, sometimes no" (*kadang ya, kadang tidak*), exemplifying the similarly hesitant ways young mothers speak of their mixed feelings toward the social-sensory configuration of the spiritual landscapes in which they live.

As Bennett writes in her case study of early motherhood in Lombok, "The reorientation of young mother's lives to new social spaces and networks is a key part of their transition from single daughters to married mothers that sadly results in shrinking social worlds for many. Young mothers express loneliness and longing for the companionship of female peers and their natal families."[30] Comments Ais made about her loneliness after marriage exemplifies a broader picture of the beginning of motherhood among Sasak women in Lombok. In such a context of pregnancy and childbirth, where social, religious, and medical concerns converge, I understood the lived realities of vulnerability that have mostly been taken for granted in previous discussions of childbirth in Asia.

It is worth noting here that as far back as the 1960s, anthropologists have observed the Sasak Muslims referring to fate and predestination as being of considerable significance.[31] Religious fatalism is another long-standing tradition in Lombok in the context of pregnancy and childbirth, and because medicine is no longer new, and there has always been room for speculation, there is an increased chance for conflict between interpretations in the aftermath of pregnancy loss and illnesses. Many informants in Raragi repeatedly claim the matter of fertility is dependent "on the hands of our God" (*izin nenek epenta*) while they engage in rich traditions of infertility care actively performed in the village as in wider regions of Lombok. As a religious teacher puts, "It is Allah who decides [*tentukan*] whatever that happens to our lives, but we can make efforts to pursue fortunes [*riski*]." In Reragi, as in the broader Islamic context, people consider life and death as predestined. The notion of the divine will powerfully and ultimately permeates their responses to life-changing misfortunes, including the death of loved ones.

Significantly, fatalistic remarks at times of death more often acknowledge specific agents beyond human control, which in Ais's case are *bakeq* as social beings, of whom people can be cautious but are ultimately powerless to control what they do. It is worth noting here that Ais's older sister-in-law Nana (who is also Uji's older sister-in-law) experienced a stillbirth in 2010 and a miscarriage in 2012 and shared her story in a separate interview in the absence of Ais.[32] Nana recalls that the nurse told her that her losses were because her "uterus was too weak." On the other hand, Nana's natal mother and mother-in-law took care of Nana and comforted her during the hospitalization and afterward, saying "Maybe she has not wanted to live with us [but] later we would be given a good one [by the God]!" As Nana resolves, "We are patient and always protect our heart. If we don't, then we would go mad. Must be patient. Always be patient. We must be patient."

It is remarkable here that Nana did not adopt the objectifying terms that she received from the nurse to address the pregnancy loss of her sister-in-law. Instead, as Ais describes, Nana and her mother advised her to stay home during the pregnancy and consoled her in the aftermath of the loss that it might have been an offense by *bakeq*. From Ais's side, this process of hearing their words and acknowledging the offense by *bakeq* involves synesthetic experiences externalizing the cause of loss from herself, where the shocking sight of the deceased child, the smell of blood, and her previously unconscious vulnerability are linked together.

As Bennett surmises and my research attests, for both ordinary Sasak women and their healers, "not only is the whole body positioned as the locus for healing, but personally undergoing the bodily experiences involved in reproduction is understood as essential knowledge."[33] While the clinic and hospital birth configure a biomedical system of knowledge adherent to modern visualist objectification and a Cartesian dichotomy of mind and body, people in Reragi actively sense and speak of *bakeq* and other agentive beings other than humans in the aftermath of illnesses and death, by incorporating their own experiences and sensations of vulnerability.

As Ingold discusses, the verbal conventions of a society do not come ready-made, nor are they simply superimposed upon the experience of its members so as to "make sense" of it. Rather, they are continually being forged and reforged in the course of people's efforts to make themselves understood—that is to "make sense" of *themselves* to others. They do this by drawing comparisons between their own sensory practices and experiences and those attributable to their fellows."[34] Indeed, as Ingold writes in a recent critique on visualism in the anthropology of senses, conventional approaches have often led to "the mistaken belief that differences between cultures in the ways people perceive the world around them may be attributed to the relative balance, in each, of a certain sense or senses over others."[35] Such critique, I suggest, is worth serious consideration as we endeavor to take olfaction seriously.

The olfactory interaction with *bakeq* is significant not because it attests to how smell is central to the conception of the world among the Sasak people but because it witnesses how it interoperates with other modalities of vulnerability. As we have seen, social-sensory experiences concerning *bakeq* encompass olfactory, visionary, auditory, and bodily sensations, including not only smell but also sickness, mental distraction, emotional insecurity, horripilation, shuddering, discomfort, belches, and more. Further, the notion of smell of vulnerability here entangles social and emotional states such as loneliness and absent-mindedness. By the divergence between "senses" and "feelings," both described in the same term as *rasa*, people strive to find an abundance of possible meanings in the aftermath of illnesses and death. Where humans, spirits, and materiality affect one another tightly like "onion skins," people in Reragi embrace the peculiarity of the body and vulnerability in the collective process of coping, countering a modern medical objectification and segregation of the body.

Conclusion

In this chapter, I delineated specific examples showing similarities and peculiarities of how people sense their vulnerability in the spiritual landscapes of Lombok. People in Reragi often acknowledge their interaction with *bakeq* spirits, which have acute olfaction, intake food by breathing with the nose and smelling, and often attack pregnant and postpartum women, as well as their children.

As we have seen, people experience synesthetic and unexpected encounters with *bakeq*. Reragi villagers routinely use intense scents such as garlic, flowers, and incense to keep *bakeq* away, considering their understanding of olfactory differences between humans and the other beings—what smells bad to humans smells good to the *bakeq* spirits and vice versa. Various illnesses, occasionally with fatal results, are regarded as the consequence of failing to avoid meeting *bakeq*. Hence, protection against their offense and healing from their attacks necessitates constant and continual relationships among people, spirits, and materiality that are unconfined to medicalized and segregated birth settings. As they cope with the mysteries of illness, envisage their moral responsibilities, and grieve, the Reragi villagers' alertness to agencies other than humans affords them abundant possibilities—making sense of pain and loss by considering the ways it "could be" rather than the way "it is" explained by biomedicine.

Although my research substantiates many of the previous studies in Lombok about the humoral and relational senses of the body-self in the region, it has not been my purpose here to rehash criticisms and practical-technical evaluations of local healthcare conditions. Instead, this chapter aims to divert at least some attention away from clinical concerns. Through delineating people's daily treatments and critical moments of pregnancy loss, I seek to counterbalance the dominant scenario in ethnographies of childbirth in Asia in which women are depicted as underpowered "patients" trapped in sociomedical disorders.

As we have seen in Ais's episode of child loss, people ground their knowledge on the peculiarity of sensory experiences, paradoxically, to bring out an abundance of possible meanings to face illnesses and losses. To this end, the ongoing processes in which people learn to be vulnerable in agentive landscapes offer a critical perspective to recent discussions of olfaction that emphasize its undeniability and pervasiveness. In Lombok, people's allusions to their relationships to *bakeq* and other agentive beings affecting their health generates or regenerates lived efforts to acknowledge differences in how we sense and what we feel. As people strive to relate their own sensations to experiences of others, empathetic efforts to extend themselves to the bodies of others do not necessitate or ground themselves in a relative priority in one sense compared to another. In other words, we do not have to smell what others smell to feel their pain and survive their loss. We should learn by ourselves and from others how to sense and search our surroundings to find personal meanings in any way that can help us cope.

In our four years of married life, I have never been able to identify the presence of *bakeq* around me the way Uji smells them. Nonetheless, his daily reminders have imprinted on me that I have to pay physical attention to the spiritual landscapes, such as by being aware of the deserted spots in the neighborhood. He accepts we cannot feel the same way—not because he recognizes how we smell is different. Instead, Uji performs his treatments with garlic, water, breath, and prayer words because he shares a fundamental understanding among Reragi villagers that it is often impossible for one to share any sensations with others.

Now expecting a child, our everyday health concerns are not limited to various dos and don'ts in medical terms. "Don't zone out!" (*ndek giran momot!*), Uji exclaims every time he catches me staring into space. He gets upset that I am unguarded from spiritual offense when my mind is blank (*kosong pikiran*). That is how I am reminded of my constant relationship with the world of "onion skins" as a pregnant self. And that is how I learn to "smell" and hold on to my body.

Notes

1. This research was supported by the Japan Society for the Promotion of Science and the JSPS Research Fellowships for Young Scientists.

2. Woodward, *Java*, 69.

3. In Reragi, both breath (*napas*) and smell are considered tangible.

4. Telle, "Feeding the Dead," 790.

5. Telle, "Entangled Biographies."

6. Ibid., 199–200.

7. People in Reragi think that pregnancy sickness and cravings derive from the conditions or wishes of the child in the womb and affect both of the child's prospective parents.

8. Hay, "Dying Mothers"; Hay, *Remembering to Live*.

9. Bennett, *Women, Islam and Modernity*; Bennett, "Early Marriage"; Bennett, "Young Sasak Mothers."

10. Hunter, "Sorcery and Science."

11. Alter, "Introduction," 20.

12. Ibid.

13. Allerton, "Introduction"

14. Ibid., 238.

15. Ibid., 24.

16. Ibid., 238.

17. Classen, Howes, and Synnott, *Aroma*.

18. *Ilmu* in the Sasak context mostly refers to agentive secret knowledge potency held by a person, operating beyond the person's control.

19. Previous ethnographies observe humoral thinking of heat and coldness dichotomy in Lombok as in many other regions in Asia. Hay witnesses a treatment "cooling the body to *mul*, the ideal temperature—neither hot nor cold" (Hay, *Remembering to Live*, 177) for an ill child in East Lombok. Telle similarly reports that "'coolness' (*embal*) carries a range of positive connotations for the Sasak" (Telle, "Spirited Places," 294).

20. People in Lombok generally consider those whose *ilmu* is considered as higher than the others and has healing formulas as *belian* or a healer.

21. Telle, "Entangled Biographies," 200.

22. Hunter, "Embracing Modernity," 294.

23. Samuel, "Introduction," 3.

24. Ibid., 7.

25. Hay, "Dying Mothers"; *Remembering to Live*; "Women Standing."

26. Before asking for an interview, I waited two weeks, as recommended by Inaq Nir and Uji, the younger brother-in-law of Ais's sister-in-law Nana.

27. Pregnancy bath (*mandiq besembet*) is typically held in the seventh month of pregnancy. Hay observes events similar to *besumbut* ritual in which "the prospective parents are ritually cleansed, the health of the child is ensured, and the pain and danger

of birth are prevented" (Hay, *Remembering to Live*, 109). I use the term *mandiq besembet*, following the spellings confirmed by my informants in Reragi.

28. Telle, "Smell of Death," 75.

29. Ibid.

30. Bennett, "Young Sasak Mothers," 257.

31. Krulfeld, "Fatalism in Indonesia."

32. The interview took place on September 2, 2017 at Nana's house. Nana, her husband Zas, and Zas's younger brother Uji were present at the interview.

33. Bennett, "Indigenous Healing Knowledge," 9.

34. Ingold, *Perception of Environment*, 285.

35. Ibid., 281.

Bibliography

Allerton, Catherine. "Introduction: Spiritual Landscapes of Southeast Asia." *Anthropological Forum* 19, no. 3 (2009): 235–51.

Alter, Joseph S. "Introduction: The Politics of Culture and Medicine." In *Asian Medicine and Globalization*, edited by Joseph S. Alter, 1–20. Philadelphia: University of Pennsylvania Press, 2005.

Bennett, Linda Rae. "Early Marriage, Adolescent Motherhood and Reproductive Rights for Young Sasak Mothers in Lombok, Eastern Indonesia." *Wacana, Journal of the Humanities of Indonesia* 15 (2014): 20–42.

———. "Indigenous Healing Knowledge and Infertility in Indonesia: Learning About Cultural Safety from Sasak Midwives." *Medical Anthropology* (2016): 1–14.

———. *Women, Islam and Modernity: Single Women, Sexuality and Reproductive Health in Contemporary Indonesia*. London: Routledge Curzon, 2005.

———. "Young Sasak Mothers—'Tidak Manja Lagi': Transitioning from Single Daughter to Young Married Mother in Lombok, Eastern Indonesia." In *Youth Identities and Social Transformations in Modern Indonesia*, edited by Kathryn Robinson,

238–61. Amsterdam: KITLV; Leiden: Brill, 2016b.

Classen, Constance, David Howes, and Anthony Synnott. *Aroma: The Cultural History of Smell*. London: Routledge, 1994.

Hay, Cameron. "Dying Mothers: Maternal Mortality in Rural Indonesia." *Medical Anthropology* 18, no. 3 (1999): 243–79.

———. *Remembering to Live: Illness at The Intersection of Anxiety and Knowledge in Rural Indonesia*. Ann Arbor: University of Michigan Press, 2001.

———. "Women Standing between Life and Death: Fate, Agency, and the Healers of Lombok." In *The Agency of Women in Asia*, edited by L. Parker, 26–61. Singapore: Marshall Cavendish, 2005.

Hunter, Cynthia. "Embracing Modernity: Transformations in Sasak Confinement Practices." In *The Daughters of Hariti: Childbirth and Female Healers in South and Southeast Asia*, edited by Santi Rozario and Geoffrey Samuel, 279–97. London: Routledge, 2002.

———. "Sasak Identity and the Reconstitution of Health: Medical Pluralism in a Lombok Village." PhD diss., University of Newcastle, 1996.

———. "Sorcery and Science as Competing Models of Explanation in a

Sasak Village." In *Healing Powers and Modernity: Traditional Medicine, Shamanism and Science in Asian Societies*, edited by Linda H. Connor and Geoffrey Samuel, 152–70. Westport, CT: Bergin & Garvey, 2001.

———. "Women as Good Citizens: Maternal and Child Health in a Sasak Village." In *Maternity and Reproductive Health in Asian Societies*, edited by Pranee Liamputtong Rice and Lenore Manderson, 295–328. Amsterdam: Harwood Academic, 1996b.

Ingold, Tim. *The Perception of Environment*. London: Routledge, 2000.

Krulfeld, Ruth. "Fatalism in Indonesia: A Comparison of Socio-Religious Types on Lombok." *Anthropological Quarterly* 39, no. 3 (1966): 180–90.

Samuel, Geoffrey. "Introduction: The Daughters of Hariti Today." In *The Daughters of Hariti: Childbirth and Female Healers in South and Southeast Asia*, edited by Santi Rozario and Geoffrey Samuel, 1–33. London: Routledge, 2002.

Telle, Kari. "Entangled Biographies: Rebuilding a Sasak House." *Ethnos* 72, no. 2 (2007): 195–218.

———. "Feeding the Dead: Reformulating Sasak Mortuary Practices." *Bijdragen tot de Taal-, Land- en Volkenkunde* 156, no. 4 (2000): 771–805.

———. "The Smell of Death: Theft, Disgust and Ritual Practice in Central Lombok, Indonesia." *Social Analysis: The International Journal of Social and Cultural Practice* 46, no. 3 (2002): 75–104.

———. "Spirited Places and Ritual Dynamics among Sasak Muslims on Lombok." *Anthropological Forum* 19, no. 3 (2009): 289–306.

Woodward, Mark. *Java, Indonesia and Islam*. Dordrecht: Springer, 2011.

CHAPTER 9

Harnessing the Stenches of Waste

Human Bodies as Olfactory Environmental
Sensors in Contemporary China

Adam Liebman

In December 2014, I joined a hiking trip in a mountainous area not far from Kunming, the capital of Yunnan Province in southwest China. The trip, sponsored by the organization Green Kunming, had the dual purpose of providing an opportunity for outdoor recreation as well as investigating a source of pollution near an area being converted into a nature park. The trail we took followed a swiftly flowing creek up a narrow valley. We started early in the morning, in a cold winter fog, and walked about eight kilometers uphill, against the current of the flowing water, stopping periodically for snacks and water, a picnic lunch, and much socializing. Some of the participants were college students or recent graduates who had yet to secure a clear social class status. The majority of the fifty or so hikers, however, were more definitively middle-class urbanites and were covered head to toe in brightly colored designer outdoor clothing. They carried elaborate backpacks equipped with dozens of straps and pockets for the many items—gadgets, snacks, and water bottles—that the outdoor gear industry promotes as necessities for the well-prepared adventurer.

In the afternoon, we started getting closer to our destination, a location previously staked out by our volunteer guide. He stopped on a high hill with a good viewpoint of the creek below and called for us to gather around him. Then he invited us all to take a deep breath and smell the surroundings. As the group complied, heads tilted and noses pointed in different directions, first taking in the smell and then quickly turning away to try to avoid it. The smell wafted inconsistently along with the swirling wind atop the hill, but when it hit our nostrils, it burned slightly with a pungent combination of rotten eggs, rotting fish, and raw sewage. As lips curled, a feeling of disgust started to pervade the group.

The guide pointed below, directing our attention to an area covered with brownish-gray muck, explaining that this was where pig feces and other waste from an upstream village "swill" pig operation collected. The muck settled into the lowest points in the landscape, filling in areas that would be covered by water once the summer rains returned. At some of the lowest spots, there was water trickling through the muck before it joined the larger creek. This sight, along with the accompanying smells, caused a shift in our perception of the flowing water that we had been following all day. What had appeared to be clean mountain water was tainted by this repulsive excess. We apprehensively walked further toward the village, despite the hikers' affective revulsion.

After converging on a dirt road and following it to the edge of the village, we stopped and gathered as our guide told us that the people living and working here—migrants from elsewhere—purchase large tubs of "swill" (*ganshui* 泔水) that include all leftover food from restaurants and cafeterias in the city, then boil the swill and feed it to pigs. He did not explain any specific concerns with hygiene, disease risks, or toxicity that come with this practice. Instead, he suggested that everyone look around and inspect the village to see for themselves what was going on. As we dispersed into the village, peeking into and snapping photos of pigpens and makeshift houses, most of the workers hid as best they could in their living quarters. A few poked their heads out and watched us with apprehension. The outdoor gear and presence of a white foreigner made it especially clear that we were from a very different world, marking but extending beyond rural-urban and social class distinctions. We were nature lovers and environmental protectors, and we were there to condemn what we took to be a group of immoral and backward environmental polluters. One hiker, overtaken by the sights and pungent stench of so much concentrated swill and pig feces, vomited on the side of a road. After we gathered and walked away from the village, another participant shouted a declaration for all who could hear: "I will never eat meat again!"

No collective effort was made to consider the situation from the perspective of the migrants working to raise the pigs, who had landed in a quite undesirable industry. I felt my anthropological sensibilities acutely as I sympathized with the workers. Not only did they have to handle and live among the stinking leftover and wasted food of urban consumers but also, on this day, they had to feel the piercing scornful gaze and disdain of a group of middle-class nature lovers.

Stench and Imperceptibility in Waste Politics

This chapter examines the shifting role that stench plays in waste politics, especially in relation to reproducing and contesting boundaries that separate who is seen as responsible for and who as unjustly suffering from environmental pollution. The chapter does so through engaging with Green Kunming activities that are focused on pollution monitoring and prevention. Waste in many different forms figures largely in the organization's work, which ranges from monitoring factory emissions to holding workshops on low-waste and low-carbon lifestyles. I describe and analyze how stench helped shape disagreements and tense encounters during two Green Kunming activities. First is the hiking trip described above, which I revisit at the end. Second is a waste incineration plant tour that was unexpectedly shaped by a local resident dramatically narrating how stench and haze from the incinerator affected her life. Broadly, the chapter extends efforts among discard-studies practitioners to take materialities more seriously[1] while demonstrating the productive questions about waste politics that emerge where olfaction and materiality meet.

In the broader research project of which this is a part, I approach "waste politics" as both a field that makes inequality livable (in terms of how environmental and broader social injustices endure) and a field for engagements that can transform common sense assumptions and open new possibilities of social existence.[2] I examine this dynamic field through two intertwined scales. First, the Chinese government's efforts to restrict waste imports since the 2010s has massively influenced recycling programs around the world. This has challenged the narrative that China must learn how to adequately clean up the polluting by-products of its modernization by reframing this pollution as resulting from a way in which China's positioning in the global political-economic structure is neocolonial: in recent decades, as China became the biggest producer of goods for the world, it not only was riddled with the polluting by-products of industrial production but also emerged as a major waste dump for the wealthier world. This presents continuities with past eras of semicolonialization when forced trade relations with foreign powers left the country weakened and with large swaths of the population addicted to opium (i.e., polluted by a potent "junk" of a different kind).

The second scale relates to the moral claims and struggles of rural migrant waste workers, which challenge narratives suggesting they engage in dirty and polluting work because they are inherently dirty and inferior. These narratives took shape within China in part as an extension of the early twentieth-century adoption of Western notions of hygiene and sanitation that were first marked as foreign and modern, and later as urban and elite (thereby marking the "unhygienic" rural Chinese populous as distinctly nonmodern). Challenging this narrative, migrant waste workers and their allies at times point to China's corrupt officials and emergent middle-class mass consumers as the wasteful, immoral, and dirty ones,[3] emphasizing their reliance on unevenly supplied waste-management infrastructure and the labor of rural others to maintain appearances of "hygienic modernity."[4]

This chapter deals with the latter inter-China scale, but from the perspective of a middle-class environmentalism with politics that serves to both reproduce injustices and challenge power. The emergence of environmentalism in China since the 1990s in part can be understood as inevitable responses to severe environmental degradation. At the same time, the globalization of environmentalism has provided some actors on the ground with rhetoric and strategies to be mobilized, remade, and redirected, instead of creating them anew.[5] As is common elsewhere, the environmentalism of privileged classes in China tends to receive more attention as such, leaving the environmental struggles of the poor underrecognized in popular discourse.[6] But it would be a mistake to dismiss middle-class environmentalism as merely reactionary, even though direct forms of "hard confrontation" are uncommon.[7] As the encounters here show, middle-class scrutiny can be directed in different directions, both "down" toward rural migrants and "up" in a way that exposes contradictions in the state's waste-management investments.

These two directions will illustrate how the political potential of stench can be mobilizing in different ways.

In the swill pig village scene above, stench plays a key role in structuring a brief but tense encounter. The encounter involved a clash of lifeworlds that both dehumanized the workers and de-animalized the pigs (reducing them both to the category of mere problematic excess/waste), even though the rural migrant workers are making a living off (and the pigs directly living off) edible food waste from the same kind of middle-class consumers whose scornful gaze suddenly penetrated the village. The stench was otherworldly, encountered as a uniquely pungent by-product of the smells of rural animal husbandry exaggerated by the excesses and contradictions of wealth and urban modernity. But the stench was also reflexively intimate, as recognizable dried red chilies skimmed off the top of slop tubs and discarded into streams of liquid feces served as a stark reminder to the hikers that these pigs' sustenance could very well be their lavish banquet meal leftovers from the day before. In the poetic words of Dominique LaPorte, author of *History of Shit*, "Beautified, ordered, aggrandized, and sublimated, the town opposes itself to the mud of the countryside. But in so doing, it also exposes itself, in the notoriously virginal face of nature, as a place of corruption. 'The bourgeois reeks!' 'He stinks of money!' . . . If the shit that glows in the fields becomes the lasting gold of city streets, the stench of shit lingers where gold sleeps."[8]

LaPorte describes the productive and intertwined waste-value and rural-urban dialectics of capitalist development as played out through stench. "Shit" as pungent fertilizer—or more generally, waste products as potential raw materials for production—are essential substances for the accumulation of value as urban or bourgeois "gold." Containing and removing these substances and their stenches provides the state with a basic justification for existence and extends its reach to modern political control over the human bodies whose excrement becomes profuse in the city.[9] Yet the lingering odors of these substances productively mark processes of value extraction with ruralness and backwardness, as they also cover up the violence, corruption, and exploitation of capital accumulation.

What changes when shit or waste is conceived not just as value potential marked by an offensive odor but also as a crucial pathway for distribution of imperceptible toxins into and between living bodies? Following the swill back to city restaurants, I sat down to speak with a cook at a popular organic restaurant in Kunming. I naively asked if he thought that the restaurant swill trade that feeds so many peri-urban pigs is a good way to reuse food waste, with environmental benefits. He replied that the problem is food waste itself has become so dirty and toxic. First, restaurant swill is full of cigarette butts, used tissues, and other disgusting things. Second, today's food is full of chemical additives, heavy metals, and other impurities.[10] He emphasized that swill pig meat is the cheapest meat on the market, and it does not meet their standards. Yet swill pig meat—which makes up a significant amount China's pork supply, 30 percent of one typical large city—is not easy for consumers to detect by appearance, taste, or smell.[11] Nor does the stench of swill pig production directly correspond with the risks it potentially spreads, including infectious diseases, pathogenic microorganisms, parasites, and toxic heavy metals such as lead and cadmium. While the legally mandated practice of boiling swill before feeding it to pigs eliminates most of these risks, heavy metal accumulations occur regardless.

Overall, the role of stench in waste politics in the industrialized and industrializing world appears to be steadily decreasing as more attention is directed to odorless substances such as DDT, PCBs, and PBDEs—synthetics built out of benzene that have been used in pesticides, paints, plastics, dish detergents, flame retardants, and other products.[12] Another key type of odorless substance, focused on below, are dioxins, primarily formed as by-products of certain industrial activities and from burning fuels or waste. Many of these chemicals have already become so-called legacy contaminants, which circulate through different scales despite efforts to reduce their production, thereby continuing to take root in and disrupt many forms of life.[13] How can individuals sense and bear witness to pollution when it is "too *tiny* or too *vast* to be fully comprehended," or when it transfers "its harmful presence to the future" through toxic lag?[14] The scales and temporalities through which toxic substances become imperceptible has made environmental sensing and monitoring technological apparatuses crucial mediators of struggles to identify and assign responsibility for environmental risks that affect different bodies.[15]

In the context of China's post-Mao reform era of rapid industrial development and capital accumulation (starting in the 1980s), waste politics have also become increasingly focused on risks that are imperceptible to human senses, including those associated with most toxic wastes. This process corresponds with the global expansion of a modern "risk society" in which social struggles increasingly focus on the distribution of (environmental) "bads" and less on the distribution of goods.[16] Given this trend, the broader questions that guide this exploration include the following: (1) Can stench still serve as a productive medium for indirectly sensing environmental risks that are as pervasive as they are unknowable and undetectable? (2) How might we productively conceive of human bodies as themselves environmental sensing technologies, especially in terms of olfactory capacities? (3) How do the particularities of historical, cultural, and political-economic context shape entanglements of the human body as olfactory environmental sensor, taking the Kunming of the 2010s and its position within China and Asia more broadly as testing ground?

China and the Spring City

Before turning to another Green Kunming activity, I briefly address the third question. Stench has come to be a sign for offenses against modern ideals of sanitation—*weisheng* (卫生) in the Chinese context. Prior to the nineteenth century, *weisheng* was associated with Daoist practices related to self-regulating internal vitality through diet, meditation, and medication.[17] However, as China was confronted with imperial forces from the West and Japan in the early twentieth century, national elites undertook a project of "awakening" the Chinese people from national subjugation. *Weisheng* was targeted for reforms and was remade to signify "modern" sanitation practices of the West—something China was imagined to sorely lack. As Warwick Anderson shows, the Western colonial gaze tended to see non-Western bodies as open, polluting, grotesque, and lacking the more contained—yet simultaneously more vulnerable—qualities of Western bodies.[18] As such, within the regime of excremental colonialism, in which the "body's orifices and its products" were used to mark social boundaries, waste politics centered around toilets and feces, with stench as an embodied mediator for judgments made according to Western standards.[19]

Excremental colonialism caused lasting effects in Asia, and its remnants can be felt in the ways that orifices and excrement continue to serve as potent sources for reproducing social boundaries both on the civilizational and municipal scales. Ethnographically, exploring waste politics in relation to stench calls for a close attention to locality. I chose to study waste politics in Kunming not because there are especially large quantities of waste in this city and broader region relative to other parts of China, although there certainly is plenty. The waste in, around, and of Kunming, however, has some unique material qualities, is entangled in unique configurations, and has unique semiotic resonances. In short, it has unique materialities. Here I evoke "materiality" in relation to waste as a way of describing a lens that captures a realm beyond stable material qualities, instead showing how different material qualities and affects of waste are made present and made to matter by the different relations in which it becomes entangled.[20]

An initial reason for conducting research on waste politics in Kunming was the prominence of environmentalism in the city, as I was interested in the shifting values that environmentalism was bringing to existing waste-reutilization practices. This environmentalism manifests in Kunming in two main ways. The first is a commodified environmentalism seen through efforts to market the city as a premier domestic travel destination. Kunming is sold to potential travelers as having a temperate, warm climate year-round, purportedly making it an ideal destination for appreciating a modern, beautiful, and ecological city. When I meet Chinese people outside of Kunming and tell them that I have lived and worked there, they often repeat Kunming's standard branding that it is a "spring city" and a very beautiful place. This notion of beauty comes not only from the climate but also from geophysical features, including forested mountains to the west, north, and east of the city, and the largest lake in Yunnan Province—Lake Dian—to the south. Since the rapid development of a domestic mass tourism market in China beginning in the 1990s, Kunming has been marketed as a modern metropolis built into a beautiful natural landscape and as a gateway for travel adventures to other parts of bioculturally diverse Yunnan Province.

The second primary way that environmentalism manifests in Kunming is through the relatively high numbers of international, domestic, and grassroots environmental NGOs that have operated in the city. Many of these NGOs have focused on biodiversity conservation, as Yunnan Province is an international hotspot for biodiversity. Kunming thus often serves as the base of their operations, but not as a focus of their conservation activities. The activities of these environmental NGOs in broader Yunnan Province have played an instrumental role in enabling Western scholars' claims that there is (or was, in the first two decades of the twenty-first century) an environmental movement in China as a whole.[21] Green Kunming stands out from most other environmental NGOs in Kunming, as they are focused not on biodiversity conservation nor nature protection per se but rather on types of pollution problems that are quite ubiquitous across contemporary China, especially in industrialized and urbanizing areas.

Incineration Tour: Sniffing for Pollution

Smell played an unexpectedly large role in another Green Kunming outing, to investigate a waste incineration plant on a northwestern urban fringe. Participants in the activity gathered at nine o'clock on a hazy Saturday morning at a bus stop not far from the plant, in an old industrial neighborhood. Most of the residential buildings in the neighborhood were affiliated with consumer-goods factories that were no longer functioning or that had been relocated elsewhere, as such local production in Kunming had declined considerably due to competition from factories on China's east and southeast coasts. In the spaces and structures that these factory work units left behind, many scrap-trading and -processing industries had filled their place—serving as crucial nodes where a portion of the waste matter of value that materialized in Kunming was concentrated, sorted, processed, and sold to the factories that could use the materials for production.

The incinerator fit in well with the neighborhood's transformation from a center of industrial production to a center of industrial salvage and waste management. The incinerator was one of five that the city had approved to meet the official goal of processing 100 percent of the city's garbage, and it was the earliest to begin operation—in 2008. The city's massive sanitary landfill in the western district had already been closed earlier that year in the transition toward "full incineration." In subsequent years, however, one landfill remained open to the northeast of the city, in part to provide a place for containing the toxic solid waste leftover from incineration.

After a group of twenty-five students, young professionals, and retirees had arrived and gathered, Green Kunming's founder, Mei Nianshu, introduced the plan for the day. She then began to ask what questions participants had about the incineration plant, which she would later do her best to address with the managers of the plant. A few local residents who were passing by stopped to listen, curious about the intentions of this group. One passerby, who heard that we were here to visit the waste incinerator, interjected that she had many complaints about the plant. Mei welcomed her to say more. The woman then went on to very loudly and agitatedly describe to us her experience living near the incinerator. She stated that the workers' housing complex where she lives is very close to the incineration plant, about one kilometer away. Everyday, there is always a layer of black smoke or dust with a foul odor inside the room, and her son and grandson do not dare to come home to visit. She had called the mayor's hotline many times to report the problem, but nothing had changed. This unplanned encounter with a local resident shaped the tone of the tour. It attuned participants' noses to possible aberrant smells, and their eyes to the haze in the air.

We proceeded to walk down a muddy road toward the incineration plant, then scrambled across four lanes of fast-moving cars, a center divider, and finally four more lanes, until we arrived at the gates of the complex. As we crossed through the gate, participants pointed up to the smoke/steam (precisely which substance was up for debate) that was billowing out of two towering chimneys. We also sniffed for, detected, and discussed a mild but distinct stench, not exactly a smell of the food rot that typically characterizes concentrated garbage but something slightly different—a sharp, sulfuric stench of rotten eggs mixed with burning plastic and other chemicals.

Soon, we were welcomed by the plant manager and chief engineer. They led us on a tour of the main control room, which was filled with computers showing graphical representations of the incineration process and monitoring the status of different stations as the two incineration boilers produced steam. Behind a line of ten or so computers was a row of six digital screens showing cameras that filmed the incineration loading process from different angles. Above them was a long red light-display board showing real-time measurements from the incineration, including the pressure, temperature, and flow of the steam produced. Some of the participants who were versed in relevant technological knowledge engaged with the managers about the numbers, but most of us merely listened in, trying to make some sense of it all. Disappointment soon spread through the group, as it became clear that we would not be seeing the environmental monitoring data that concerned us the most.

After leaving the main control room, we walked to a room directly overlooking the factory floor, where garbage was moving toward the furnace area on a conveyor belt. Two employees were looking for large objects that needed to be broken into pieces before entering the furnace. We were told that a few large pieces of construction waste would also be pulled out and sold for their scrap value. However, participants were surprised to watch as the two employees mostly stood by idly watching the stream move past them, without making any effort to sort out post-consumer paper, plastic, and glass that could also be sold as scrap and recycled. Participants were hoping to see a more professionalized version of the kind of sorting performed on the streets by rural migrant scrap traders, one that matched their aesthetic visions of modern environmental management. In the end, they saw very little sorting at all.

To finish the tour, we were led to a meeting room with a large table surrounded by plenty of chairs for the whole group. Mei took the lead in asking the plant managers over twenty questions from the list she had made earlier, with her own inquiries added in. One theme was the economics and operation of the plant. The managers complained that the city government did not always allocate promised subsidies and, more crucially, that they had approved *too many* incineration plants for the city. They said that the supply of garbage provided by the city's sanitation department was not enough to meet the demands of five incinerators and that, based on the current situation, they worried it would take them over twenty years to recoup their costs and become profitable (fig. 9.1). In this sense, incineration had given unsorted garbage a new materiality as raw materials (i.e., goods, commodities) for the production of electricity and potential generation of value. Even though the managers claimed that they hoped urban residents and the city waste workers could do a better job sorting garbage, especially in terms of keeping out plastics that could be recycled, and thereby minimize the production of dioxins, the fact that there was not enough garbage to satisfy the economic needs of the city's five incineration plants presented a significant contradiction.

The next theme of the discussion was pollution control. The managers spoke about their cooperation with the environmental protection bureau (EPB) in monitoring emissions from smokestacks, including sulfur dioxide, nitrogen oxide, and dust (fig. 9.2). However, most participants wanted to hear about dioxins, which the managers were reluctant to address, beyond describing the activated carbon-scrubbing technologies they used to limit dioxins from being released into the air. Finally, they admitted that dioxin emissions were difficult to monitor. Only a few laboratories in China, including one located in eastern Jiangsu Province, were equipped to test it, they claimed. Thus, they invited the Jiangsu laboratory to help them test for dioxin once per year, which most recently gave them the results of 0.08 nanograms per cubic meter. Bragging a bit, the manager said that not only did this result meet the national standard of 1 nanogram per cubic meter but also met the stricter European standard of 0.1 that would soon be the new standard in China as well.

However, other employees who were asked about the dioxin levels earlier in the tour reported that the levels were 0.3 nanograms per cubic meter. Even though this number also met the current national standard, the discrepancy raised the suspicion of dishonesty. Mei asked if the plant planned to make its emissions data available to the public, in accordance with a new national

Fig. 9.1   Incineration plant monitoring equipment. Photo: Adam Liebman, 2013.

Fig. 9.2   The incinerator's main smokestack. Photo: Adam Liebman, 2013.

environmental law that was set to go into effect the next month (January 2014). The manager said that they planned to install a sign outside of the factory showing emissions data as well as put the data on the company's website. However, regarding dioxin emissions, they said that they still needed to consider whether they would make that data public, since it was only tested once per year.

The last main theme of the discussion was environmental complaints and public participation. Mei asked if the plant had received many complaints from Kunming residents in the last few years. She described the resident that we encountered by the bus stop and how she had major complaints about the smell and smoke from the factory that built up in her home and had caused her children to move elsewhere and refuse to visit. The manager first clarified that complaints are made to the EPB and claimed that the factory fully cooperates with the bureau. He recounted that once, in 2011, a large number of inmates from the nearby prison mysteriously lost consciousness, and they shut down the incineration plant for sixty-four hours while the EPB investigated. But eventually the source of pollution was discovered to be from a small chemical factory located further in the hills. The shutdown cost the factory over 200,000 yuan—a loss for which they were never compensated, he complained.

This victimizing story set the stage for contesting the resident's complaint that we had heard earlier. The manager asked if we smelled any odor on-site, expecting the answer to be no. But Mei and others instead nodded and suggested that they had indeed sensed a bit of a stench. The manager shook his head and said, "There isn't any. Only on rainy or cloudy days there will be a bit." He continued by emphasizing how good the environment is within the factory premises, and he asserted that the supposed "dust" was not from the factory but rather from the third ring road that we had crossed to get to the plant, mentioning that heavy transport trucks kicked up a lot of "yellow dust," which could be seen clearly as the source of the problem from the flowers and grass on the side of the road that were caked with dirt. Following this line of reasoning, the manager suggested that the complaining resident we encountered was simply mistaken. In a report about the trip that Green Kunming published, they described this debate and added the following: "The resident reported black dust [*heihui* 黑灰] not yellow dust [*huanghui* 黄灰]. Although the factory area has a lot of greenery and the environment looks good, the smoke and gas are discharged through a very tall smokestack. It drifts for some distance before coming down, and does not come down right below the smokestack. The good environment of the factory does not mean that the surrounding environment is good. Therefore, our volunteers [the participants of the Green Kunming tour] did not express full approval of the above answer."[22]

After the discussion with the managers concluded, we left the premises with warm goodbyes and vague promises for productive exchanges in the future. The group of participants gathered again outside of the factory gate to summarize what we had learned that day and to discuss lingering pollution concerns both perceptible and imperceptible in nature. Noses were rechecking the air now that we again stood some distance away from the smokestacks. Eyes studied the haze, seeing if it was possible to visually differentiate the yellow dirt kicked up by passing trucks from a more generalized black haze possibly coming down from the incinerator's smokestacks. Dioxins, which have no smell or color, loomed as the biggest concern, but participants nevertheless tried to attain some kind of sensory, experiential grip on the pollution problems.

The Green Kunming report on the trip concludes with some "additional information," focused on both the perceptible and the imperceptible emissions of the incineration plant. First, it summarizes relevant national policies related to regulating the smells of waste incineration. It states that, for dealing with odorous pollutants such as ammonia, hydrogen sulfide, methanethiol, and other odors not taken into consideration in environmental risk assessment results, incineration plants should be sited at an appropriate distance from residential areas and public facilities such as schools and hospitals, no less than 300 meters.[23] The report goes on to include a long quotation from a nationally well-known environmental scientist and critic of incineration, Zhao Zhangyuan.[24] The quoted text from Dr. Zhao begins with an explanation of how the national standard minimum distance was originally 1,000 meters but became reduced little by little as managers complained about how difficult it was to meet the requirement, until the standard of 300 meters was set. Zhao goes on to explain how dioxins accumulate in the body, easily entering fat cells and leading to cancer. According to a study from Japan, he notes, people living within 1.2 kilometers of an incineration plant had twice the rates of cancer compared to people living outside of that radius.

The Green Kunming report concludes that, according to experts, only at a distance of one to two kilometers, or perhaps even further, can it be safe to live near an incinerator. "Safety," in this concluding statement, is primarily gauged in relation to dioxin exposure. Yet, since dioxins are imperceptible to human senses, distance and safety can be at least partially gauged and sensed through the mild stench of other waste-related substances—such as ammonia, hydrogen sulfide, and methanethiol—emanating from the plant. The firsthand sensory experience provided by the Green Kunming tour, through which human bodies were acting as environmental sensors in a way that emphasized distrust in the plant's technological monitoring system, plays a crucial role complementing the data from Dr. Zhao and embracing his critical position on incineration.

Theorizing Garbage and Swill from the (Nonontological) Ground

To productively bring the stories together in another way, here I take a closer look at "swill" and its relation to the broader category in which it generally is placed: municipal solid waste (garbage, trash, rubbish, etc.).

In 2014, I spent a day in Hong Kong with Janet, a native Hong Konger who had previously lived and worked in Kunming, but at the time was the local sales representative of a Swedish company manufacturing food-decomposing machines that quickly convert food waste into soil. The electric machines function by using a patented microorganism mixture. This biotech business venture thus targeted one of the most challenging difficulties of managing municipal solid waste with high post-consumer content: that organic food waste tends to be mixed with nonorganic materials. Organics and nonorganics pollute each other, diminishing their respective reusability and value. Further, organics are responsible for methane emissions that contribute to global warming. Keeping "wet" municipal waste separate from "dry" garbage is thus a top priority of waste reformers around the world, which in turn has created business opportunities for innovative compost technologies.

Although the Swedish company had found some success in Asia by marketing the machines to canteens and high-rise housing estates in Hong Kong, Janet spoke of her difficulties breaking into the mainland Chinese market. In the mainland, there is a lack of specific policies similar to those in Hong Kong that incentivize investment in the machines, and most food waste from restaurants, canteens, and cafeterias is sold daily to swill dealers, who in turn sell to pig farmers. Within the mostly unregulated markets through which swill is traded, it is thus a waste matter of value.

Many people in mainland China were in fact quite interested in the technology, Janet told me, but another difficulty involved the nature of mainland Chinese food waste, which generally has high levels of liquid and oil. The oil suffocates the microbes by limiting their access to oxygen, causing them to die. One of Janet's coworkers also added that food waste is unique in this way: unlike cardboard and plastics, which essentially have standard compositions everywhere, food waste varies regionally and culturally, depending on what and how people eat. The oil content of food waste tended to be particularly high in southwest China, and Janet emphasized that the machines struggled to adequately process the food waste there. The topic of oily food led us into a discussion of the increasing popularity across China and beyond of Sichuan-style hot pot restaurants (which provide a large pot of boiling broth for customers to self-cook meats and vegetables) and whether anyone present in the conversation could handle the thick layer of numbing-spicy (*ma la*) red oil that sits on the top of the broth. We could almost smell the spiciness as we sat in their workshop, along with the damp smell of the forest that surrounded us, mixed with the slightly sweet smell of finished compost.

Ontologically, waste and garbage are ungrounded objects, operating more as "floating signifiers" capable of being filled with almost any content—that is, any type of thing, substance, or body, with any material qualities, can become waste if deemed worthless and disposable in a specific social context.

Only as rejected and discarded things are brought together and grow in quantity, becoming what Joshua Reno calls "mass waste," does municipal solid waste become an object of global comparability and of environmental governance.[25] And only through this process does garbage become quantifiable and emerge to have standard measurable properties such as moisture content and plastic composition. Food waste in the form of *ganshui* (imperfectly translated here as "swill") mimics the characteristics of garbage as mass waste in that it can be composed of a heterogeneous assortment of substances, although mostly restricted within the subcategory of edible organics. A similar heterogeneousness characterizes standard categories for "recycling" such as e-waste, plastic, and metals, whereas the international scrap-trading business is carried out through the use of standardized commodity codes with precise specifications and contamination standards.

The symbolic-structural approach to waste as essentially "matter out of place," and as a by-product of schemes of classification, is limited in what it reveals.[26] Indeed, precisely due to its "floating" semiotic nature and lack of ontological grounding, waste as such is rarely a direct object of inquiry for the environmental sciences. Rather, scientists and engineers deal with specific waste streams and waste-disposal techniques, especially landfilling and incineration, which function as reservoirs for chemical compounds that leak into the air, water, and soil. For example, the accumulation of suspected carcinogens PBDEs in and around landfills is one such common measurable and globally comparable object of scientific inquiry. This chapter takes a cue from the environmental sciences by attending to the particular substances, mostly imperceptible, that occur within and are released by waste streams, and that are of biggest environmental concern. But the chapter also does not leave behind the broad and ontologically ungrounded categories of waste and swill, as it is precisely these categories and sensorial experiences they provide that grounds, or perhaps orients, the human body as olfactory environmental sensor.

What then can we learn from this exercise of dwelling on the role of stench in the two activities that are the basis of this chapter? I return to the hiking tour to sketch out some potential conclusions.

Stench and Bodies

The hiking trip to the swill pig village shocked me, and not only due to unpleasant olfactory inputs. I had not expected to be thrown into a situation where a group of disadvantaged poor were treated with such disrespect, and I was quite uncomfortable with the apex of that particular Green Kunming activity. It initially illustrated to me how middle-class environmentalism in China entails a lens of valuation that greatly differs from the dominant lens of valuation in the socialist Mao era—that is, labor.

In the socialist past, labor was seen and promoted by the state as the key for generating value—by transforming matter into useful products and thereby helping the nation develop. Waste matter also took on special importance in the context of resource scarcity due to its use-value potential.[27] In relation to the realm of pig husbandry, this manifested in campaigns to improve the collection of swill from urban sources to supply more food for pigs raised in villages outside of the city. At the same time, pigs themselves were celebrated by the Communist Party for their ability to serve as both "small-scale, organic fertilizer factories" and "treasure bowls"—that is, providers of delicious, protein-rich meat.[28] Yet this view of swill collection and usage has shifted under the more recently emerged environmentalist lens, through which manual labor and production, while still generative of economic value, are now seen as often generating pollution and threatening the environment. The hard work and thriftiness needed to make good use of food waste related to the capacities of pigs is not only no longer valued by the state and new middle class, it is increasingly despised.

Pigs that are fed *ganshui*—and the meat that they become after being slaughtered—have also experienced a major revaluation. Kunming locals told me that in the past "swill pigs" were considered to have the most flavorful meat and were thus highly prized. But the proliferation of unsafe food in an industrializing food system, marred and contaminated by agrochemical residues and harmful additives and substitutes, means that swill pigs are increasingly seen by middle-class consumers as sites where food safety risks accumulate, becoming more concentrated, yet remaining difficult to detect. Thus, recent contestations over swill pigs, and the shifting status of swill pig meat, highlight changing valuations of bodies, both human and livestock. In the socialist era, human bodies were valued for their capacity to perform productive labor for the state, while livestock was valued for possessing an inherent productivity that could be activated by the thrift and hard work of humans. However, through recent concerns with food safety, and the risks of *ganshui* in particular, both types of bodies are being reimagined and reclassified in terms of how they can function as potential agents and pathways for spreading harmful substances that proliferate amid an industrializing food system and inadequate food safety regulations.

Later, as I reflected on both the hiking trip and the incineration tour, I began to think more about the olfactory ways in which pollution and toxicity in Kunming were sensed and served to reproduce social boundaries in urban and peri-urban life. Although the substances that constitute these problems and health risks are most often imperceptible, widespread concern over such risks can lead middle-class urban dwellers to attune their noses to atmospheric anomalies, which in turn can generate revulsion, avoidance, and even contestation. Green Kunming thus takes a two-sided approach to environmental pollution. On the one hand, the staff and volunteers use environmental monitoring technologies to collect numerical data. For example, they regularly perform tests on surface water for ammonia and "chemical oxygen demand," which quantify the levels of oxygen consuming organics in water (mostly coming from urine and fecal content) that kill fish and cause algae blooms.

Yet, on the other hand, Green Kunming operates with an inherent awareness that such efforts to quantify pollution are often insufficient for achieving their mission of "using the *participation of the masses* and policy advocacy techniques to solve environmental problems in our local valley" (as stated on their official social media accounts [emphasis added]).[29] Numerical data, which can be abstract, cold, and only partially comprehensible to laypeople, is therefore often an incomplete motivator. Further, such data is open to contestation by entities who strategically speak from the side of scientific method and its institutionalized procedures for verification.[30] Thus, Green Kunming also harnesses opportunities for middle-class Kunming residents to experience pollution with their senses, as they guide them to spaces where they can take in whatever stenches can potentially be linked to pollution and to act as they see fit.

The lack of ontological grounding of waste (both swill and municipal solid waste) thus does not limit the capacity of its multiple materialities but rather is a characteristic that shapes and expands its affective and political potential. As such, the work of Green Kunming illustrates how the stenches of waste, as well as the capacity for human bodies to serve as olfactory environmental sensors, can be harnessed to help bring about heightened awareness of and contestation over more ontologically grounded, yet less perceptible, waste-related pollutants, such as carcinogenic dioxins.

Notes

1. Liboiron, "What and the Why of Discard Studies."
2. Mouffe, *On the Political*; Rancière, *Disagreement*; de la Cadena, "Indigenous Cosmopolitics."
3. Goldstein, "Remains of the Everyday."
4. Rogaski, *Hygienic Modernity*; Lai, *Hygiene, Sociality, and Culture*, 74–75.
5. Weller, *Discovering Nature*; Hathaway, *Environmental Winds*.
6. Guha, *Environmentalism*.
7. Wang and Wang, "Soft Confrontation."
8. LaPorte, *History of Shit*, 39.
9. Ibid.
10. Yan, "Food Safety," 705–29.
11. Xu, "Foshan."
12. Altman, "Benzene Tree."
13. Altman, "Time-Bombing"; Armiero and Fava, "Of Humans, Sheep, and Dioxin," 67–82.
14. Davies, "Introduction to Part II," 120.
15. Ibid.
16. Beck, *Risk Society*.
17. Rogaski, *Hygienic Modernity*.
18. Anderson, "Excremental Colonialism."
19. Ibid., 643.
20. Hawkins, "Plastic Materialities."
21. See Hathaway, *Environmental Winds*.
22. "Uncovering All Kinds of Problems."
23. See Zhang, "Rational Resistance" on homeowners' struggles against incineration.
24. Johnson, Lora-Wainwright, and Lu, "Quest for Environmental Justice."
25. Reno, *Waste Away*.
26. Liboiron, "Waste."
27. Goldstein, "Remains of the Everyday"; Liebman "Reconfiguring Chinese Natures."
28. Schmalzer, *Red Revolution, Green Revolution*.
29. See Green Kunming's WeChat public account, available online at https://mp.weixin .qq.com/s/uic-pjVyunz-UWUxSxsrsg. Accessed January 25, 2023.
30. Davies and Mah, *Toxic Truths*.

Bibliography

Altman, Rebecca. "How the Benzene Tree Polluted the World." *The Atlantic*, October 4, 2017. https://www.theat lantic.com/science/archive/2017/10 /benzene-tree-organic-compounds /530655/.

———. "Time-Bombing the Future." *Aeon*, January 2, 2019. https://aeon.co/ essays/how-20th-century-synthetics -altered-the-very-fabric-of-us-all.

Anderson, Warwick. "Excremental Colonial ism: Public Health and the Poetics of Pollution." *Critical Inquiry* 21, no. 3 (1995): 640–69.

Beck, Ulrich. *Risk Society: Towards a New Modernity*. Sage, 1992.

Cadena, Marisol de la. "Indigenous Cosmopolitics in the Andes: Concep tual Reflections Beyond Politics Beyond Politics as Usual." *Cultural Anthropology* 25, no. 2 (2010): 334–70.

Davies, Thom. "Introduction to Part II." In *Toxic Truths: Environmental Justice and Citizen Science in a Post-Truth Age*, edited by Thom Davies and Alice Mah, 119–23. Manchester: Manches ter University Press, 2020.

Davies, Thom, and Alice Mah. *Toxic Truths: Environmental Justice and Citizen Science in a Post-Truth Age*. Manches ter: Manchester University Press, 2020.

Goldstein, Joshua. "The Remains of the Everyday: One Hundred Years of Recycling in Beijing." In *Everyday Modernity in China*, edited by Made leine Yue Dong and Joshua Goldstein, 260–302. Seattle: University of Wash ington Press, 2006.

Guha, Ramachandra. *Environmentalism: A Global History*. New York: Longman, 2000.

Hathaway, Michael. *Environmental Winds: Making the Global in Southwest China*. Berkeley: University of Cali fornia Press, 2013.

Hawkins, Gay. "Plastic Materialities." In *Political Matter: Technoscience, Democracy, and Public Life*, edited by

Bruce Braun and Sarah J. Whatmore, 119–38. Minneapolis: University of Minnesota Press, 2010.

Johnson, Thomas, Anna Lora-Wainwright, and Jixia Lu, "The Quest for Environmental Justice in China: Citizen Participation and the Rural-Urban Network Against Panguanying's Waste Incinerator." *Sustainability Science* 13 (2018): 733–46.

Lai, Lili. *Hygiene, Sociality, and Culture in Contemporary Rural China.* Amsterdam: Amsterdam University Press, 2016.

La Porte, Dominique. *History of Shit.* 1978. Cambridge, MA: MIT Press, 2000.

Liboiron, Max. "Waste Is Not 'Matter Out of Place.'" *Discard Studies*, September 9, 2019. https://discardstudies.com/2019/09/09/waste-is-not-matter-out-of-place/.

———. "The What and the Why of Discard Studies." *Discard Studies*, January 1, 2018. https://discardstudies.com/2018/09/01/the-what-and-the-why-of-discard-studies/.

Liebman, Adam. "Reconfiguring Chinese Natures: Frugality and Waste Reutilization in Mao Era Urban China." *Critical Asian Studies* 51, no. 4 (2019): 537–57.

Marco, Armiero, and Anna Fava. "Of Humans, Sheep, and Dioxin: A History of Contamination and Transformation in Acerra, Italy." *Capitalism Nature Socialism* 27, no. 2 (2016): 67–82.

Mouffe, Chantal. *On the Political.* New York: Routledge, 2000.

Rancière, Jacques. *Disagreement: Politics and Philosophy.* Minneapolis: University of Minnesota Press, 1999.

Reno, Joshua. *Waste Away: Working and Living with a North American Landfill.* Berkeley: University of California Press, 2016.

Rogaski, Ruth. *Hygienic Modernity: Meanings of Health and Disease in Treaty-Port China.* Berkeley: University of California Press, 2004.

Schmalzer, Sigrid. *Red Revolution, Green Revolution: Scientific Farming in Socialist China.* Chicago: Chicago University Press, 2016.

"Uncovering All Kinds of Problems with Waste Incineration on December 14." Green Kunming online report, December 19, 2013. Archived by the author; no longer available online.

Wang, Xinhong, and Yuanni Wang. "Soft Confrontation: Strategic Actions of an Environmental Organization in China." In *Toxic Truths: Environmental Justice and Citizen Science in a Post-Truth Age*, edited by Thom Davies and Alice Mah, 220–34. Manchester: Manchester University Press, 2020.

Weller, Robert. *Discovering Nature: Globalization and Environmental Culture in China and Taiwan.* Cambridge: Cambridge University Press, 2006.

Xu, Jiajia. "Foshan: 7000 Swill Pigs in a Hidden Shanty Town." *China Economy Net*, March 20, 2013. http://district.ce.cn/newarea/roll/201303/21/t20130321_24219951.shtml.

Yan, Yunxiang. "Food Safety and Social Risk in Contemporary China." *Journal of Asian Studies* 71, no. 3 (2012): 705–29.

Zhang, Amy. "Rational Resistance: Homeowner Contention Against Waste Incineration in Guangzhou." *China Perspectives* no. 2 (2014): 45–52.

CHAPTER 10

The Smell of a Corpse

Olfactory Culture in a Singaporean Funeral Parlor

Ruth E. Toulson

I grew up in a funeral parlor in the northwest of England. My father was the town undertaker. But the first time I smelled death was not in the viewing room, the "Chapel of Rest," which smelled of furniture polish, dust, and stagnant water. Nor was it in the mortuary out back, a cramped, windowless room, which smelled only of formalin and bleach. The first time I smelled death was on Saddleworth Moor in the Dark Peak. It was April 1985 and I was eight years old.

My father, mother, brother, and I had taken the bus to Dovestones Reservoir and set out up the steep path toward Pots and Pans monument, the cenotaph for Saddleworth's war dead, high on the moor. My father insisted that we hike each weekend, no matter the weather, to "blow away the cobwebs." It is for good reason that the Peak District is described as "the lungs of the industrial north."[1] To hike was to escape from our mill town in the valley, where the air was thick with soot and tobacco. From the window of my box room upstairs in the funeral home, my view was of the looming slag heap of the spent coal mine and behind it the hulking mass of the Benson and Hedges's cigarette factory, which had replaced the colliery as the main employer of the town's men. But I would raise my eyes and look beyond this to the freedom of the heathered moor.

We were not a family to discuss politics. It was one of a long list of things not to be brought up at the dinner table. I learned early that what happened in the voting booth was as unmentionable as the events of the bedroom or the confessional. But I understood even then that to hike on the moor was a political act. The Dark Peak was the site of the Kinder Scout Trespass. In 1932, about five hundred men and women had taken to the hills in defiance of the law. For my father to walk here was to exert the working man's right to roam, to give the proverbial middle finger to the wealthy landowner who would prefer his land empty for his grouse shoot or his fox hunt.

"Do Not Swim" signs had been erected at the reservoir's entrance. They had not been there the week before. My father remarked that a child had drowned over the Easter weekend, his foot trapped in an abandoned shopping cart hidden deep beneath the water's surface. "Took the police divers four days to find him, the poor sod. Definitely a closed-casket job."

"His poor mother. Poor woman. Who got the body? The Co-op?" my mother asked. The Co-Operative Funeral Business was the largest in town, rival to our small family firm.

"Yes, Glossop Co-op. They wouldn't have taken anything for it. Can't make money off the death of a kiddie."

I ran ahead, not wanting to think about drowning boys. The air was ripe with the scent of sun-warmed peat, cut through by the herbaceous note of crushed heather beneath my feet. Then suddenly, the smell I was soon to label death.

Overwhelming, both fetid and sweet.

I turned to follow the smell, more curious than repelled, jumping from millstone grit boulder to millstone grit boulder up a narrow stream. There, caught behind a large rock, was a ewe on her back, stiff-legged and bloated, her wool a fleece of flies. The ewe's vulva was turned toward me, swollen, the grievous purple of a bruise, already studded with maggots like pins. And from her emerged her half-born lamb, ruddy-bodied, still bound in the liquid universe of its placenta. The stench of death, of blood and of terror, was undercut with the smell of lanolin from her fleece, caught there between the rocks. It was a well of scent almost too thick to breathe in. On a stone, a crow cocked its head, as if curious as to why I was there, before it went back to pecking at the ewe's dumb eye.

Why begin here? The context for this chapter, after all, is not my childhood town, nor my father's funeral business, but Singapore. Since 2003, I have conducted ethnographic fieldwork in this Southeast Asian city-state, in funeral homes, cemeteries, and crematoria, trying to understand what it means to die and to grieve here. I begin with the stench of death on the moor because it raises a question: Why is the smell of a corpse quite so troubling? In Singapore, the possibility that a dead body might smell disturbs to the extent that, nearly without exception, bodies are embalmed. This happens despite the fact that they are, again nearly without exception, cremated only a few days later. As I will describe, embalming is skilled, time-consuming work. It is also peculiar, unnecessary work, always on the verge of failing. After all, the body in the mortuary would, given the chance, smell the same as the dead ewe, the same as the half-born stillborn lamb. Its smell is indistinguishable from the deer carcass at the side of the road, from the green-tinged lamb chop left too long at the back of the refrigerator, from the compost heap too infrequently turned. The corpse, without the mortician's intervention, smells like the overcrowded yard of a factory farm, like the rubbish bin at the height of summer. But this stench is purposefully excluded from the dense olfactory culture of a Singaporean Chinese funeral, where the air is thick with incense, sandalwood, and smoke, each put to particular ritual work.[2] My task here is to understand the reasons for this exclusion.

The answer to the question "Why are Singaporean morticians quite so determined that their corpses should not smell?" might seem so obvious that it is peculiar to ask it. My disgust that day on the moor was visceral. I gagged. My stomach turned. It would be easy for the reader to presume that, in beginning on the moor, I am suggesting that there is something shared about disgust at the smell of a corpse, a commonality that links northern England more than three decades ago with contemporary Singapore. And that, therefore, there is something innate and therefore universal about responses to smell, particularly to those that prompt revulsion. My argument, however, is quite the opposite.

There are, of course, multiple points of overlap between cultures. My father, an English undertaker of the old school, would share a Singaporean mortician's resolution that a corpse should not smell. His concern for the drowned boy on the moor was that the child's parents would be denied the comfort of viewing their son in an open casket. "Suitable to view" also meant suitable to smell. Indeed, there are remarkably few cultures that make ritual use of the smell of a rotting corpse. (See, for example, Beth Conklin's careful work on mortuary cannibalism in Amazonia.)[3] But there is something particularly Singaporean here, too, something particular to Singapore's distinctive olfactory culture, a culture constructed and maintained through complex social work.

Ideas about how a funeral should smell reveal tensions at the heart of sensory moral economies, a term I borrow from Kelvin Low's recent article examining the nascent literature theorizing sensory cultures in Asia.[4] What I hope will become clear is that "not smelling"—something possible only because of the laborious and highly skilled work of morticians—is also a social act, one that signals the nature of the sociality that continues to exist between the living and the dead. As I will describe, Singaporean Chinese funerals offer an olfactory overload, so that which is preventing from smelling matters every bit as much as that which is encouraged to smell. Both smelling and the purposeful absence of smell are guided by the same principles.

At the heart of this paper, too, is an examination of a particular quality of smells, their ability to leak and the struggle to contain them. A corpse that smells is a corpse that leaks. Any mortician will tell you that. Why is leakiness so problematic here? Because, I argue, Singapore (like multiple societies but it is particularly central here) is a society built upon the very idea of containment. But containment, again, like the idea that corpses could be prevented from smelling, is an impossibility, a process always in the act of failing. I begin with a brief history of attempts to control smells in colonial and early postcolonial Singapore.

Odors of the Colonial and Postcolonial Other

There is a history of Singapore that could be told through smells and attempts to contain them, part of a broader body of scholarship that understands colonialism as an intimate sensory interface. One can read for smells, for example, in Brenda Yeoh's *Contesting Space in Colonial Singapore: Power Relations and the Urban Built Environment*, with its accounts of overcrowded housing, overflowing cesspools, and heaping night soil.[5] It is easy to imagine the smell as one reads James Warren's *Rickshaw Collie: A People's History of Singapore, 1880–1940*, with its detailed documentation of coroner's court reports, that tell of the noisomeness of overcrowded coolie living quarters,

the sickly tang of the opium den—brown sugar and liquorish, cut with vine-
gar—and the fetid funk of the abandoned corpse.

For the British colonizer, the stench and ripeness of the tropics was an
afront to the senses, causing European women to faint and "civilized" men
to fall ill.[6] Indeed, early attempts to prevent the spread of disease in the colonies, such as the creation of the Schools of Tropical Medicine in Liverpool
(1898) and London (1899) were "but one of many means . . . for curtail-
ing the toll of our fellow citizens in those insalubrious, over-seas territories
of the empire."[7] Disease theories in the nineteenth century were largely
miasmatic: experts believed that disease spread through the escape of putrid
vapors, and therefore, disease was imagined as rooted in geography, in the
urban environment, in the "disposition of various quarters, their humidity
and exposure, the ventilation of the city as a whole, its sewage and drainage systems, the siting of abattoirs and cemeteries, [and] the density of the
population."[8] Control of the environment was the solution to disease.

While colonized workers lived in overcrowded slum dwellings that edged
Singapore's port, colonial officials lived purposefully upwind. Their "Tubor-
bethan" bungalows, the "black and whites," were set high in Singapore's
inland leafy center. The bungalows were a triumph of colonial design: their
wide verandas and deep eaves keeping out the sun, their terracotta-tiled
floors retaining the night's coolness, and their steep roofs channeling stale
air out of the house.[9] Still, there were times when colonizers could not avoid
the malodor of "the other." Such was the pungency of the coolie that it was
recommended that women carry a scented handkerchief to hold to their noses
if they were to ride in a rickshaw.[10] The introduction of electrically powered
fans in the grand Raffles' Hotel was greeted with considerable excitement,
sparing diners the stink of the armpit of the servant who had previously
wielded the fan.[11] There is far less in the literature on what the colonized
thought of the smell of the colonizer. (But see McLagan on "butter-stinkers"
as a historical term used by Japanese to refer to Europeans based on their
distinctive smell[12] and Margaret Weiner's description of the Balinese view
of the colonizing Dutch as "milky."[13])

In contrast to the airy "black and whites," Singapore's Asian communities
lived in overcrowded conditions that could not help but stink. In more ways
than one, this was a city built on the principle of divide and rule, separated
into a Chinatown, a Little India, an Arab Street, and a Malay Kampong—
each area kept separate from the "good class European housing." It was a
city built on separation of those who smelled differently. Yeoh, for example,

drawing on Simpson's 1907 *Report on the Sanitary Conditions of Singapore*, describes the tenements of Sago Lane, residences of Chinese rickshaw drivers and hawkers. Each floor was divided into multiple cubicles, "windowless rooms, dark and cheerless, receiving neither light nor air direct from the outside."[14] Much of each space was taken up by the occupants' goods, "Professor Simpson discovered a general goods hawker in one of the cubicles sleeping on a bench 18 inches below a shelf containing boots, shoes, pipes, whistles, soaps, towels, lamps, and tooth powder, whilst in another cubicle, a fruit and food hawker shared his tiny space with apples, eggs, preserved pig, mangoes (many overripe and rotten), and other kinds of fruit," all this occurring amid "immense quantities of rubbish and filth."[15]

The residents of these overcrowded dwelling houses shared brick-lined privies that drained into cesspools, constructed in such a way that allowed "the escape of noxious gases from their filth encrusted interiors into the dwelling rooms of the houses."[16] Feces and urine were emptied into pails then collected by Chinese syndicates who organized the transfer of night soil to market gardens and plantations on the edge of town. The smell of the filth was regarded as as much a danger as the filth itself. The author of an 1896 "Report on the Pollution of the Singapore River" noted, "Privies and privy drainage, with their respective stinkings and soakings, and the pollution of air and water which are thus produced have in innumerable instances been the apparent causes of outbreaks of enteric fever. . . . Filth and disease are apparently enabled to run their course, with successive inoculations from man to man, by the instrumentality of molecules of excrement, which man's carelessness lets mingle in his air and food and in drink."[17]

It was not merely that these foul-smelling methods of dealing with filth threatened the health and therefore the productivity of the coolie; "it infused the public environment with the pungent smells of disease."[18] In 1896, *The Straits Times* described Singapore's market gardens as "vegetable horrors, reeking with decomposed excreta and totally unregulated by the Municipality. . . . There are many roads in Singapore that, in themselves, are picturesque and convenient, and very suitable for the erection of good European houses, but they are rendered undesirable, if not positively unhealthy, by the fact that market gardens, plentifully manured with extremely evil-smelling manure, abut upon those roads."[19]

Disease was identified by smell, too. Cholera, for example, left a sweetness about the body. Tuberculosis made the breath foul and left the taint of stale beer on the skin. The odor of typhoid fever was that of baked bread, while yellow fever made one stink of the butcher's shop. Diphtheria left the breath sweetish and putrid, smallpox, sweetish and pungent. And it was not only the living who made a stink. Early discussions over the need to clear Chinese cemeteries were grounded in the fact that passersby could smell the improperly buried dead and that these smells were a danger to the living.[20] "'All smell is disease,' Edwin Chadwick told a British parliamentary inquiry, and nothing smelled worse than a putrefying corpse. One could be more precise: specific diseases were blamed on the dead. Typhus fever owed its origins to 'the escape of putrid vapors,' and 'overcrowded burying grounds would supply such effluvia most abundantly' testified the eminent physician W. F. Chambers."[21] It is clear that these examples of rejection and regulation are not merely about imposing a colonial sensory script on colonized subject—"the progressive narrative of modernity where otherness is connoted through filth and stench that requires eradication from the viewpoint of colonizers"—but also about marking difference in moments of unavoidable intimacy. Centrally, they display power relations at work.[22]

Following independence, the new state's urgent concern was to solve these problems made evident by stench, problems of water supply and sewage disposal, of disease, of improper burial and slum housing. The state began to construct HDB apartment blocks.[23] These were initially emergency units built quickly to replace the tuberculosis-teaming "Chinatown," the overcrowded "Little India," and the malarial kampong. But the destruction and replacement of these cities-within-the-city did not bring an end to the colonizer's vision of a city kept peaceful, as it was divided on racial lines. Instead, it miniaturized it, again creating racial harmony via containment. Each floor in each HDB apartment block is assigned on principles of racial balance—following the composition of the nation, ideally each apartment floor will have seven Singaporean Chinese families, two Malay, and one Indian—in order to avoid the re-creation of ethnic enclaves. But principles of separation and containment continue to be central to Singapore's much vaulted ethnic harmony and not merely in the frequently tiny separate units that comprise each HDB block. Even the HDB void deck—the empty area in the ground floor of most HDB tower blocks, a space available for community events, often viewed as the pinnacle of Singapore's multiethnic engineering—is based on the false hope of containment. Its blank concrete form, entirely unadorned, makes it a suitable setting for both a Chinese funeral and a Malay wedding. But conflicts emerge when smells leak out, when Malay wedding guests smell Chinese funeral joss. Harmony rests on the (always impossible) erasure of the prior presence of the other.

Even the legislation that tightly controls the construction of funeral parlors, which cluster together in three main parts of the island, hidden away in industrial estates in Sin Ming, Geyland Bahru, and Lavender Street, is built on concern for the senses. No funeral business may exist within 400 meters of any dwelling place, precisely so that no one need look down from their HDB balcony and see a body arriving on a gurney or departing in a casket, or hear the discordant cacophony of funeral music, or have their lungs filled with smoke and joss. The most troublesome of these disturbances are smell and noise, precisely because they are so difficult to contain. After all, one can close one's eyes or turn one's head far more easily than one can stop smelling or hearing (blocking one's ears only does so much). It is notable that, side by side with funeral parlors are other dirty businesses, such as laundromats and car-repair shops. The problem with these businesses is also their smell and noise, rather than that they are distressing to view.

There is much more that could be written on Singaporean smells, both in the colonial period and after independence. I share this brief history here for two reasons. First, to direct you to the work of Yeoh who, at far greater length, articulates Singapore's particular history of governmental rule through the control of the urban form. And second, to begin to articulate an argument that becomes pivotal later in this chapter: centrally, that Singapore—both historically and today—is a place whose governance rests on the (im)possibility of containment. Something that smells, in its leaky nature, challenges. And, as by definition, a corpse that smells is a corpse that leaks, we begin to understand why smelling corpses might trouble.

The Olfactory Culture of a Singaporean Chinese Funeral

Leave behind Singapore's history for the moment, a history built on the attempted containment of difference, that difference often signaled by smell, and turn to the olfactory particularities of a Singaporean Chinese funeral. The corpse's lack of smell—or to be more accurate, the fact that the smell of the decaying corpse is not part of ritual performance, that the only acceptable way for a corpse to smell is of nothing at all—is striking because Chinese funeral ritual is marked by olfactory overstimulation. A "traditional" Chinese funeral in Singapore is a heady challenge to the senses.[24] It is an excess of texture and color, of heat and noise, of smoke and incense, of movement and emotion. While mourners wear muted tones, generally casual clothing in white, navy, or dark green—or, for the most "old-fashioned" of mourners, gowns and hoods of dull sackcloth and hemp—the corpse is dressed in layers of vividly colored silk, perhaps with a glittering pearl attached to its lip. Within the caskets—traditionally glazed with crimson shellac and lettered with gold leaf, although most now are varnished wooden veneer engraved with gold and lined with white silk—the body is draped in a saffron blanket embroidered with red, then nearly buried in heaps of folded metallic prayer paper. The space for the funeral, whether within a purpose-made funeral parlor or in the HDB void deck, is demarcated with billowing drapes of silk, in saffron to signify that the rites performed are Buddhist, bright blue for Daoist, or white for Christian. Altars are crowded with statues of the Buddha and with bowls of fruit, flowers, tea lights, and joss. In "traditional funerals," paper funeral goods, houses, cars, and bank safes, crafted in vivid florescent crepe paper, necessities for an afterlife understood as a material world, are piled outside the funeral venue, then, on the last night, set alight, filling the air with sparks and ash.

During the "hot and noisy" nights of the funeral, saffron-clad monks lead the mourning party in circles round the coffin. Daoist officiants chant and leap over buckets of hot coals. Late in the night, at the point of exhaustion, women sob loudly—partly weeping, partly speaking—and men try to choke back their tears. At times, daughters and daughters-in-law fall onto the casket, faces pressed to the plastic guard that is inserted after the third day to seal in the corpse. The plastic guard ensures that the body will not be swarmed by coffin flies, which are drawn to the merest whiff of decay, and also serves to keep any odors in. Relatives pull the women back, wrestling with their unsteady weight to the point that they sometimes fall, a tangle of bodies on the floor beside the casket, grief beyond control. When led away from the casket, a woman, perhaps the widow, will faint and fall to the ground, so predictably that the funeral director's men wait to rush in with a chair. The air is filled with chanting, the sounding of cymbals, and wailed grief.

At dawn on the final day of the funeral, the casket is placed in the hearse and conveyed to the crematorium or, far more rarely as burial is highly discouraged in land-scarce Singapore, to the cemetery. In front of the hearse, a brass band sometimes leads the parade, its discordant music designed to scare ghosts who might linger. Behind the hearse, the family walk in stocking feet, making visible again that grief is pain. But once the family arrive at the crematorium, there is a change of tone, signaled again by changes in color, light, smell, and noise. Tears are purposefully stemmed when, immediately after the casket disappears behind the screen, the family is led from the windowless cremation room, down the stairs, and into a sun-flooded reception area. There, the funeral director's workers will have set up a light buffet: elegantly glazed French pastries and savory hors d'oeuvres, each one no more than a mouthful, and cartons of iced green tea. The atmosphere changes instantly. Children are no longer hushed; they run in the bright corridor, whooping. The attendees mingle, conversations now punctuated with laughter unthinkable mere minutes ago. In part, this shift of attention is possible because the body is no longer present and thus no longer the unavoidable point of focus. Only the photograph of the deceased remains, set on a side table in a flower-filled basket. But the incense that had been lit before it for the length of the funeral, making visible the presence of the dead, is now extinguished. These rooms at Mandai Crematorium are the first places since the death that do not smell of joss or of smoke and sweat.

At the doors, as guests leave, the funeral company's female workers hand out packets of tissues, bound with a red string, and sprinkle the guests' hands with water in which chrysanthemum blossoms float, again signaling in sensory form that the ritual has come to an end. Both the red string and the water have continuity with early ritual practices, but in this iteration, it is not clear whether the pouring of water is an acknowledgment of the danger of contact with a polluting corpse or closure via cleansing or whether the red thread-bound tissues are a sign of pollution dispersed or a departing gift.

Look closely and there is more to all this than mere sensory excess. Each element—color, light, noise, and smell—is carefully orchestrated, put to work to structure ritual. This is not a surprise. Classen, Howes, and Synnott, writing on the power of smell within ritual, note that "The boundary-crossing nature of smell . . . is often made use of to help the participants in a rite of passage—for example, a funeral—cross over from one stage to the next: they are symbolically wafted along with the olfactory flow."[25] If Chinese funeral ritual is an act of making and breaking ties,[26] shifts in light, sound, sensation, and smell signal the transforming relationship between the living and the dead. They facilitate the release of the corpse and forge the beginning of a new bond between the living and their emergent ancestors. The heady overstimulation of the last night, particularly in contrast to the calm of the final moments at the crematorium, signal that funeral ritual is dangerous but necessary work—and then, with the joss that signals the soul's presence finally extinguished, that that transformative work is done.

Why then, in the midst of this, is there so much insistence that the smell of the corpse is not part of this ritual overload? Again, theorizing that corpses cannot smell because such a thing would be, well, highly unpalatable, does not get us very far. The funeral consists of a surfeit of sensations, many of them unpleasant. Clouds of incense and smoke from the constant lighting of joss sticks and the burning of paper goods cloud the air and catch in the throat. The noise, heat, and humidity are overwhelming. Relatives, who are forbidden from washing during the multiday wake, reek of the sickly sweetness of sweat and despair. Above all, the dominant emotion of a funeral is often fear, particularly fear of the polluting corpse that, no matter how disfigured and horrifying, remains at the ritual's center. But in the midst of this, there is no space for the malodor of a decaying body.

A Mortician's Work

A great deal of work is involved in preventing a corpse from stinking. Morticians—some Filipino migrant workers, some Singaporean locals who have trained in the United States, Australia, New Zealand, or the United Kingdom, a decreasing number of Americans, Australians, New Zealanders or British citizens of European descent—spend perhaps four hours working on a body, far more if the body is autopsied, disfigured, or already decomposing.[27] They are fighting an always-eventually-lost battle against decay. The mortician begins by washing and drying the body. Then they expose and raise the arteries—in the unautopsied adult body, the choice is between the common carotid, the femoral (external iliac) and the axillary (brachial) arteries, although any major artery will do, and begin to replace the blood with embalming fluid. The larger the artery, the higher the pressure it can sustain and the quicker the fluid will flow, emptying out through a nick in the corresponding vein, most frequently the internal jugular or the femoral, until blood pools at the end of the sloped steel table. To delay rot from within, the morticians pierce the organs with a sharp trocar, forced in just above the navel, then pumped through with highly concentrated cavity fluid. The body is washed, then washed again. Finally, the now embalmed body is dressed and makeup is applied to even out the skin tone. Workers take great care to style the dead's hair and arrange the clothing and jewelry and, for deceased women, to apply more makeup, lipstick, and eyeshadow, if they wore it in life. Yet this attention to detail does not extend to the application of the recently dead's favorite perfume or aftershave. A corpse must smell of nothing at all.

By law, within twenty-four hours, any corpse must be cremated or buried, embalmed or refrigerated. The Singaporean Chinese preference for multiday funerals and for the open casket means that embalming or refrigeration are the only options. And, as no Singaporean funeral parlors are equipped with refrigerators, embalming is the only real choice.[28] Embalming here, therefore, is never intended to bring long-term preservation and thus there is a delicate balance to be struck between longevity and appearance. Too high a proportion of formaldehyde in the embalming fluid and the body takes on an unearthly cast, the dark gray-green of a river rock, which morticians label "embalmer's gray." The skin becomes tight, the face bloated and monstrous. But too low a concentration and the body does not "hold." The features of the face begin "to soften." Or at least that is how a mortician would describe it, although the descriptor troubles me, as there is nothing gentle about decomposition. The features of the face collapse, making visible what is bone, what is cartilage, and what is flesh. The body is no longer a whole but a composite of layers—each decaying at a different rate. Because of its softness, the eyeball is the first part of the body to putrefy, so the eyelids must be held closed, whether with glue or a plastic spiked cap. But still, as the eyeball liquefies, it may leak out, causing the corpse to shed a foul-smelling gelatinous tear. Any orifice presents a risk. Morticians will carefully check the body for fluid leaking from an incorrectly sutured orifice or autopsy scar. Each injection point leaves a hole to plug and another place to leak. If the viscera are not sufficiently treated, the contents of the stomach and bowels may bubble up to the mouth, something morticians label "purge," leaving a foul-smelling discharge the color and texture of coffee grains on the dead's lips. Purge from the lungs, meanwhile, is often frothy, its smell slightly fishy and sweeter. As morticians inspect a body, their most powerful tool is their nose. A corpse that leaks cannot help but smell, and the nature of the odor, always unpleasant but marked by subtle differences, is evidence that embalming has not held back the inevitability of decay. What is death but the process by which complex proteins and carbohydrates become simple compounds, amino acid, ammonium carbon dioxide, hydrogen sulfide, methane, and mercaptans? Each of these gases has a smell of its own: hydrogen sulfide smells like rotten egg, hydrogen phosphate like garlic, and ammonia smells urinous. It is ironic, perhaps—the mortician's curse—that overexposure to formaldehyde kills one's sense of smell.

Theorizing the Trouble with Smell

Why is a smelly corpse so troubling? Perhaps because, as morticians know well, a corpse that smells is one that is undeniably, irrevocably set on the path to decay. Katherine Verdery,[29] writing on the hyperpreserved bodies of political leaders (and on statues, which she regards as the hyperpreserved corpse par excellence, a body now made of stone), notes that keeping the corpse of a dead leader is intended to suggest the continuing relevance of their ideological regime. The scentless body, one that embalming ensures gives no evidence of decay, acts as a similar holding place—not for the person's ideas but for the web of relationships in which they persist. During the days of the funeral, the bereaved do not have to face the absolute reality of death. In large part, this stems from the fact that, in Chinese folk religion, death marks not the termination of a relationship but its transformation, a transformation from alive to corpse and ancestor, which depends on the ritual actions of the family. During the period of the funeral, the dead are therefore treated as if they still live. They are offered food, spoken to, dressed, and blessed. Becoming an ancestor is a social act; it is a gift given to the dead by the living, and such acts need time.

Even for those who have little belief in ancestors and their creation, the harsh reality of dying, as evidenced by the corpse's decay, may well be too much to bear. Ritual, spread across days, and structured through light and dark, noise and quiet, heat and cool, smell and absence of smell, provides an experience separate from chronological time, a holding point, a stillness. The continual smell of incense not only signals the ongoing presence of the dead, but it creates a sense that this is a time out of the ordinary. Seligman, Weller, Puett, and Simon[30] write of ritual as presumptive, suggesting that through ritual we attempt to create the world as we wish it were. If the scentless body allows the bereaved to temporarily deny the physical realities of death and decay, so be it. In other places, I have examined how funeral directors often view the work of embalming—particularly the work of hiding injuries and reviving bodies racked by illness—as an act of tender deceit.[31] The body that does not smell, and therefore does not decay, is an example of that deceit, too. It is an act of fundamental dishonesty, performed by funeral staff, which is also an act of kindness.

Rather than being at odds with the excess of smell (and of noise, heat, and emotion) that marks a Chinese funeral, the scentless corpse is actually more of the same. It acts in parallel ways. What do I mean by this? The work of smells, of incense and smoke in particular, of noise, of light and dark, and of heat, is profoundly social. All are forms of communication between the living and the dead. When a funeral band plays, it is a way of speaking to the wandering dead, stressing that the living acknowledge their presence but warn them against threatening the newly deceased or taking offerings meant for them. The music is meant to provide a distraction. Late on the penultimate night of the funeral or at the columbarium when the remaining funeral offerings are burned, relatives throw white prayer paper, the smallest denomination notes of the Bank of Hell, into the air and shout "fortune," again meant as a placating offering to the neglected dead so that these hungry ghosts do not take the gold and silver meant for the newly dead.

The lighting of incense in front of the funeral portrait is a way of summoning the dead's wandering soul. It says, "Stay here, for all you may wish to wander." And after cremation, extinguishing the incense suggests that this place is no longer a hook for a soul, indeed that the soul must now depart and find its own path. In a sophisticated analysis of the use of candles, incense, paper money, and firecrackers in Chinese rituals, G. Fred Blake suggests that each element is prized because of its contrasting qualities. At moments of ritual disaggregation, candles and incense are used, as they burn slowly, steadily, and quietly. While in moments of ritual reaggregation, paper and firecrackers are burned because they burn rapidly, flaringly, and noisily. He suggests that "the departure from mundane time and entrance into sacred time is accomplished by slowing down, increasing quietude, entering a dreamtime,"[32] hence it is marked not by firecrackers or paper money but by candles and incense. At each point, each sensory element signals ritual's purpose at that moment and articulates the shifting relationship between the living and the dead.

Preventing the dead from smelling is similarly, I would suggest, an act of communication about the purpose of ritual and, centrally, the nature of sociality. This insight comes from Anne Allison's writing on "lonely death" in Japan. Allison describes the noxious odors that leak from the bodies of those "without intimate others to do the work of not letting them die abandoned."[33] The smell of a corpse is, she suggests, "promiscuously social . . . a rotten smell that both lingers and seeps into surroundings: depreciating property and angering neighbors. And far more noticeable than the resident whose isolation had gone unnoticed before that." The smell of the undiscovered corpse is the "smell of social decay." It is evidence of the dead person's disconnection from family. It is their loneliness and abandonment made visceral.

Allison describes the careful work of those who clean up after these lonely deaths, whether dealing with bodies themselves or with the household objects they leave behind. Elders who may be at risk of lonely deaths are urged to make their preparations to avoid this, whether working to strengthen alternative social connections or working with a company to clear as many of their belongings as possible before death. Centrally, to allow one's dead body to go undiscovered, to become something that smells, becomes a profoundly antisocial act. In a Singaporean funeral, a corpse that smells is an embarrassment—as embarrassing as it would be for the living person to stink. Family members interviewed in the days after a funeral where an incorrectly preserved corpse began to purge, leak, and stink compared it to "my deodorant failing on a hot day. Lifting my arms and realizing I stank," to "being the person who had farted in the elevator." It is an embarrassment for the mortician, who is presented with the undeniable evidence of the failure of their work, and for the family and their guests, who now have intimate and unwanted awareness of their relative's incontinence. Above all, it is an embarrassment for the corpse itself.

The Problem of the Incontinent Corpse

Describing the smelling corpse as incontinent brings us again to the particular quality of smells, which is central here, the quality with which we began: the fact that smells break boundaries, leak, and are difficult to contain. An unpleasant smell emanating from a corpse is, above all, evidence of that body's leakiness. For the embalmer, a bad smell is evidence of an actual leak. It is evidence that, uncontrolled, something is seeping from somewhere— perhaps from an orifice insufficiently plugged, perhaps from an incision too loosely stitched. While highly culturally variable, it is common to be troubled by things that leak from the body, to be squeamish about snot, mucus, saliva, or menstrual blood, uncontrollable boundary crossers one and all. In a sensitive ethnography of hospice care, Julia Lawton probes the social squeamishness that surrounds the most troubling of deaths and finds leakiness, not death itself, the thing that troubles. Lawton notes that the root of the word palliative is "to cloak" or "to veil," but she asks: What *exactly is it* that is cloaked? Centrally, she queries the suggestion of earlier researchers, Mellor and others, on palliative-care nursing—that the dying are sequestered within the hospice because death itself is feared. After all, in the English context in which Lawton conducted her research, a significant proportion of the terminally ill now die at home.³⁴ Instead, she suggests that only a certain kind of death happens in the hospice: death that a community cannot accommodate, whether practically or symbolically.³⁵ These are the dying who, most frequently because of cancer's spread, suffer from the loss of control of the body's physical boundaries, from incontinence, from seeping ulcers, from bursting and fumigating tumors, from uncontrollable vomiting or bleeding.

In Lawton's work, social death often occurs before physical death. She describes how, when a dying patient's body deteriorates in a way that society cannot accommodate, when their body begins to leak and smell, family often withdraw. She details a case of a man she calls Sydney, who was admitted directly to a single room rather than a shared ward because of the smell of his fungating tumor. Lawton notes that "the smell in fact proved to be so repellent that his wife refused to go into his room from the time of admission until his death six days later."³⁶ Though they had been married for many years, such was the disruption of smell that their relationship—in its social form—ended well before physical death. She also describes how patients, at the point they were aware of their incontinence and its stench, would ask to be sedated, orchestrating their own social deaths days before their physical ones. The Singaporean Chinese funeral's production of a deodorized body upends this. It allows the dead to remain in the social realm for a little longer, for at least the time of their funeral. Again, this echoes Allison's analysis: to smell is antisocial. By purposefully not smelling, the corpse can remain in the social realm for at least a little while.

A further point—although I make my argument more tentatively here. Lawton argues that in the English context about which she writes, leakiness troubles because the physically bounded body is "an aspect of embodiment which is central to selfhood."³⁷ Here, she draws on Marcel Mauss and on Mary Douglas and on the

> well-rehearsed argument within the anthropological and sociological literature that the body, and experiential modes of embodiment, are culturally elaborated and culturally embedded products. Following on from Mauss' observations on "techniques of the body," Douglas for example has argued for a dialectical relationship between the body and the society within any cultural milieu. Whist the body can act as a "model for society" by affording "a source of symbols for other complex structures." Douglas also suggests that the "social body constrains the way the physical body is perceived." Hence, it

is through the body, and the ways in which the body is deployed and modified that socially appropriate self-understandings are created and reproduced.[38]

In classic symbolic anthropological analysis, Douglas writes on texture and fluids, on mucus and blood, both clotted and free-flowing, on vomit and excretion. (See also McClelland in this volume.)[39] These substances trouble because they cross the body's boundaries. The central idea here is that a body resembles a world, and hence the unbounding of the body suggests the troubling unbounding of the world (and its opposite, that the body provides an imaginary for the world). You can exchange "modern 'West'" here simply for "modern" and thus apply it to Singapore. Is it too much to suggest that, this place, a society built on containment, on separation, on fear of leakiness, as evidenced by its geographic enclaves and control of racial ratios, might find the threat of a leaky body particularly troubling?

Theorizing Smell: Before and Beyond Symbolic Analysis

If contemporary Singaporean Chinese corpses do not smell, it is clear that they once did. But you will find nothing in the academic literature that mentions this, despite the fact that, with funerals of the past lasting perhaps forty days and with neither refrigeration nor embalming, these bodies could not have helped but stink. As I write, a well-worn copy of James Watson and Evelyn Rawski's edited volume *Death Ritual in Late Imperial and Modern China* is beside me on my desk. It is the preeminent text on Chinese funeral rites and remains the central reference work for the field. And yet, in its multiple richly detailed chapters, on everything from the meaning of offerings on funeral altars, to the laments of Hakka women, to the preservation of the body of Mao, there is no mention of smell or its control. The reasons for this are clear: the volume reflects the theoretical concerns of the time—namely, structuralism and symbolism, particularly Levi-Straussian structuralism, which encouraged a focus on the structure hidden beneath the everyday, the patterns found in symbolic action, which became central to British symbolic anthropology in the 1960s, '70s, and '80s. It is therefore little wonder that the volume pays such attention to ritual action, to the maintenance of social structure (the influence of functionalism evident there too), to pollution, articulated as something symbolic, and to gender, understood as binary.

Although we have moved away from the structuralist and symbolic anthropology of that period, there is a way that smell—particularly smell that disgusts—and, more broadly, problematic leakiness continues to be theorized that is inescapably bound to that era and is undergirded by such theorizing. But that, I would suggest—although I am guilty of this myself, in my arguments thus far—restricts our understandings. I remember a discussion with a colleague. We were talking about a particular chapter in *Death Ritual*: Watson's chapter on funeral specialists in Cantonese society. "Those who come with the coffin" are treated "like lepers—or worse," Watson states.[40] Coffin handlers, those who have the closest contact with the corpse and thus are most exposed to its pollution, are beyond the pale of standard human interaction, considered "the ultimate form of human degradation." Death pollution is described by Watson's interlocutors (and by older interlocutors of mine) as "killing airs," "released at the moment of death like 'an invisible cloud.'"[41] It emanates not from bones but from decaying flesh, which explains the practice of secondary burial in some southern Chinese societies. Could it be, I wondered aloud, that "killing airs" were actually smells? That people were afraid and distressed because corpses smelled revolting? My colleague laughed, suggesting that I was missing the point, thinking more like a funeral director than an anthropologist.

When we theorize why something troubles, Douglas, writing in the 1960s and '70s, entrenched in the French structuralism of that moment and in the functionalism of her Oxford training, taught us that the issue is not the thing itself. Dirtiness or disgustingness are not qualities of a thing but systems of classification, ways of marking the boundary, drawing a line. They are symbolic. In *Purity and Danger*, Douglas's example is the Jewish food laws as they are expressed in Leviticus. One might imagine that Jewish prohibition against eating pork comes from a problem with the pig itself, perhaps that pigs were particularly dirty, disease-ridden creatures in Old Testament times. This isn't the issue, stresses Douglas. Instead, the pig, which has cloven feet but does not chew the cud, falls between categories. The prohibition is symbolic. In creating a categorized, symbolically bounded plate, one creates a symbolically bounded world.

These ideas—that pollution is symbolic rather than inherent and frequently the result of the breaking of rules of categorization, of being "matter out of place"—are frequently applied to the corpse. People fear corpses and are repulsed by their decay, and therefore their smell, but not because they understand that corpses can spread disease, as such beliefs existed far earlier than scientific understandings of the complexity of disease transmission. Indeed, as Thomas Laqueur points out, a dead body is the *result* of an epidemic far more frequently than it is its *cause*:

> This does not mean that corpses are always innocuous: fleas on buried bodies can spread typhus and plague; fetal material from a cholera victim can get into water supply; the exhalations from a body that had tuberculosis can still be infectious and doctors are encouraged to cover the faces of corpse and keep autopsy rooms well ventilated; special precautions must be taken in caring for the bodies of those who had blood-borne diseases. But in every such case a living body is more dangerous than a dead one: fleas abandon a corpse; bacteria . . . viruses die quickly once their host is dead. Putrefying, stinking bodies are even more innocent than fresh ones, which are innocent enough: bacteria do not thrive in the alkaline conditions of decomposition. Rotting flesh may be disgusting, but it is not a good vector of disease.[42]

On the one hand, this emphasis on the symbolic has power when we try to understand the squeamishness that surrounds the corpse. Watson writes that community members in the society he studied said that death workers stank. "Those who come with the coffin" were believed to hold garlic clothes in their mouths to disguise the smell of death that settles upon them. Contemporary funeral workers, too, are often described as "smelling of death," and are frequently told that the dead can be smelled, particularly on their hands. To be clear, while the death workers of whom Watson writes may well have smelled, my interlocutors, many of them polished young professionals who see the funeral business as a service industry like any other, do not. And, as I have taken pains to stress, a well-treated corpse should not smell at all. Again, this is about the symbolic, about marking difference, just as Low's earlier ethnographic material on the fact that Singaporeans of Chinese descent perceive Singaporeans of Malay and Indian descent as having distinct and unpleasant aromas tells us more about racial prejudice than the reality of odors.[43]

But I would argue this race to symbolic analysis, for all its power, misses something. There is a suggestion within it that, because something is symbolic, it is not also "real." I note that the same thing happens when thinking about the body—in this case, the embalmed body. We are so quick to read the body as symbol that we forget that it is also material, something that leaks, putrefies, fizzes, and softens. Mary Douglas's analysis of the body as "symbol of society"[44] and "cultural text"[45] sidesteps the body's materiality. This is also evident in other symbolic analyses such as those of Robert Hertz[46] and Victor Turner.[47] More broadly, I have read far too many books on death where it is clear that the author has never seen a dead body. My suggestion here—that symbolic analysis often leads to a neglect of the physical—has broader applications. We are leaving a period in scholarship when we were so keen to read the body as symbol that we forgot that it was also, simultaneously, something material, something weighty, and if not treated correctly, something that rots and putrefies. One perspective need not exclude the other.

In conclusion, it is not as obvious as it may at first seem that corpses should not stink. In a ritual world that makes abundant use of smell—and of heat, light, and noise—the fact that corpses do not smell, and the fact that this happens only with considerable human effort, requires analysis. The deodorized corpse, surprisingly enough, does much the same ritual work as incense, smoke, and sweat. It serves to make possible the ongoing relationship between the living and the dead and articulates the shifting nature of that relationship. But the embalmed body is, above all, a social construction, standing peculiarly as part person, part product (see Troyer[48] for further discussion of this). It is therefore central that, in attempts to analyze it, in focusing on its clear symbolic power, we do not also forget its materiality.

Notes

1. Allison, "The Kinder Scout Trespass."
2. While Singapore's population is multiethnic, consisting of Chinese, Malay, Indian, and other Singaporeans, my work focuses on Singapore's Chinese majority, as the funeral industry is largely divided on racial and religious lines.
3. Conklin, Consuming Grief.
4. Low, Scents and Scent-sibilities, 620.
5. See also the work of Ruth Rogaski, who examines Tianjin, China, also a treaty port city. Both Yeoh and Rogaski illuminate the fact that governmental modernity is always a hygiene project.
6. Bashford, Imperial Hygiene; Howes, Empire of the Senses; Rotter, Empire of the Senses; Senior, Caribbean; Yip, Disease; see particularly Manderson and Jolly, Sites of Desire, Rice and Manderson, Maternity; Manderson, Sickness and the State; Ram and Jolly, Maternities, for discussion of the role of colonial women.
7. McGregor cited in Yeoh, Contesting Space, 85.
8. Yeoh, Contesting Space, 87.
9. Ballantyne and Law, "Genealogy."
10. Bilainkin, Hail Penang!
11. Brown, Indiscreet Memories; Edwards and Keys, Singapore. There is a great deal of literature concerned with sweat and its odor. See, for example, Ann Stoler's work (Carnal Knowledge, 173) on Dutch imperialism

in late colonial Indonesia. Dutch children were not to be held by their local domestic servants, as Dutch parents were afraid of the consequences of their children being soaked in the "powerful" sweat of the Javanese. See also Stoler, "Embodying Colonial Memories."

12. McLagan, *Fat*, 9.

13. Weiner, *Visible and Invisible*.

14. Simpson cited in Yeoh, *Contesting Space*, 96.

15. Ibid., 96–97.

16. Ibid., 191.

17. Ibid., 193.

18. Ibid.

19. Ibid.

20. Ibid., chapter 8.

21. Laqueur, *Work of the Dead*, 230.

22. Low, "Theorising Sensory Cultures," 620.

23. HDB refers to the Housing Development Board Authority and is used as a shorthand for the state-provided-but-citizen-owned high-rise apartments in which some 80 percent of Singaporeans continue to live. The provision of HDBs is perhaps the most substantial commitment to public housing (and, paradoxically, to home ownership) ever made by any state.

24. What I gloss as "traditional" here Singaporean funeral directors and mourners would label Buddhist. Scholars would describe such practices as examples of Chinese folk religion, a complex blending of Buddhism, Daoism, and ancestor worship particular to the region. For Christian funerals (and for Soka Buddhist funerals, a global Buddhist movement that began in Japan and is growing in Singapore, and "free-thinker" funerals, the Singaporean label for those unaffiliated with a particular religious tradition), tenting, altar dressing, and casket blankets are white. Such funerals are also less noisy and lack joss and smoke.

25. Classen, Howes, and Synnott, *Aroma*, 123.

26. See Stafford, *Separation*.

27. In 2021, Singaporean funeral directors began a training and certification program for embalmers with the aim of moving away from dependence on "foreign talent." This is a significant shift in the industry.

28. Some strict adherents of particular Buddhist sects refuse embalming on the grounds that it causes pain to the still sentient body. By law, such bodies must be cremated within twenty-four hours.

29. Verdery, *Dead Bodies*.

30. Seligman, *Ritual and Its Consequences*.

31. Toulson, *Coffin Shop Polity*.

32. Blake, *Burning Money*, 88.

33. Allison, *Being Dead Otherwise*.

34. Lawton, *Dying Process*, 123.

35. Ibid.

36. Ibid., 136.

37. Ibid., 124.

38. Ibid., 137.

39. Douglas, *Purity and Danger*.

40. Watson, "Funeral Specialists," 109.

41. Ibid., 112–13.

42. Laqueur, *Work of the Dead*, 231–32.

43. Low's careful ethnography of the perception of smell in Singapore is full of descriptions that can only be read as grounded in the racial divisions of Singaporean society, where ethnic Singapore's Chinese majority hold much of the nation's power. Chineseness in Singapore operates in the way white privilege operates in many European societies. In descriptions that are often painful to read, Singaporean Chinese respondents speak at length about their perception of their Singaporean Malay, and particularly their Singaporean Indian, compatriots as unpleasantly smelly.

44. Douglas, *Natural Symbols*.

45. Douglas, *Purity and Danger*.

46. Hertz, *Death and the Right-Hand*.

47. Turner, *Forest of Symbols*.

48. Troyer, *Technologies*.

Bibliography

Allison, Ann. *Being Dead Otherwise*. Durham: Duke University Press, 2023.

Allison, Eric. "The Kinder Scout Trespass: Eighty Years On." *The Guardian*, April 17, 2012. https://www.theguardian.com/society/2012/apr/17/kinder-scout-mass-trespass-anniversary.

Ballantyne, Andrew, and Andrew Law. "Genealogy of the Singaporean Black-and-White House." *Singapore Journal of Tropical Geography* 3, no. 23 (2011): 301–13.

Bashford, Alison. *Imperial Hygiene: A Critical History of Colonialism, Nationalism, and Public Health.* London: Palgrave, 2003.

Bilainkin, George. *Hail Penang! Being the Narrative of Comedies and Tragedies in a Tropical Outpost, Among Europeans, Chinese, Malays, and Indians.* London: Sampson Low, Marston, 1932.

Blake, C. Fred. *Burning Money: The Material Spirit of the Chinese Lifeworld.* Honolulu: University of Hawai'i Press, 2011.

Brown, Edwin A. *Indiscreet Memories.* London: Kelly and Walsh, 1936.

Buckley, Thomas, and Alma Gottlieb, eds. *Blood Magic: The Anthropology of Menstruation.* Berkeley: California University Press, 1988.

Classen, Constance, David Howes, and Anthony Synnott. *Aroma: The Cultural History of Smell.* London: Routledge, 1994.

Conklin, Beth. *Consuming Grief: Compassionate Cannibalism in an Amazonian Society.* Austin: University of Texas Press, 2001.

Douglas, Mary. *Natural Symbols: Explorations in Cosmology.* London: Barries and Rockliffe, 1970.

———. *Purity and Danger: An Analysis of the Concepts of Pollution and Taboo.* London: Ark, 1984.

Edwards, Norman, and Peter Keys. *Singapore—A Guide to Buildings, Streets, Places.* Singapore: Times Books International, 1988.

Hertz, Robert. *Death and the Right-Hand.* London: Routledge, 2006.

Howes, David, ed. *Empire of the Senses: The Sensual Culture Reader.* London: Routledge, 2004.

Kipnis, Andrew. *The Funeral of Mr. Wang: Life, Death, and Ghosts in Urbanizing China.* Berkeley: University of California Press, 2021.

Laqueur, Thomas. *The Work of the Dead: A Cultural History of Moral Remains.* Princeton: Princeton University Press, 2015.

Lawton, Julia. *The Dying Process: Patients' Experiences of Palliative Care.* London: Routledge, 2000.

Low, Kelvin E. Y. *Scents and Scent-sibilities: Smell and Everyday Life Experiences.* Newcastle upon Tyne: Cambridge Scholars, 2009.

———. "Theorising Sensory Cultures in Asia: Sociohistorical Perspectives." *Asian Studies Review* 43, no. 4 (2019): 618–36.

Low, Kelvin E. Y., and D. Kalekin-Fishman, eds. *Everyday Life in Asia: Social Perspectives on the Senses.* London: Routledge, 2016.

Manderson, Lenore. "Race, Colonial Mentality, and Public Health in Early Twentieth Century Malaya." In *The Underside of Malaysian History: Pullers, Prostitutes, Plantation Workers . . . ,* edited by Peter J. Rimmer and Lisa M. Allen, 193–213. Singapore: Singapore University Press, 1990.

———. *Sickness and the State. Health and Illness in Colonial Malaya, 1870–1940.* Cambridge: Cambridge University Press, 1996.

Manderson, Lenore, and Margaret Jolly, eds. *Sites of Desire / Economies of Pleasure: Sexualities in Asia and the Pacific.* Chicago: The University of Chicago Press, 1997.

McLagan, Jennifer. *Fat: An Appreciation of a Misunderstood Ingredient.* Berkeley: Ten Speed Press, 2008.

Ram, Kalpana, and Margaret Jolly. *Maternities and Modernities: Colonial and Postcolonial Experiences in Asia and the Pacific.* Cambridge: Cambridge University Press, 2009.

Rice, Pranee Liamputtong Rice, and Lenore Manderson, eds. *Maternity and Reproductive Health in Asian Societies.* London: Routledge, 1996.

Rotter, Andrew. *Empires of the Senses: Bodily Encounters in Imperial India and the Philippines.* Oxford: Oxford University Press, 2019.

Seligman, Adam B., Robert P. Weller, Michael Puett, and Bennett Simon. *Ritual and Its Consequences: An Essay on the*

Limits of Sincerity. Oxford: Oxford University Press, 2008.

Senior, Emily. *The Caribbean and the Medical Imagination, 1764–1834*. Cambridge Studies in Romanticism 119. Cambridge: Cambridge University Press, 2018.

Stafford, Charles. *Separation and Reunion in Modern China*. Cambridge: Cambridge University Press, 2000.

Stoler, Ann Laura. *Carnal Knowledge and Imperial Power: Race and the Intimate in Colonial Rule*. Berkeley: University of California Press, 2010.

———. "Educating Desire in Colonial Southeast Asia: Foucault, Freud, and Imperial Sexualities." In *Sites of Desire / Economies of Pleasure: Sexualities in Asia and the Pacific*, edited by Lenore Manderson and Margaret Jolly, 27–47. Chicago: Chicago University Press, 1997.

Stoller, Paul. "Embodying Colonial Memories." *American Anthropologist* 96, no. 3 (1994): 634–48.

Strivens, Maila. "Modernizing the Malay Mother." In *Maternities and Modernities: Colonial and Postcolonial Experiences in Asia and the Pacific*, edited by Kalpana Ram and Margaret Jolly, 50–80. Cambridge: Cambridge University Press, 2009.

Toulson, Ruth E. *Coffin Shop Polity: Life and Death in a Chinese Funeral Parlor*. Unpublished manuscript.

———."The Meanings of Red Envelopes: Promises and Lies at Singaporean Chinese Funeral." *Journal of Material Culture* 18, no. 2 (2013): 155–69.

Troyer, John. *Technologies of the Human Corpse*. Cambridge, MA: MIT Press, 2020.

Turner, Victor. *The Forest of Symbols: Aspects of Ndembu Ritual*. Ithaca: Cornell University Press, 1967.

Verdery, Katherine. *The Political Lives of Dead Bodies: Reburial and Postsocialist Change*. Columbia: Columbia University Press, 2000.

Warren, James. *Rickshaw Coolie: A People's History of Singapore, 1880–1940*. Singapore: National University of Singapore Press, 2003.

Watson, James. "Funeral Specialists in Cantonese Society: Pollution, Performance, and Social Hierarchy." In *Death in Late Imperial and Modern China*, edited by James Watson and Evelyn Rawski, 109–34. Berkeley: California University Press, 1990.

Watson, James, and Evelyn Rawski, eds. *Death in Late Imperial and Modern China*. Cambridge: Cambridge University Pres, 1990.

Weiner, Margaret J. *Visible and Invisible Realms: Power, Magic and Colonial Conquest in Bali*. Chicago: The University of Chicago Press, 1995.

Yeoh, Brenda S. A. *Contesting Space in Colonial Singapore: Power Relations and the Urban Built Environment*. Singapore: National University of Singapore Press, 2003.

Yip, Ka-che. *Disease, Colonialism, and the State: Malaria in Modern East Asian History*. Hong Kong: Hong Kong University Press, 2009.

Contributors

JEAN DURUZ is Adjunct Senior Research Fellow in UniSA Creative, an academic unit within the University of South Australia, and Affiliated Professor of the University of Toronto's Culinaria Research Centre. Duruz's research interests focus on cultural connections of place and identity in postcolonial global cities, such as London, Mexico City, New York City, Sydney, and Singapore, with an emphasis on sensory landscapes. Her most recent article (with Angela Giovanangeli, Alice Loda, and Nicholas Manganas) is "Emotional Scapes in Mediterranean Port Cities: Walking Barcelona, Marseille and Genova" in *European Journal of Cultural Studies* (2022).

HANNAH GOULD is a cultural anthropologist and Melbourne Postdoctoral Fellow in the School of Social and Political Sciences, University of Melbourne. Gould is the author of multiple articles and book chapters on death, religion, and material culture, with a regional focus on Northeast Asia and Australia. Her manuscript *When Death Falls Apart*, forthcoming in 2023, explores the making and unmaking of material traditions around death and dying based on extensive fieldwork in the Japanese Buddhist deathcare sector.

QIAN JIA is a PhD candidate at Stanford University, completing her dissertation titled "Sensing the Broadening World: The Birth of Incense Culture in Song Dynasty China (960–1276)." Her research interests lie in middle-period Chinese literature and culture, genre conventions, sensory studies, material culture, gender studies, knowledge production, and the idea of the empire.

SHIVANI KAPOOR is Assistant Professor at the Centre for Writing Studies, O. P. Jindal Global University. She has a doctorate in political science from the Centre for Political Studies, Jawaharlal Nehru University, New Delhi. Her work is located at the intersection of caste, sensory politics, and labor and examines the relationship between caste and the senses in the leather industry in contemporary Uttar Pradesh. Her earlier work examined debates around the representations of "untouchable" selves through self-writing and its circulation of Hindi Dalit autobiographies from Uttar Pradesh. She has published several journal articles and book chapters on these issues. She has previously taught at Ambedkar University Delhi, University of Delhi, and Shiv Nadar University and has been a Visiting Fellow at the Centre for the Study of Developing Societies (CSDS), New Delhi.

GAIK CHENG KHOO is Associate Professor at the University of Nottingham Malaysia. Focusing on Malaysia, Gaik has written on independent cinema and filmmaking, food identity, and Korean migrants. Her research concerns the durian supply chain, where she argues for a more integrated and ecologically sound practice for the Malaysian durian industry. She recently published "Adjusting to Slow Times and Happiness: South Koreans in Malaysia" in *Korea Journal* (2022).

ADAM LIEBMAN is Assistant Professor of Anthropology at DePauw University. He is interested in waste politics, infrastructure, embodiment, and junk art. He is the author of "High Metabolism Infrastructure and the Scrap Industry in Urban China" in *China Quarterly* (2022).

LORENZO MARINUCCI is Associate Professor of Aesthetics at Tohoku University. His research interests include Japanese aesthetics and poetics, phenomenology, intercultural philosophy, and the study of atmospheres. He is currently working on a book exploring Japanese olfactory paradigms from such a philosophical approach. He is also an active translator of nonfiction, fiction, and poetry from Japanese, English, and German. A recent publication is "Iro 色: A Phenomenology of Color and Desire" in the *European Journal of Japanese Philosophy* (2020).

GWYN MCCLELLAND is Senior Lecturer in Japanese Studies at the University of New England. His monograph *Dangerous Memory in Nagasaki* (2019) composed a collective biography of nine Catholic *hibakusha* in Nagasaki. An Asian historian, Gwyn has recently published "Valuing the Urakami Cathedral After the Atomic Bombing: Fundraising and Social Rupture in Nagasaki" in the *Journal of Cultural Economy* (2022). He is a past Japan Foundation Fellow and a current National Library of Australia Fellow, supported by the Harold S. Williams Trust. His research interests include memory studies, oral history, emotion in testimonial narration, and engagement with sensory studies.

PETER ROMASKIEWICZ is a PhD Researcher in the UC Santa Barbara Department of Religious Studies. His research interests span Buddhist Studies, Medieval Chinese Religions, Sensory Studies, and Composition and Rhetoric. His dissertation research explores the convergence of medieval Chinese religions and the sense of smell and is tentatively entitled "Sacred Smells and Strange Scents: Olfactory Imagination in Medieval Chinese Religions."

SAKI TANADA is Curator at the Toyama Glass Art Museum, Japan. Her research interests lie at the intersection of the body and craft. Her fascination with material culture developed during five years of doctoral field research in Indonesia, where she studied local practices of weaving and wearing cloth take a key role in social and reproductive wellbeing for the Indigenous Sasak People in Lombok Island. Her most recent publication is a bilingual exhibition catalogue "Kirstie Rea: The Breadth of Stillness" (カースティ・レイ：静けさの地平) for the Toyama Glass Art Museum, 2021.

AUBREY TANG is a Lecturer in Film Studies at Chapman University, California. Tang's research interests include film theory, phenomenology of perception, as well as Chinese and Sinophone cinemas. Before entering academia, she was a published short-story author, a columnist, a translator, a radio host, and a wedding singer in Hong Kong and the United States. Raised by her blind grandmother in Hong Kong, she finds her passion in phenomenology. A recent publication by Tang is "The Parasites of Language: 'President Trump, Please Liberate Hong Kong'" in *Language and Dialogue* (2022).

RUTH E. TOULSON is a cultural anthropologist and a mortician. She is a Professor in the Division of Liberal Arts, Maryland Institute College of Art, Baltimore, Maryland. Toulson is the author of multiple articles and book chapters on death, grieving, and material culture, which draw on her research in the funeral industry in Southeast Asia and Mainland China. She is the editor, with Zahra Newby, of *The Materiality of Mourning: Cross Disciplinary Perspectives* (2018) and, with Sarah Wagner, of the *Cambridge University Press Handbook of the Anthropology of Death* (forthcoming). Her current book project draws on multi-year fieldwork in Chinese funeral parlors in Singapore to examine the causes and consequences of rapid transformation in the way death is ritualized and grieved.

Index

Italicized page references indicate illustrations. Endnotes are referenced with "n" followed by the endnote number.

www.ingramcontent.com/pod-product-compliance
Lightning Source LLC
Chambersburg PA
CBHW032125020426
42334CB00016B/1071